Allegory and the
Work of Melancholy

72

Internationale Forschungen zur Allgemeinen und Vergleichenden Literaturwissenschaft

Redakteure:
Norbert Bachleitner & Alfred Noe

Anschrift der Redaktion:
Institut für Vergleichende Literaturwissenschaft, Berggasse 11/5, A-1090 Wien

Allegory and the Work of Melancholy

The Late Medieval and Shakespeare

Jeremy Tambling

Amsterdam - New York, NY 2004

Cover photo: Albrecht Dürer - Melencolia I
Bequest of William P. Chapman; Jr., Class of 1895
Courtesy of the Herbert F. Johnson Museum of Art, Cornell University

Le papier sur lequel le présent ouvrage est imprimé remplit les prescriptions de
"ISO 9706:1994, Information et documentation - Papier pour documents -
Prescriptions pour la permanence".

The paper on which this book is printed meets the requirements of " ISO
9706:1994, Information and documentation - Paper for documents -
Requirements for permanence".

ISBN: 90-420-1018-5
©Editions Rodopi B.V., Amsterdam - New York, NY 2004
Printed in The Netherlands

CONTENTS

ACKNOWLEDGEMENTS

Though it may not seem to reflect much perspicacity, *Allegory and the Work of Melancholy: The Late Medieval and Shakespeare* was a hard title and subtitle to choose. That is partly because, with regard to the texts chosen, I aim not at an imaginary comprehensiveness, but try to contribute to a theme perceptible because of contemporary theory, which then enables a reading and re-placing of that theory. (*Theory of the Medieval* could have been a title for the book.) I work with medieval materials but, as a comparativist with an interest in empirical research as much as in theory, I do not speak only or even primarily to medieval specialists, my hope being to open up areas of study: i.e. not letting the medieval be corralled in a separate world from the modern. I believe medievalists are more wide-ranging in their materials than critics who work in the modern period (empirical observation suggests this, and Paul de Man confirms it when he says in *Blindness and Insight* (2nd edition, (Minneapolis: University of Minnesota Press 1983) p. 157) of the seventeenth-century quarrel between the Ancients and the Moderns that "the modern camp not only contained men of slighter literary talent, but .... their arguments against classical literature were often simply against literature as such"). Since the drift of Walter Benjamin's argument, which draws on medieval materials, is to see modernity in terms of the ruin, or disaster, I write for 'modernists', hoping to direct them towards material which is akin to Blanchot's 'writing of the disaster', and perhaps neglected.

Some of the material developed in this book comes out of my previous and ongoing work on Dante - who appears here, however, only as source of one of Chaucer's Monk's 'modern instances'. Discussion of the texts, interest in which goes back a long way for me, also emerges from a fascination with Benjamin and history and with a death-state as inseparable from life which appears in most recent form in my book *Becoming Posthumous* (Edinburgh: Edinburgh University Press 2001).

I have accumulated many debts which, like this book, go back a long way: from first reading *The Knight's Tale* with Brian Worthington, to undergraduate teachers of English Medieval and Renaissance literature, Elizabeth Salter, Philippa Tristram and Derek Pearsall, Karen Sterne, Bob Jones and Philip Brockbank, to a Chaucer conference at Kent in 1991, where Richard Neuse invited me to present work on *The Monk's Tale*, and for an opportunity to present work on Hoccleve and Henryson at Cornell in 1994, for which I thank Winthrop Wetherbee: the discussion afterwards persuaded me that I must include *Yvain* in my work. I thank those who have read chapters: Kit Givan, whether in Hong Kong or Oklahoma, Priscilla Martin, Clayton McKenzie, Wimal Dissanayake and James Simpson.

I owe him thanks for the conference on Langland he organized at Cambridge in 1993 (my part in that came out in my "Response to Mary Carruthers," *Yearbook of Langland Studies* 9 (1995), 114-116) and, more recently, for generously agreeing to read my work on *Piers Plowman* and for commenting on it. I thank Ackbar Abbas, who has always been in front of me with his readings of Benjamin in my own department of Comparative Literature. And I thank David Lawton, who accepted a version of my work on Hoccleve for the adventurous annual *New Medieval Literatures* 6 (2003), and who has allowed me to reprint the work here. Also Peter Cunich who has given me help with my history, and invited me to give a History department seminar on apocalyptic thinking. And thanks to all others, such as Jonathan White, whose discovery that while I have been working on Dante, or the moderns, I have also been pursuing work in other areas of the medieval, has produced interesting conversations. Here I particularly recall Francis Barker, who was always insightful on any topic, not least, of course, on the early modern period. And also Jonathan Hall. Thanks also to students who have listened, especially on the subject of Derrida and Blanchot. A big debt to Pauline, whose enabling power this book represents, and whose, therefore, it is.

Research for this book has taken place in many libraries, but I single out two for thanks and acknowledgement: the Warburg Institute in London, and the Hong Kong University library, which is always wonderfully helpful in its staff and well-stocked. Thanks to Bob Tsang Hon Hei for preparing the book for the press, as a research assistant working with money thoughtfully granted by the Hong Kong University Grants Committee.

INTRODUCTION

Benjamin's *Trauerspiel*

> It is not a question of a return to the Middle Ages or anything like it. The mistake of postulating an absolute historical time: There are different times *even though* they may be parallel. In this sense, one of the times of the so-called Middle Ages can coincide with one of the times of the Modern Ages. And that time is what has been perceived and inhabited by painters and writers who refuse to seek support in what surrounds them, to be 'modern' in the sense that their contemporaries understand them, which does not mean that they choose to be anachronistic; they are simply on the margin of the superficial time of their period, and from that other time where everything conforms to the condition of *figure*, where everything has value as a sign and not as a theme of description, they attempt a work which may seem alien or antagonistic to the time and history surrounding them.[1]

> Majesty of the allegorical intention: destruction of the organic and living - the extinguishing of appearance.[2]

> The work is the death mask of its conception.[3]

I – *MELENCOLIA I*

Studying one topic usually requires thinking simultaneously about another. Take, for example, the two terms on the front cover of Angus Fletcher's classic study, *Allegory: The Theory of a Symbolic Mode*.[4] The paperback's cover gives the title and displays Dürer's engraving of 1514, *Melencolia I*. The engraving's title can be discerned within the banderole held out by the flying bat. *Allegory* appears on the title of Fletcher's book, and *melancholy* in the title of the picture. Aligning the title with the otherwise unexplained picture makes the image of melancholia allegorical of allegory and the two concepts as if in a montage. Fletcher does not refer to the picture, but beginning with emblematic poems, he quotes Erwin Panofsky:

> Writing of Dürer, Panofsky thus defines emblems: 'images which refuse to be accepted as representations of mere things but demand to be interpreted as vehicles of concepts; they are tolerated by most modern critics, as a rule, only if incorporated in a work so rich in 'atmosphere' that it can, after all, only be 'accepted' without a detailed explanation (as in Dürer's engraving of *Melencolia I*)'. (Fletcher, 25)

---

[1]   Julio Cortázar, *Hopscotch*, trans. by Gregory Rabassa (New York: Pantheon Books, 1966), p. 480.

[2]   Walter Benjamin, 'Central Park', *New German Critique*, 34 (1985), 32-58 (p. 41).

[3]   Walter Benjamin, *One Way Street and Other Writings*, trans. by Edmund Jephcott and Kingsley Shorter (London: Verso, 1979), p. 65.

[4]   Angus Fletcher, *Allegory: The Theory of a Symbolic Mode* (Ithaca: Cornell University Press, 1964): papberback edition 1970. Hereafter Fletcher and page-number.

Nothing else is said on *Melencolia I*, leaving an undecidable relationship between *Melencolia I* and allegory, which, 'in the simplest terms' 'says one thing and means another' (2). It is *allos* (other) and *agoreuein* (to speak openly, in the agora, in the market-place). Allegory, speaking differently, was seen in Roman times as "inversion" (2), where something is said that differs from its literal meaning. *Inversion* was linked to *translation*, the Latin translation of the Greek *metaphor*.

Later, Fletcher refers to the Greek word "enigma" – recalling I Corinthians 12.12: 'For now we see through a glass, darkly (in an enigma, in a riddle)'. The words, in Latin, are alluded to by Langland, earlier than the OED, which gives 1539 for 'enigma' in English. Fletcher cites the Elizabethan Henry Peacham, 'aenigma: a kind of allegory, differing only in obscurity, for Aenigma is a sentence, or form of speech which, for the darkness, the sense may hardly be gathered' (Fletcher 8). Giorgio Agamben recalls Aristotle's definition of the enigma in the *Poetics* (58a): *ta adynata synapsai*: 'a putting together of impossible things'.[5] Riddles and emblems are tropes which put together impossible things. Lope de Vega paired the enigma with allegory, saying 'an enigma is an obscure allegory that is understood with difficulty'.[6] The cover of *Allegory* is an enigma.

An Italian lawyer, Andreas Alciatus, in *Emblematum liber* (1531), said an emblem had three parts. The motto was above the picture (or ikon), and underneath the ikon came the epigram (*subscriptio*). Dürer's *Melencolia I*, is earlier, however, than the emblem-books. In its left-hand upper part is a sea, the bat flying overhead. A rainbow, enframing a comet, shines above the sea which has flooded the land. In front of the sea, visible on the far left, is an alchemist's crucible, with a fire burning below. The right-hand lower part of the picture shows a woman, seated on a step. She has drooping wings, a wreath of bitter-sweet herbs on her head; her left arm supports her drooping head, though her eyes turn upwards. Her right hand holds, idly, a pair of compasses. At her feet is a saw, a ruler and lathe and a pair of pincers; under her skirts is the mouth of a pair of bellows, and there are nails on the floor. To her right, almost central, a *putto* sits on a millstone, or knife-grinder's stone, writing on a tablet.

In the down-left-hand side is an uninscribed round globe, and a lean dog, asleep. To its right is an inkpot. Behind the dog, centre

---

[5] Giorgio Agamben, *Stanzas: Word and Phantasm in Western Culture*, trans. by Ronald L. Martinez (Minneapolis: University of Minnesota Press, 1993), p. 139.

[6] Quoted, José Antonio Maravall, *Culture of the Baroque: Analysis of a Historical Structure,* trans. by Terry Cochran (Minneapolis: University of Minnesota Press, 1986), p. 222.

left, is a huge stone polyhedron, and under one of its overhanging sides, a hammer. Behind the woman, is a building, seen in perspective. The ladder with seven rungs for Panofsky 'seems to emphasise the incompleteness of the edifice'.[7] A pair of scales hang from the wall retreating away from the viewer. On the facing wall appears an hour-glass, a magic square, and above it a bell. The Viennese iconologist Karl Giehlow said that the magic square was Jupiter's, as if it was there to counteract Saturn's melancholy: Walter Benjamin quotes this in *Ursprung des deutschen Trauerspiels* (*The Origin of German Tragic Drama*).[8] There is ambiguity within melancholy, since Jupiter's geniality contests another spirit of heaviness. The picture does not deliver one message, but more than one. What makes melancholy melancholic is an ambiguity within it, so that like bi-polar depression, it includes excitation and carnival. Perhaps the bell over the magic square is magic, for evoking good spirits. The magic square gives the date 1514.

Klibansky, Saxl and Panofsky interpret the key hanging from the woman's belt, and the purse on the floor, saying that 'the key signifies power, the purses riches'.[9] They connect that with the Medieval melancholic, avaricious and miserly. Judas Iscariot, in the Gospels, carried the purse, and his melancholy was suicidal (286). The head resting in the hand implies grief, fatigue, or thought; though for Agamben it is despair.[10] The hand, however, is not open, since a clenched fist is brought up against her cheek, and this is interpreted as having been, for the medieval illustrator, the sign of someone under certain delusions, but, for the Renaissance, 'the fanatical concentration of a mind which has truly grasped a problem, but which at the same time feels itself incapable either of solving or of dismissing it' (319). Two types of melancholia, then.

Benjamin's analysis discusses Dürer's sleeping dog, whose posture suggests uneasy dreams. He links the polyhedron in the centre to *acedia*, dullness of heart, like sloth (155), quoting Aegidius Albertinus, writing in 1617:

> acedia or sloth is comparable in kind to the bite of a mad dog, for whoever is bitten by the same is immediately assailed by horrible dreams, he is terrified in his sleep, becomes estranged and senseless, rejects all drink, is afraid of water, barks like a dog, and becomes so

---

[7] Erwin Panofsky, *The Life and Art of Albrecht Dürer* (Princeton: Princeton University Press, 1955), p. 156

[8] Walter Benjamin, *The Origin of German Tragic Drama*, trans. by John Osborne (London: Verso, 1977), p. 151. Hereafter *Origin* plus page-reference.

[9] Raymond Klibansky, Fritz Saxl and Erwin Panofsky, *Saturn and Melancholy* (London: Dent, 1964), p. 284. Further references in text.

[10] Agamben, *Stanzas* p. 10.

fearful that he falls down in terror. Such men die very soon if they receive no help. (156)

Through this polyhedron, the engraving distorts the ability of perspective to establish a single-subject position for the viewer. A distorted cube, its six sides are diamond-shaped, not square, with the two diagonally opposite corners cut off to produce two more sides triangular in shape on which it stands. It has been read as a three-dimensional anamorphosis. Since none of its angles is 90 degrees, it is an optical illusion, impossible to construct in three dimensions, and the shape, which is complexly related to the magic square's numbers, appears cubic, but the shape is distorted. Terence Lynch sees the polyhedron, in its deceptive appearance, as the deep design of the engraving.[11] Maravall discusses the baroque anamorphosis as an example of interest in illusion, where the reality of the world under test– as it is in *Don Quixote*. When Don Quixote discusses the bones of giants he adds, climactically, 'as geometry evinces beyond all doubt'[12] but whether this is Quixote's lucidity or madness is questionable, for anamorphosis makes geometry illusory, like the baroque's perception of life as a dream.[13] It implies an impossible space, a denial of the viewer's single-subject position.

Dürer's engraving is at the heart of *The Origin of German Tragic Drama* which reads the *Trauerspiel* - plays of mourning - as a contrast to the Enlightenment which succeeded them. Their mourning records history as failure and fragmentation, and only to be thought through allegory. Enlightenment history, as with Hegel, has repressed such a reading of history in favour of developmental progress and the belief in mimetic representation, using not allegory but symbolism. This would also mean the end of melancholia. Allegory as a form loses status in the early modern. John MacQueen traces it through Roman literature, as with Quintilian (35-95 CE) in the *Institutio Oratoria* (VIII.vi.44-59). Quintilian takes allegory to have two forms; either comprising one thing in words and another in meaning, or 'something absolutely opposed to the meaning of the words' [*aut aliud verbis aliud sensu ostendit aut etiam interim contrarium*]. This includes irony, sarcasm, (*asteimos*), and proverbs. Allegory

---

[11] Terence Lynch, 'The Geometric Body in Dürer's "Melencolia I"', *Journal of the Warburg and Courtauld Institute* 45 (1982), 226-31.

[12] Miguel de Cervantes, *Don Quixote*, trans. by Charles Jervis (Oxford: Oxford University Press, 1992) 2.1. p. 530. (Translation first published 1742.)

[13] Maravall, p. 223. He refers to the work of Baltrusaitis, whom Lacan also quotes in his discussion of Holbein's *The Ambassadors* (1533); see his *The Four Fundamental Concepts of Psychoanalysis*, trans. by Alan Sheridan (Harmondsworth: Penguin, 1977), p. 85. Baltrusaitis sees the highwater mark of the anamorphosis as 1630-50, and Paris as a centre for its study. For the world as illusion, see Maravall, pp. 198-99.

dominates in Prudentius (348-410 CE) in the *Psychomachia* – 'the battle in, or fight for the soul'. Prudentius is contemporary with Augustine (354-430), whose *Confessions* are a psychomachia. Allegory is the mode of Guillaume de Lorris (c.1230) and Jean de Meung (c.1270) in *Le Roman de la rose*, of Dante in the *Commedia* and of Spenser's *The Faerie Queen*; MacQueen cites no examples after the seventeenth century.[14] Allegory becomes a casualty of Enlightenment thought, and so of modernity. If allegory appears in modern texts, it is as other to dominant narrative modes, repressed by a newer form of writing marked by a will to truth in historical representation.

Adorno, however, links Dickens's *The Old Curiosity Shop* (1841-42) to Baroque allegory.[15] Dickens begins 'Night is generally my time for walking'. For contact may then be disavowed and the city can hardly be read. But the night-walking narrator meets Nell, and restores her to her home, the warehouse of curiosities. Her grandfather leaves her there to go out into the night, and the narrator reflects upon the isolated girl in her bed, as she is surrounded by the contents of the shop, that 'she seemed to exist in a kind of allegory'.[16] Nell asleep, surrounded by medieval relics, was illustrated by a woodcut made by Samuel Williams, of which Thomas Hood wrote, in the *Athenaeum*:

> Look at the Artist's picture of the Child, asleep in her little bed, surrounded, or rather mobbed, by ancient armour and arms, antique furniture, and relics sacred or profane, hideous or grotesque: - it is like an Allegory of the peace and innocence of Childhood in the midst of Violence, Superstititon, and all the hateful and hurtful Passions of the world. [...][17]

---

[14] John MacQueen, *Allegory* (London: Methuen, 1970). I have cited pp. 49-50, 59-60. For an example of the nineteenth-century's rejection, see Henry James' critique of Hawthorne's allegory: Henry James, *Hawthorne* in *Literary Criticism: Essays on Literature: American Writers, English Writers* (New York: Library of America, 1984) pp. 336-8. On modern allegory, see Willen von Reijen, ed, *Allegorie und Melancholie* (Frankfurt: Suhrkamp Verlag, 1992). It contains essays by various hands on Adorno and Benjamin, on allegory in art and on Benjamin and Paul de Man.

[15] Theodor Wiesengrund Adorno, 'An Address on Charles Dickens's *The Old Curiosity Shop*', trans. by Michael Hollington in *Charles Dickens: Critical Assessments* ed, Michael Hollington (London: Helm Information, 1995) vol 2 of 4, p. 363. See also Benjamin in the *Arcades* project trans. Howard Eiland and Kevin McLaughlin (Cambridge Mass.: Harvard University Press, 1999), p. 208. Benjamin relates the novel to the collector and continues by citing Adorno's piece.

[16] Dickens, *The Old Curiosity Shop*, ed. by Angus Easson (Harmondsworth: Penguin, 1972), pp. 43, 56.

[17] Harvey, pp. 122-3.

12

The picture evokes *Melencolia I*, repeating its heap of unsorted items on the floor, suggesting a drunken architecture with the pillar leaning uselessly to the right, and with, to the left of the sleeping girl, the dead world appearing in the form of a mask, like a gargoyle. The girl sleeps in a museum of strangeness, the objects allegorizing her dreams. For Hood, she is alive and the world dead: Dickens's London is an old curiosity shop, full of dead things, relics of medieval history (empty suits of armour, pointless weapons). But Nell is marked for the death of which her sleep is the allegory. The text annihilates the dream of peace and innocence: the solitary walker walks only by night, and has fantasies of bodies 'dead yet conscious' condemned to lie in a 'noisy churchyard' where they hear footfalls. The picture dramatises melancholy, since the objects are like dream-images, reminders of things that there can be no relationship to; yet as enigmatic, 'curiosities', they evoke curiosity. Identifying with Nell, the text kills her, marking her out for dead from the beginning for it identifies too with the threatening mask, or the shadows of men in armour. The textual desire is to both dead *and* conscious. 'She seemed to exist in a kind of allegory': life is allegorical; not quite animate since death and the inanimate are also animate.[18]

In Baudelaire's 'Le Cygne', [The Swan] in *Les Fleurs du Mal*:

> Paris change! mais rien dans ma mélancolie
> N'a bougé! palais neufs, échafaudages, blocs,
> Vieux fauborgs, tout pour moi devient allégorie,
> Et mes chers souvenirs sont plus lourds que des rocs.[19]

> (Paris changes! But nothing in my melancholy has shifted! New palaces, scaffolds, stone blocks, old suburbs, all for me becomes allegory, and my dear memories are heavier than rocks.)

In Haussmann's modernizations of Paris, new palaces appear as old neighbourhoods disappear; wooden scaffolds veil stone blocks for new monumental architecture, but these alienate, because the subject lacks relationship with these emblems of modernity. 'Tout pour moi devient allégorie' means a devaluation of appearances; what has disappeared from the new Paris is more visible. 'Le cygne' reads the old – 'le vieux Paris' - in the new, which instead of being new, awakens memories. Baudelaire makes allegorical thinking the modern artist's condition of thought. 'Baudelaire's genius, which drew its

---

[18] For discussion of this passage, see Richard Maxwell, *The Mysteries of Paris and London* (Charlotteville: University Press of Virginia, 1992), pp. 112-115.

[19] Charles Baudelaire, "Le Cygne", *Les Fleurs du Mal* no. 91, translation mine. For an historical note on the relation of Baudelaire to Dürer, see James S. Patty, 'Baudelaire and Dürer: Avatars of Melancholia', *Symposium* 38 (1984), 244-257.

nourishment from melancholy, was an allegorical one', writes Benjamin, '[...] the allegorist's gaze, which falls upon the city is ... the gaze of alienated man'.[20] Alienation, etymologically related to allegory (what is alien belongs to the other) also means madness: the OED gives a first citation of 1482 for this. It becomes part of being modern, imposing demands on how to see, how to read, while showing the impossibility of doing either of these things.

II – READING *THE ORIGIN OF GERMAN TRAGIC DRAMA*

The monuments of the bourgeoisie are ruins, and this allegorical insight is possessed by Benjamin's 'Angel of History': 'where we perceive a chain of events, he [the Angel of History] sees one single catastrophe which keeps piling wreckage upon wreckage, and hurls it in front of his feet'.[21] Under this gaze the past ceases to exist as tradition, or as a chain of events, as in post-Hegelian history writing, but appears as ruins. In antiquity, the god associated with time was Saturn, embodiment of melancholy. An allegorical character incarnates melancholy, and the melancholic gaze is allegorical, robbing the past of the appearance of cohesion. Benjamin 'came into the world under the sign of Saturn – the star of the slowest revolution, the planet of detours and delays'.[22] So the "Epistemo-Critical Prologue" to the *Origin of German Tragic Drama* defines thinking by 'digression' [so that] '[...] the process of thinking makes new beginnings, returning in a roundabout way to its original object' (*Origin* 28). We cannot *possess* knowledge (as in possessing data as acquired property, or possessing 'the truth'). The mind must work with fragments of historical phenomena, such as individual works of art. Benjamin questions how these may be associated in a way revealing or configuring a pattern, an idea, which he calls a 'mosaic' or a 'constellation'. 'Ideas are to objects as constellations are to stars' (34). The tragic dramas he discusses point to, or produce, a constellation; which is the non-paraphrasable idea they suggest. A constellation, assemblage of isolated fragments is not a totality, or a complete truth, nor does it have definite status. The word relates back to classical mythology and to the gods faintly remembered in its name and approximate shape. That keeps the notion of the

---

[20] Walter Benjamin, *Charles Baudelaire: A Lyric Poet in the Era of High Capitalism*, trans. by Harry Zohn (London: New Left Books, 1973), p. 170.

[21] Walter Benjamin, 'Theses on the Philosophy of History', in *Illuminations* trans. by Harry Zohn (London: Jonathan Cape, 1970), p. 259. Hereafter *Illuminations* plus page number in the text.

[22] Gershom Scholem, 'Walter Benjamin and his Angel' in Gary Smith, *On Walter Benjamin: Citical Essays and Recollections* (Cambridge, Mass.: MIT Press, 1988), p. 59. The quotation comes from a piece called 'Aegesilaus Santander', (written in Ibiza, 1933), which Scholem discusses.

constellation within the sphere of allegory. But a constellation is also for the guidance of shipping; its fictitious nature supports an objective reality.

As allegorical thinking is not positivist, ideas do not amount to positivist knowledge. An idea is not 'knowledge'. But in a constellation, 'phenomena are subdivided and at the same time redeemed' (34). The combination of such constellations is what Benjamin calls 'truth', which appears not through the Enlightenment 'will to truth' but through 'total immersion and absorption'; since 'truth is the death of intention' (36). Benjamin, whose work is a text of German modernism (55), reads in the *Trauerspiel* elements suggesting a different sense of history from the Hegelian, and responding to failure and fragmentation in both mourning (*Trauer*) – compare Freud's 'work of mourning' (*Trauerarbeit*) - and melancholia. The title *The Origin [Ursprung] of German Tragic Drama* implies that there is a knowable truth which is the 'source' of the drama Benjamin studies, but in the 'Epistemo-Critical Prologue' the origin is what history will reveal; it is discovered or created by a history which itself constitutes the origin. The 'origin' appears posthumously and is inseparable from the constellation or mosaic which is revealed when texts are put together.

The Origin of German Tragic Drama came from a *Habilitations* presented to the University of Frankfurt in 1925. The examiners did not understand it: Benjamin never became a University teacher. The *Trauerspiel*, or tragic drama, means the plays of lamentation or mourning of Lutheran writers and dramatists, many from Silesia, such as Martin Opitz (1597-1639), Andreas Gryphius (1616-64) and Daniel Lohenstein (1635-83), who followed on from the Dutch writer Joost van den Vondel (1587-1679). Gryphius had been influenced by Vondel while he was staying in Leiden (1638-44). Their common context was the Thirty Years' War, (1618-48), which began in the territories of Bohemia, Moravia and Silesia, when the Protestants overthrew the regents of the Catholic Ferdinand II and set up the Calvinist Elector Palatine Frederick V (1596-1632), the 'Winter King', in his place. Many of the plays which constitute the *Trauerspiel* appeared after the Thirty Years' War, meditating upon it. Opitz's poems written between 1620 and 1630, called 'Poems of Consolation in the Adversity of War' (*Trostgedichte in Widerwertigkeit dess Krieges*), saw the War as punishment for original sin. They drew on the Medieval Wheel of Fortune, Lydgate's theme, saw Fortune's favour as delusory, and quoted from Jeremiah's Lamentations.

For the rest of this Introduction, I shall give a reading of part of Benjamin's *Trauerspiel* book: it furnishes many of the terms appearing throughout this study.

'TRAUERSPIEL AND TRAGEDY'

The first chapter, 'Trauerspiel and Tragedy', contrasting these two forms, speaks of melancholy as the dominant emotion of the Lutherans amongst the German dramatists (138). It was not the motivating force of Greek tragedy. Benjamin quotes often from Berlin-based theorists of that drama, such as Herbert Cysarz: the book virtually works by assembling diverse passages which readers must unpick.[23] This drama is differentiated from Aristotle's influence, for Benjamin quotes Martin Opitz, (Calvinist critic and poet, who wrote about the Thirty Years' War, and whose authority was Julius Caesar Scaliger [1484-1558]), that *Trauerspiel* shows the fall of kings:

> [it] is equal in majesty to heroic poetry, except that it seldom suffers from the introduction of characters of lowly estate and ignorable matters: because it deals only with the commands of kings, killings despair, infanticide and patricide, conflagration, incest, war and commotion, lamentation, weeping, sighing and suchlike. (62)[24]

These plays engage with history, with the state (65) and with the sovereign as the incarnation of history. Many deal with the medieval subject of 'the fall of princes'. Benjamin refers to *Maria Stuarda*, the name of a play by Haugwitz, (1647-1706), which was also a play by Vondel, called in the MS, 'Martyred Majesty' - *gemartelde majesteit*) (63). He refers to *Leo Armenius* (Gryphius's first play, of 1646), and to *Catharina von Georgien* (Gryphius, 1647), and to *Carolus Stuardus* (Gryphius's play of 1649 on Charles the First).

---

[23]   Benjamin said of the *Trauerspiel* study that it 'consists almost entirely of quotations. The drollest mosaic technique one can imagine' - quoted in Gary Smith (ed.) *Benjamin: Philosophy, Aesthetics, History* (Chicago: University of Chicago Press, 1989) p. xxxix n.111.

[24]   On the *Trauerspiel* see: Bernhard Ulmer, *Martin Opitz* (New York: Twayne, 1971); Peter Skrine, *The Baroque: Literature and Culture in Sevententh-Century Europe* (London: Macmillan 1978); Jane O. Newman, *The Intervention of Philology: Gender, Learning and Power in Lohenstein's Roman Plays* (Chapel Hill: University of North Carolina Press, 2000); Erika A. Metzger and Michael M. Metzger, *Reading Andreas Gryphius: Critical Trends 1664-1993* (Columbia, SC: Camden House, 1994); Blake Lee Spahr, *Andreas Gryphius: A Modern Perspective* (Columbia SC: Camden House, 1993); Gerald Ernest Paul Gillespie, *Daniel Casper von Lohenstein's Historical Tragedies* (Athens: Ohio State University Press, 1965); Judith Popovich Aikin, *German Baroque Drama* (Boston: Twayne, 1982). The only English edition of the plays is Gerald Gillespie (ed.) *German Theater Before 1750* (New York: Contiunuum, 1992); with a cut version of Gryphius's *Leo Armenius* and Lohenstein's *Sophonisbe*.

There is *Papianus* (Gryphius 1659) and *Agrippina* (Lohenstein).[25] Hallmann, who became a Catholic convert, wrote a play, *Dying Innocence: Or Her Excellency Catherine, Queen of England* (1669-73) which also appears in Benjamin's discussion. The *Trauerspiel* included the drama of the tyrant and the martyr-drama, and these two could be identified with one another, as they unite in the characters of Shakespeare's Richard II, or Henry VI.

Two key Benjaminian terms, *catastrophe* and a *state of emergency* (66) appear within the pattern of the king versus history (tragedy pitted the hero against the gods). *Catastrophe* implies the reverse of the world of beautiful appearance: a fragmented state (Hamlet's 'the time is out of joint'). 'The ruler is designated from the outset as the holder of dictatorial power if war, revolt, or other catastrophes should lead to a state of emergency' (65). But this decisionism is modified because of the discovery of the ruler's vacillating, Hamlet-like (melancholic) state: 'The prince who is responsible for making the decision to proclaim the state of emergency reveals at the first opportunity that he is almost incapable of making a decision' (71). The *state of emergency* comments on the European seventeenth-century, about which it has been said that only seven years (to be precise, 1610, 1669-71 and 1680-82) were without war. Maravall, in *Culture of the Baroque* says baroque culture reacted to crisis-conditions felt at the heart of the state. But Benjamin's phrases comment also on the state of emergency that marked modern Germany from 1918 onwards. The medieval; the Thirty Years' War, and the prelude to the Second World War, link through images of the past.

The *Trauerspiel* contains three topics: first, madness, focussed through Herod the tyrant, figure of also hubris (70). Madness appears through a stress on man as a beast, like Nebuchadnezzar (86). Herod appears in a quotation from Hallmann (1640-1704) in his 1670 play touching on Herod, *Mariamne* (94). Madness reappears in discussion of the representation of the emotions in the Renaissance and the Baroque, where the emotions are emphasised at the expense of action (this compares with *Hamlet*).

> The tempo of the emotional life [in the baroque] is accelerated to such an extent that calm actions, considered decisions occur more and more infrequently. The conflict between sensibility and will in the human norm, which [Alois] Riegl has demonstrated so beautifully in the discord between the attitude of head and body in the figures of Giuliano and Night on the Medici tombs ... extends to the drama. It is particularly striking in the person of the tyrant. In the course of the

---

25 For useful brief comments on these, see Roy Pascal, *German Literature in the Sixteenth and Seventeenth Centuries: Renaissance, Reformation, Baroque* (London: Cresset Press, 1968), pp. 114-119.

> action his will is increasingly undermined by his sensibility: and he
> ends in madness (99).

The use of the Viennese art-critic Riegl compares with the earlier
citation Benjamin has made from him, on his interest in decadent
periods – such as the baroque – as contrasted with the 'classical'
Renaissance (55). Baroque art is tortured, fragmented, out of shape,
decadent: outside classical form.[26] Michelangelo's statues for the
Medici tombs express distortion and so are allegorical, expressions
of extremity and of non-balance – since madness is disturbance of
'the balance of the mind' – and illustrate a decadent / baroque
tendency towards the clash of the will and sensibility. From this
failure of integration, which allegory expresses, comes madness.

A second topos is life as a theatre. As the drama ensures that 'full
robes, crown and sceptre' are not wanting when the king appears on
stage (69), so that he is in presentation pictorial-allegorical, so 'el
gran teatro del mundo' - the title of a play by Calderón (1641)-
pervades the *Trauerspiel*. It exists especially in *La vida es sueno*
(1636) - Calderón's *Life is a Dream*.

> In the drama the play-element was demonstratively emphasised, and
> transcendence was allowed its final word in the worldly disguise of a
> play within a play. (82)

Benjamin also quotes from Lohenstein's *Sophonisbe* (1666):

> our brief life is nothing but a poem. A play in which now one man
> enters and another leaves; with tears it begins and with weeping ends.
> (83)

Tragedy and *Trauerspiel* are distinguished in that the former was
produced on a fixed stage, itself a tribunal, a place for justice, the
sense of injustice being one aspect of the tragic (102-120).
Trauerspiel was 'travelling theatre' (119), for touring troupes acted
these plays, as much as they were performed by Silesian Protestant
gymnasia. The stage in these representations was temporary, set up
for a spectacle connecting mourning and ostentation. The earth is
figured as 'a stage for mournful events' and Gryphius's *Leo Armenius*
is quoted: 'Such a *Trauerspiel* springs from thy vanities! Such a
dance of death [*Todten-Tantz*] is cherished in the world' (120).
Vondel, an Anabaptist who converted to Catholicism, saw the world
as a stage, where each plays his role and gets his share. The trope
makes life allegorical. Peter Skrine emphasises that in Gryphius,
words such as *Traum*, *Wahn* and *Phantasie*, (seldom found in the

---

[26] For Riegl's influence on Benjamin, see Michael W. Jennings, *Dialectical
Images: Walter Benjamin's Theory of Literary Criticism* (Ithaca: Cornell
University Press, 1987), pp. 152-163.

German Bible), indicate how Gryphius's drama, whose subject is transience, focuses on illusion.[27]

A third recurring point is the drama's lack of motivation - as madness may be a symptom of that. Benjamin refers to the 'isolation of times, scenes and types' (75): as in allegory where several different characters are needed to present one person, qualities are kept separate from each other, as distinct entities. The same page refers to the dominance of intrigue, or 'the corrupt energy of schemers' (88) - an invocation of Iago-like qualities. 'Discontent is the classic motive' for the drama (88): it is the word in the first line of *Richard III*, casting light back on the *Henry VI* plays, and it was apparently a new word for the 1590s. Discontent is focussed in the courtier, who provides 'the gloomy note of intrigue' (97), a point repeated in the discussion of 'ministerial intrigue' (125); 'intrigue', too, is a word of the seventeenth century.[28] Calderón distinguishes 'passion' from a 'psychological motive to action' (133). Characterisation is not derived from psychological penetration: Benjamin draws Shakespeare into the *Trauerspiel* by seeing *Othello*'s Iago and *Hamlet*'s Polonius as modelled on the demonic fool (127). In the martyr-drama 'the very estate of man as creature ... provides the reason for the catastrophe' (89) implying that the figures of the drama are 'merely creaturely' so that 'even the life of apparently dead objects secures power over it' (132).[29] To be under the dominion of a object, like Hamlet with the skull of Yorick - then, presumably, a real skull - asks where is life: in the figure or the emblem?

Madness, life as a theatre, and indecision connect with the relationship Benjamin makes between baroque drama and the medieval passion play (75-76). The latter brought on 'tyrants, devils and Jews' as figures of wickedness whose motivations needed no justifying; Benjamin can cite Vincent of Beauvais as a medieval figure whose sense of tragedy and comedy is valid for the seventeenth century (77). Drawing out differences, however, Benjamin suggests that the *Trauerspiel* avoids the subject of fate, or destiny being controlled by the stars, and reads in that a history of

---

27 Cp. 'The dialogue contains interpretive references to the fact that what is happening on the stage is to be understood as an example, that the stage is a metaphor for the world'. Anthony J. Niesz, *Dramaturgy in German Drama: From Gryphius to Goethe* (Heidelburg: Carl Winter: Universitätsverlag, 1980), p. 40.

28 See the discussion by Samuel Weber, 'Genealogy of Modernity: History, Myth and Allegory in Benjamin's *Origin of the German Mourning Play*' *MLN* 106 (1991), 465-500 (p.477).

29 See Charles Rosen, 'The Ruins of Walter Benjamin', in Gary Smith, ed., *Walter Benjamin: Critical Essays and Recollections* (Cambridge, Mass.: MIT Press, 1988), pp. 129-175.

the astrological having been suppressed by respectable Christianity. Pagan tragedy was read in astrological terms by Hildebert of Tours in the eleventh century, and so it could be taken entirely mechanistically (130-31).

PROTESTANT MELANCHOLY

The Counter-Reformation returned to medieval thought about melancholy, while the Reformation, denying the value of good works, returned to yet another earlier, non-Renaissance state, showing the dominance of fate in people's lives. 'Something new arose: an empty world', and in this state:

> mourning is the state of mind in which feeling revives the empty world in the form of a mask, and derives an enigmatic satisfaction in contemplating it. (139)

There is a loss of relationship between the subject and what is outside. For Freud, 'in mourning it is the world which has become poor and empty; in melancholia it is the ego itself'.[30] Both states, mourning and melancholia, seem true here. Perhaps they are, despite Freud's division, indivisible. Benjamin speaks of an increased distance and of 'deadening emotions' coming 'between the self and the surrounding world to the point of alienation from the body'.[31] In this 'pathological state' 'the most simple object appears to be a symbol of some enigmatic wisdom because it lacks any natural, creative relationship to us'. In *Melencolia I* 'the utensils of active life are lying around unused on the floor, as objects of contemplation'. The melancholic turns the signs of activity into objects contemplated from an alienated view. The description half-quotes a description of the setting for Eternity's Prologue in Gryphius's play *Catharina von Georgien*: 'a whole collection of stage properties are lying scattered about the floor' (124). Dürer's *Melencolia I* anticipates the baroque. Unable to relate to the outside, 'the baroque explores libraries. Its meditations are devoted to books' (140), books therefore being markers of alienation.

The prince is the 'paradigm of the melancholy man' (142), and is associated with madness. An emotional state such as Jealousy relates, in Lohenstein's *Sophonisbe*, to the passion of the 'insane melancholic' (145), for a passion, or emotional state, is seen as a mental disorder; Benjamin quotes the Munich writer Aegidius Albertinus that the melancholic should be chained, as mad. In the

---

[30] Freud, 'Mourning and Melancholia', *On Metapsychology : The Penguin Freud 11* (Harmondsworth: Penguin 1977), p. 254.
[31] Compare Benjamin on Kafka: 'the most forgotten alien land is one's own body', *Illuminations* p. 132. See also Maravall's discussion of alienation, in relation to baroque *furor*, p. 213.

Renaissance understandings of melancholy, Benjamin notes a 'conventional' (Aristotelian) link between madness and melancholy (147). To explicate that he turns to Panofsky and Saxl, and to Karl Giehlow (149). Drawing on this research, melancholy becomes ambiguous, associable with sloth and dullness, like Medieval *acedia*, or with intelligence and contemplation. It can be sublime, or sluggish and depressed.

The argument recalls the physiological explanations for melancholy which were provided by the idea of the 'humours'. This mode of thinking about the body developed from Hippocrates (5c. BCE) to the Pergamon-born Galen, of the second century. Author of *De locis affectis* ('Of the Affected Parts'), Galen became the main medieval authority. He made the brain the centre of the nervous system, affected by the humours that rise into it. In 'humours' psychology, digested food passes into the liver which produces four humours, blood, yellow bile, phlegm and black bile, which make up the body's liquid content. Blood is hot and moist, choler (yellow bile) hot and dry. Phlegm is cold and moist, black bile (Greek *melaina chole*) cold and dry. Blood and choler produce a warm and wet temperament, sanguine, appropriate for the spring of the year, and like fire. The opposite is phlegm and water, (the wintry phlegmatic person). A temperament dominated by yellow bile is choleric, hot and moist being characteristic of air and of summer. Dry and cold produce black bile: melancholy (autumn, the dominance of the cold, dry earth).

Perhaps *choler* and *bile* come from common Greek sources. 'Atrabile' was 'anciently used for an imaginary fluid, thick, black, and acrid, supposed to be secreted by the renal or atrabiliary glands, or by the spleen, and to be the cause of melancholy' (OED). Hence 'atrabilious'. The spleen, spongy and of loose texture, soaked up the black bile. In Gower's *Confessio Amantis*, 'The Splen is to Malencolie / Assigned for herbergerie' [lodging].[32] It also produces laughter and mirth, so that it implies passion, speaking either in jest, or from the heart, or in caprice, or demonstrating a hot or proud temper, or violent ill-will, or ill-humour, or moroseness. Most of these uses appear in Shakespeare; spleen as 'excessive dejection' appears in 1644 (OED). Melancholy was 'choler adust', or 'melancholia adust'. 'Adust' means browned, as if scorched by fire, and was expresed in the body's dryness, its symptom sallowness. 'Melancholia adusta' was burnt black bile, or came from the burning of yellow bile to black. Michael Dols says that Galen developed an

---

[32] *Confessio Amantis* 7. 449-50 in *The Complete Works of John Gower* 4 vols, ed. by G.A. Macaulay (Oxford: Clarendon Press, 1901).

'incinerator principle' based on a unidirectional transformation of the humours: cooking could transform one humour to another, 'phlegm could become blood, blood could become yellow bile and yellow bile, black bile'.[33]

But Aristotle had linked genius with madness within the concept of melancholy; melancholy furthered a prophetic ability (147). Hence the pseudo-Aristotelian argument of *Problemata* XXX: 'Why is it that all those who have become eminent in philosophy or poetry or the arts are clearly melancholics, and some of them to such an extent as to be affected by dreams caused by black bile?' Marsilio Ficino linked creativity and melancholia with Plato's 'divine frenzy' where the soul is in an ecstasy which petrifies and almost kills the body.[34] Benjamin quotes Ficino that the melancholy god (Saturn) 'seldom imprints his mark on ordinary characters and ordinary destinies, but on men who are different from others, who are divine or bestial, happy or bowed down under the profoundest misery' (149-150). Saturn, or Cronos, is both the God of the golden age, of the Saturnalia and carnival, god of agriculture and the earth - as melancholy is of the earth - but also mournful, dethroned and dishonoured.

So doubleness pervades melancholy: Benjamin contrasts the Ficino-like melancholy of Melanchthon with the negative state of Luther's, the dominant spirit of the Reformation and Counter-Reformation (138). Baroque melancholia broke with the Renaissance and, reverting to the humours model, showed an affinity with the medieval (145). Three forms making up 'saturnine man' co-exist in Dürer: humoural melancholia, melancholy as furor and genius, melancholy as *acedia*. Doubleness shows since 'melancholy betrays the world for the sake of knowledge. But in its tenacious self-absorption, it embraces dead objects in its contemplation, in order to redeem them' (157). Benjamin thinks of the betrayal of courtiers in intrigue-drama. Desire for knowledge is melancholic since requiring a mortification of objects, but the world as 'dead objects' in *Melencolia I* fascinates: things are sundered from meanings and have lost their place, and allegory starts in contemplating death.

'ALLEGORY AND TRAUERSPIEL'

The second chapter introduces the Romantic discrimination against allegory and for symbolism: in Goethe, Schopenhauer or Yeats, or, here, Coleridge:

---

[33] Michael W. Dols, *Majunun: The Madman in Medieval Islamic Society* (Oxford: Clarendon Press, 1992), p. 19.
[34] On this, see Panofsky, p. 165.

an allegory is but a translation of abstract notions into a picture-language, which is itself nothing but an abstraction from objects of the senses [...] on the other hand a symbol [...] is characterized by the translucence of the special in the individual, or of the general in the special, or of the universal in the general; above all by the translucence of the eternal through and in the temporal. It always partakes of the reality which renders intelligible; and while it enunciates the whole, abides itself as a living part in that unity of which it is the representative.[35]

Abstract notions become picture-language, but this language is also abstract, and dead, separate from the immediacy of the symbol. Benjamin argues for the relevance of allegory by differentiating it from the symbol as sign; allegory is 'not essentially different from writing' (162), and so, as in deconstruction, outside the intention imposed in symbolism:

Whereas in the symbol destruction is idealized and the transfigured face of nature is fleetingly revealed in the light of redemption, in allegory the observer is confronted with the *facies hippocratica* [death's head] of history as a petrified primordial landscape. Everything about history that, from the very beginning has been untimely, sorrowful, unsuccessful, is expressed in a face - or rather in a death's head. (166)

The contrast is between *nature* and *history*. Symbolism by its idealism and quality of being spontaneous, seems to arise from nature whose 'face' it celebrates as capable of redemption. Benjamin speaks of 'natural history' (47), one not idealized, or given symbolic status - becoming a history of humanist progress - which would imply development away from nature. In allegory, history means not humanist progress or redemption but sorrow and fragmentariness, and it is a 'petrified primordial landscape' - and if petrified, under the Medusa's stare. There can be no movement in the lifeless object such as Yorick's skull - bone being akin to stone - handed to Hamlet by the gravedigger who started to dig graves on the day that Hamlet was born. Allegory as an art of death recalls death, and:

death digs most deeply the jagged line of demarcation between physical nature and significance. But if nature has always been subject to the power of death, it is also true that it has always been allegorical. (166)

The first sentence distinguishes nature and allegory. Death separates physical nature and significance: nothing in nature has an inherent significance, hence the need for allegory, but to speak about nature, or death, requires allegory, for neither can be brought into representation. The symbol makes Nature 'natural', feminine,

---

[35] The statement from *The Statesman's Manual* (1816) is quoted by Michael Davitt Bell, *The Development of American Romance: The Sacrifice of Relation* (Chicago: University of Chicago Press, 1980), p. 131.

maternal, but these are no more than allegories. The history of the disappearance of allegory after the seventeenth century is that of Enlightenment and post-Enlightenment thought making nature seem *less* allegorical, becoming the basis by which 'the natural' is established, as if this was outside history. But Benjamin reads history as more 'primordial' than nature, constructing nature which is 'imprinted by history' (173).

The second section (167-174), discusses the origins of baroque allegory. While maintaining continuities with the medieval, it draws out differences, since it follows Giehlow in returning to the Renaissance emblem and its debt to the *Horapollo*. Discovered in 1419 and printed in 1505, this document of the 4th century CE, attempted to read Egyptian hieroglyphics as a secret writing. Post-Ficino scholars took the hieroglyph as an image of divine ideas, whose significance was its non- 'natural' interpretability, and power of instruction. The word 'rebus' for which the OED gives 1512 as a first use, is used by Benjamin here, and it is a reminder that allegory connects with Freud; dreams are allegorical since a dream is a rebus.[36] Renaissance emblems instructed because everything in nature was seen as an 'emblematic representation',' 'irremediably different from its historical realization. In moral fables and in catastrophes, history served only as an aspect of the subject-matter of emblematics' – whose signifying value was thus in excess of history.

Whereas 'medieval allegory is Christian and didactic – in the mystic and natural-historical respect the baroque is descended from antiquity' (171). Benjamin showed that the baroque recalled the 'grotesque', the atmosphere of old Roman burial chambers whose secrets were being uncovered, and whose buried forms provided emblems. The OED gives Lydgate for an early use of the 'emblem'; the Renaissance made all nature emblematic, where an emblem is inlaid or engraved work, like the inscription on a coin. So, 'where nature bears the imprint of history, that is to say, where it is a setting, does it not have a numismatic quality?' (173). What inscribes nature is history, indeed, Benjamin writes elsewhere that 'the range of life must be determined by history rather than by nature'.[37] Life is not a pregiven, outside history; history is both life and inscription.

Yet in allegorical interpretation, quoting Giehlow, 'one and the same object can just as easily signify a virtue as a vice, and therefore more or less anything' (174). The following section (174-177) evokes this: if 'any person, any object, any relationship can mean absolutely anything else' - a potential since 'truth is the death of intention' (36)

---

[36] Freud, *The Interpretation of Dreams: Penguin Freud 4* (Harmondsworth: Penguin, 1976), p. 382.
[37] 'The Task of the Translator', *Illuminations*, p. 71.

including intention in writing - then there is a refusal of idealization, within the 'profane world' which is marked by the Fall, and so death. And this giving up of the 'detail' of the world (175) because of death, allows in 'ambiguity' - which Benjamin discusses by comparing allegory as *script* to the symbol as *picture*.

> In the field of allegorical intuition, the image is a fragment, a rune. Its beauty as a symbol evaporates when the light of divine learning [which would remove it from that which can be understood 'naturally'] falls upon it. The false appearance of totality is extinguished. For the *eidos* disappears, the simile ceases to exist, and the cosmos it contained shrivels up. The dry rebuses which remain contain an insight which is still available to the confused investigator [the 'introvert', the brooder (140) of *Melencolia I*]. ... Classicism [the spirit of the Renaissance, reappearing in the Enlightenment] was not permitted to behold the lack of freedom ... the collapse of the beautiful, physical nature. But beneath its extravagant pomp, that is precisely what baroque allegory proclaims. (176)

Nature is dead, history is life, but in the form of ruins. The word 'ruin' runs through the next section (177-182), as in: 'allegories are in the realm of thoughts what ruins are in the realm of things' (178).[38] Thoughts, too, are ruins, marked by death; no thought exists as complete, or total. Benjamin quotes Borinski, writing in 1924, that 'antiquity in the modern world is only to be seen in its material form, as a picturesque field of ruins'. Borinski cites Renaissance pictures such as one by Domenico Ghirlandaio where the birth of Christ is set in the ruins of an antique temple. But for Benjamin, the modern world shows (not progress but) ruins.[39] In the baroque, the allegorist 'pile[s] up fragments ceaselessly, without any strict idea of a goal' (178). Nature is 'eternal transcience', 'and here alone did the saturnine vision of this generation recognize history. Its monuments, ruins, are, according to Agrippa von Nettesheim, the home of the saturnine beasts. In the process of decay ... the events of history shrivel up and become absorbed in the setting. The quintessence of these decaying objects is the polar opposite to the idea of transfigured nature as conceived by the early renaissance'. (179-80). In the Renaissance, nature seems to signify but in baroque allegory nature is fallen, and 'bears the imprint of the progression of history'.

---

[38] For the ruin, compare Maravall, pp. 186-8.

[39] However much "ruin" links with the catastrophic effects of Fascism, for Benjamin to see the modern world as ruins is not simply negative (whereas to see everything in terms of progress would be): see *Charles Baudelaire: A Lyric Poet in the Era of High Capitalism*, trans. by Harry Zohn (London: New Left Books, 1973), p. 176. The *Trauerspiel* study, nonetheless, emphasises what there is of mourning in the concept of the ruin.

Symbolism affirms the permanence of nature ('the symbol ... remains persistently the same'); but 'the object becomes allegorical under the gaze of melancholy' and 'melancholy causes life to flow out of it and it remains behind dead ... exposed to the allegorist ... unconditionally in his power' (183). The 'gaze' may be Medusan, petrifying a conception of the primacy of nature as life. The object 'is now quite incapable of emanating any meaning or significance of its own; such significance as it has, it acquires from the allegorist'. (183-4). So allegory, in the last section, is the melancholic's only pleasure (185).

Medieval allegory had thought of 'the futility of the world events and the transience of the creature as stations on the road to salvation' (81). Baroque allegory saw the same as 'stations of [the world's] decline' (166). Yet this is not an absolute difference between the medieval and the baroque, and the melancholy actuating allegorical thinking is not only Protestant.[40] Its genealogy is in the medieval. The allegory which fragments, emptying and divesting the world of meaning while piling up the allegorical fragments 'in desolate, sorrowful dispersal' (186), depends upon melancholia's power. The 'primacy of the thing over the personal' and 'the fragment over the real' is a 'confrontation between the allegory and the symbol' (187). Benjamin adds a point from Cysarz, on allegorical personification as the ultimate non-spiritualization of things.

The last part (215-235) focuses on the corpse, 'the key figure of the early allegory',[41] quoting from a seventeenth century piece on emblematics: 'The whole body cannot enter a symbolical icon, but it is not inappropriate for part of the body to constitute it'.[42] For the body gives only an illusion of a substantial unity, while body parts emphasise differences which render that unity unreal; pain is that which shows up difference within the body. The most complete example of the fragment in the plays is the corpse, as opposed to the classical statue, feature of symbolic art. Both speak of death, but differently: the corpse is the 'pre-eminent' emblematic property (218), since the body is the 'other' of the subject and the production of it as the fragmented corpse - fragmented already when divided from the animating spirit - is that for which characters die. Nor is the corpse barren of meaning: hair and nails still grow from it. The live body has the appearance of the symbol, (here meaning is repressed or

---

[40] Heinz-Dieter Kittsteiner, 'The Allegory of the Philosophy of History', in Michael P. Steinberg, *Walter Benjamin and the Demands of History* (Ithaca: Cornell University Press, 1996) says that this stress on melancholy came from Florens Christian Rang (p. 54).

[41] Walter Benjamin, 'Central Park', *NGC* 34 (1985), 32-58 (p. 53).

[42] For death in the baroque, see Maravall, pp. 65 and 164.

tamed as hair and nails are cut), but the dead body, the fragment, is allegorical since it points to the loss of that symbolic meaning, while still continuing to signify something.[43] The body, from which the self had seemed alienated (140), reappears in its difference. It is as if this is what history, in an anti-Hegelian manner, has worked to produce: the body visibly presents ruin.

The corpse invites comparison between the Baroque and Medieval Christianity. Three affinities appear: the struggle against the pagan gods, the triumph of allegory and the torment of the flesh. The pagan gods represent the triumph of the flesh, their lives and the myths surrounding them being preserved only in allegory, which is 'an appreciation of the transience of things and the concern to rescue them for eternity' (223). But allegory is also associated with relating guilt to such pagan gods (recast as idols) and to the 'flesh' which allegory, as dualistic, stigmatizes. Western allegory cuts deep because it is inseparable from the existence of a sense of guilt, more intense in the Baroque because of the Renaissance revival of the repressed pagan gods (226). The medieval had bound the material world and the demonic together, concentrating demonic powers into one Satanic figure, who at the same time frustrates interpretation - creating melancholia in his turn. Benjamin refers to the 'devilish jocularity of the intriguer, his intellectuality, his knowledge of significance' (227). The devil as diabolic 'throws down', - annihilates - the neatness of allegorical division, brings systems of thought to nothing. Such a figure as Shakespeare's Richard III becomes allegorical himself, like the devil. Richard has two powers: causing 'terror in mourning' and initiating men into knowledge, which, as a form of alienation, separating the self which contemplates from the object of knowledge, engenders melancholia, and, as seen before, death: hence Benjamin speaks of 'mourning, which is at once the mother of allegories and their content' (230).[44]

---

[43] On this, see Gerhard Richter, *Walter Benjamin and the Corpus of Autobiography* (Detroit: Wayne State University Press, 2000), pp. 58-63.

[44] In 'On Narcissism: An Introduction' Freud writes:

> The complaints made by paranoics also show that at bottom the self-criticism of conscience coincides with the self-observation on which it is based. Thus the activity of the mind which has taken over the function of conscience has also placed itself at the service of internal research, which furnishes philosophy with the material for its intellectual operations. This may have some bearing of the characteristic tendency of paranoics to construct speculative systems. (*On Metapsychology*, p. 91)

In 1914, Freud has not yet spoken of the superego, but he sees its activity, nontheless, as constructing systems of thought, which also turn on itself. Knowledge, then, including self-knowledge, comes from the self that makes a

The last pages discuss the futility of this knowledge, which shows the climax of subjectivity. Allegory anticipates that awareness of futility by being allegorical, its symbols being allegories of transience (232) - which means the transience of its own form of knowledge.

> It is to misunderstand the allegorical entirely if we make a distinction between the store of images, in which this about-turn into salvation and redemption takes place, and that grim store which signifies death and damnation. For it is precisely visions of the frenzy of destruction, in which all earthly things collapse into a heap of ruins, which reveal the limit set upon allegorical contemplation, rather than its ideal quality. The bleak confusion of Golgotha [the charnel house] which can be recognized as the schema underlying the allegorical figures in hundreds of the engravings and descriptions of the period, is not just a symbol of the desolation of human existence. In it transitoriness is [...] displayed as allegory. (232)

This makes allegory born of melancholia, a form of madness, or 'frenzy' in the desire to abolish meaning, and to promote death, or the ruin. It enables a reading of the allegorical presentations of death which run through the art of the late medieval. 'Macabre', (1376, OED) seems to have first appeared in Jean le Fèvre's *Respit de la Mort*, where the author claims to have written a work called *la danse Macabré*. There was the new urban charnel-house. The OED cites *Piers Plowman* (BVI. 48-9) for 'charnel': 'For in charnel at chirche cherles ben yuel [hard] to knowe, / Or a knyght from a knaue'.[45] (The medieval city has the literal charnel house, the modern city the old curiosity shop, an allegorical charnel-house.) There was the Dance of the Dead motif, prominent in Paris in 1424, including verses which Lydgate translated. It extended to Holbein's *The Dance of Death* woodcuts (1538). The *ubi sunt* motif, the *transi* tomb, the skulls within Renaissance art and drama, as in Holbein's *Ambassadors* (1533), or *Hamlet*, and as in the chapel in Milan whose walls are wholly built out of skulls may have a mad impulse within them, but they make the subject-matter of the text vanity, or emptiness, allegory ruining meaning. The death's-head in *The Ambassadors*, like the rest of the picture a triumph of Renaissance perspectivalism, allegorizes the emblems of learning and knowledge (products of the skull) showcased on the shelves in the picture. Renaissance learning

---

difference between itself and the other, and therefore, the primary knowledge is of evil: a suspicion of the other. Benjamin's melancholic works in the same way; the desire to know is one that sets up a split within perception.

[45] William Langland, *The Vision of Piers Plowman*, ed. by A.V.C. Schmidt (London: Dent, 1987) p. 67.

as the modern is undercut by the older medieval, ghosting the terms of the new.[46]

Inadequacy in allegory to give anything objective nullifies the material content of the *Trauerspiel* which turns thereby into an image of redemption of the profane world, which was pronounced of no value. These last pages battle with two propositions by which Benjamin vindicates this art: the significance of the allegorical insight and of melancholy, and allegory's lack of power to be other than an image. Everything then depends on the idea that allegory presumes an afterlife. Its life begins from the assumption of its own deadness in its time. The writings and the art that produced the art of death seemed to know that. And that which as the art of death takes itself out of an idealist, progressive view of history as developmental has the potential of 'living on' - the title of an essay of Derrida's, to be discussed in chapter 1 - whereas that which assumed its life existed in a past historical moment has by that been replaced within history.

III – ALLEGORY AND MELANCHOLY: AFTER BENJAMIN

The *Trauerspiel* reads modernity as ruins. Belief in the power of the ahistorical and timeless symbol denies or represses this perception. Reading back to Benjamin's material in the baroque means picking up on its relatedness to 'the middle ages'. Transitions between the medieval and the baroque produce images which illuminate present modernity. Langland and Chaucer, Hoccleve, Lydgate and Henryson are my figures for this transition, and the final chapters discuss early Shakespeare.

The mosaic, which fragments into particles, and the philosophical treatise, Benjamin says, are products of the middle ages. They are comparable. Thinking of the crumbled mosaic, Benjamin speaks of the value of 'fragments of thought' (29). These compose themselves as images: the medieval world is not a single complete 'discarded image' to looked at nostalgically, but fragments for use; and 'truth content is only to be grasped through immersion in the most minute details of subject-matter'.

A 'frenzy of destruction', a desire to fragment, to bring about death may be a secret drive in medieval texts, producing something more intense than appears in Johann Huizinga's study with the English title *The Waning of the Middle Ages* (more neutrally, *The Autumn of the Middle Ages*, *Herfsttij der Middeleeuwen* - except that

---

[46] On this picture, see Jurgis Baltrusaitis, *Anamorphic Art*, trans. by W.J. Strachan (Cambridge: Chadwyck-Healey, 1977), pp. 91-114.

autumn is the time for melancholia so that the title is still not neutral). Huizinga's work may be compared with Benjamin, who comments on it in the *Arcades* project.[47] Huizinga rejects Burkhardt's 'northern renaissance', and reads the period of 'the waning of the middle ages' as revealing a psychic split. As in Malory, there is a holding on to ideas of chivalry when political realities (the ending of the Crusades, the development of a new urban world, the collapse of chivalric ideals in such campaigns as the Hundred Years' War and the Wars of the Roses) made these no more than an empty form. But they are grasped the more minutely the more they became formalistic. A double standard of ideal chivalry and of low expediency resulted in 'pessimism and the ideal of the sublime life', and 'the violent tenor of life' - two of Huizinga's chapter-titles - and, in a society which cannot think through its contradictions, 'the marked tendency of life to embody itself in images'.[48] That is the allegorical impulse. Medieval images, which put Biblical events into then contemporary fashions, thus doubling the image, are inherently allegorical. For, as Craig Owens, who sees the image as a rebus, a pictorial image which is also writing, says, 'allegory occurs whenever one text is doubled by another'.[49] This reading could extend to allegories such as Bosch's paintings, and here it might be noted that these are also fascinated by fragmentation - that of the body, at the moment when the whole body, in portraiture, was entering into early modern visual culture.[50] Fascination with the fragment, which includes a desire to produce it, and the impulse to allegorize, map onto each other, and the tendency of life to *embody* itself in images implies a desire for only half-legibility, for the image as enigmatic, secret.

---

[47] *The Waning of the Middle Ages: A Study of the Forms of Life, Thought and Art in France and the Netherlands in the Fourteenth and Fifteenth Centuries* appeared in 1919; its English translation by F. Hopman in 1924. See Margaret Aston, 'Huizinga's Harvest: England and the Waning of the Middle Ages', *Medievalia et Humanistica* n.s. 9 (1979), 1-24 and Edward Peters and Walter P. Simons, 'The New Huizinga and the Old Middle Ages', *Speculum* 74 (1999), 587-620. For Benjamin on Huizinga, see *Walter Benjamin: The Arcades Project*, trans. by Howard Eiland and Kevin McLaughlin (Cambridge Mass.: Harvard University Press, 1999), pp. 210, 376, 402, 481-2.

[48] Huizinga, p. 147. For a reading of the fourteenth century in the spirit of Huizinga, see Jacqueline Cerquiglini-Toulet, *The Color of Melancholy: The Use of Books in the Fourteenth Century*, trans. by Lydia G. Cochrane (Baltimore: Johns Hopkins University Press, 1997).

[49] Craig Owens, 'The Allegorical Impulse: Toward a Theory of Postmodernism', in *Beyond Recognition: Representation, Power and Culture* (Berkeley: University of California Press, 1994), p. 53; see also p. 57.

[50] See Lacan's interest in this: Jacques Lacan, *Ecrits: A Selection*, trans. by Alan Sheridan (London: Tavistock, 1977), pp. 4, 11-12.

Huizinga's middle ages, which could not be escaped from into a renaissance, and so received no closure, attempted to 'act the vision of a dream' (p. 39) in a society motivated by violence, anxiety and, because of the dominance of the chivalric ideology, by the lack of values that were not empty forms.[51] The melancholic implications at times, as with Langland and Hoccleve, shade into madness - perhaps 'mania' in medieval terms. Freud's work of mourning (*Trauerarbeit*)[52] extends to the *Melancholiearbeit* and even the *Allegoriearbeit* - the work of melancholy and the work of allegory. Where the cross-over between madness and melancholia lies is uncertain, but perhaps it is not necessary to accept a definition of madness which works within a modern clinical framework. Perhaps madness is always a form of melancholy – the universal disease which no one escapes, according to Burton in *The Anatomy of Melancholy*. *Acedia* is the affect undoing all others, while its negativity is also structuring them. The *Melancholiearbeit* destroys systematicity, though it may, in paranoid forms, be inseparable from the impulse to systematize. Ambivalent, it sets up an adversarial relationship with that which is also productive of melancholia: the writing of allegory. Since allegory extends to nature, mad and non-mad behaviours relate to a non-determinate state, which begins to collapse the systemic structures allegory is commonly taken to support. The *Allegoriearbeit* relates to melancholia since it brings into representation emotional states, but undoes them as single forms of existence.

Freud's *Trauerarbeit* relates to the *Trauerspiel*, and both necessitate my drawing on two writers who have done much, not necessarily through conscious influence, to extend Benjamin's and Freud's thinking about death: Blanchot and Derrida. Links between these are also made through Paul de Man.[53] Derrida's work supplements Benjamin's, and in relation to the texts here, constellating death, melancholy and mourning, and allegory, proposes

---

[51] See Edward Peters and Walter P. Simons, 'The New Huizinga and the Old Middle Ages', *Speculum* 74 (1999), 587-620.

[52] *Mourning and Melancholia*, p. 253.

[53] See Jacques Derrida, 'Force of Law: The Mystical Foundation of Authority' in Drucilla Cornell, Michel Rosenfeld and David Gray Carlson, eds., *Deconstruction and the Possibility of Justice* (New York: Routledge, 1992), pp. 3-67; *Spectres of Marx: The State of the Debt, the Work of Mourning and the New International*, trans. by Peggy Kamuf (New York: Routledge, 1994); Paul de Man, 'The Rhetoric of Temporality' in *Blindness and Insight*, 2nd edn (Minneapolis: University of Minnesota Press, 1983), pp. 187-229 and '"Conclusions": Walter Benjamin's "The Task of the Translator"', in *The Resistance to Theory* (Minneapolis: University of Minnesota Press, 1986), pp. 73-105.

the theme: how the work of allegory writes death in late medieval texts, where death is subject and cause of melancholia.

In Langland, death is part of allegorical representation; within Chaucer, death arrests the knight (as in the 'modern instances' of *The Monk's Tale*) and concludes *The Knight's Tale*; in Hoccleve, death is at the core of madness, because of the blanks in his memory; it is at the heart of Lydgate's *Fall of Princes* and it exists in the condition of life in Henryson; in Shakespeare's *Henry VI* plays it opens the trilogy. In the first chapter (Langland), allegory, madness and the identity of the subject who speaks of himself autobiographically, seem to have fused. I continue with the knight in Chaucer, regarding him as ultimately figural of the death he discusses in his *Tale*. Melancholy links here to the dominance of Saturn. The knight whose ethos is the maintenance of order shows also its subversion, and his vulnerability appears through a backward look from Chaucer at Yvain's madness in Chrétien de Troyes. His world is also discussed in relation to Dürer's *The Knight, Death and the Devil*, where the knight guards himself against the other, the engraving a parallel and contrast to *Melencolia I*.

The third chapter discusses Hoccleve, one of the first in English whose *Complaint*, an autobiographical account of his madness, articulates subjectivity and a state of madness. Allegory constructs his subjectivity, through the agency of Thought, personified and split off as part of himself. Autobiographical writing is haunted by allegory, and there seems an intimate relationship between thinking allegorically and thinking obsessionally, being held by allegory and being held by madness. The following chapter is on Lydgate, on the catastrophes of *The Fall of Princes*, a collection of medieval tragedies, like the *Trauerspiel*'s 'moral examples and catastrophes' (170). Lydgate's writings are not mad, but the spirit collecting them may be read symptomatically. The attraction of the death-state appears in the chapter on Henryson's *Testament of Cresseid*. His text embodies another form of melancholia, from age, or exhaustion, as though identifying with Saturn, the figure of decay.

The last chapter examines Shakespeare's *Henry VI* plays and the conclusion to everything looks at *Richard III* (c.1592). Their narrative time relates to the period in which Lydgate wrote, and they relate to texts such as the *Mirror for Magistrates* (1559) which revised Lydgate. Here, life in the court is as life in the theatre, and there is also a fascination with decay: a word the OED dates to 1460. Women undo the chivalric world: Joan la Pucelle, Eleanor of Cobham, Margaret of Anjou. Jack Cade represents the 'churles rebellynge', potent threat in Chaucer: this is analogous to madness and carnival and the dance of the dead. But the rebellion feared is exceeded by the frenzy of destruction instinct in the allegorical trickster, and the theatrical figure, Richard III, embodying confusion and frenzy in himself. The plays desire the apocalypse they begin with.

Here are fragments of a 'history of the (European) subject', where the subject must think in terms of personal responsibility which constitutes it as primordially guilty, and so melancholic, and death-marked.[54] In these texts we keep revisiting the use of the mirror and see how the face and the portrait become part of a fixing of being, seeing the power of the internalized demand to confession, and to the sense of death as inside and outside the subject, to the body as abject and to the subject as constructed by complaint - that strange Chaucerian word - and lamentation. Thinking about the individual intensifies, as in the allegorical dialogues which the subject holds with itself, and the Shakespearian soliloquy. These, melancholic, speak a divided relationship to the objectified body.

I began with Cortazar's *Hopscotch*, on novel-writing. The avant-garde writer Morelli says that the Middle Ages saw art as 'a series of images'. This was replaced in the modern period by art as 'the representation of reality', which Manet reversed:

> [A]t the very moment in which the representation of reality was becoming objective, and ultimately photographic and mechanical, a brilliant Parisian who wanted to be realistic should be moved by [Manet's] formidable genius to return art to its function as the creator of images.

If these late medieval texts offer images, more than a narrative that Enlightenment thought has pulled away from, they may be put alongside the image of the present. They cannot be excluded save by the post-Enlightenment idea of an historical continuous narrative which has laid the past to rest. Reading those images, 'one of the times of the so-called Middle Ages can coincide with the times of the Modern Ages' and move our perceptions of how we theorize the modern.

---

[54] Jacques Derrida, *The Gift of Death*, trans. by David Wills (Chicago: University of Chicago Press, 1995), p. 50. See also p. 3 (for the history of sexuality), and p. 51 for guilt as originary.

CHAPTER 1

Triumphs of Allegory: *Piers Plowman*

Piers Plowman by William Langland, written near the end of the fourteenth century, is not an easy text to begin with. That is so, however attractive the poem's opening is, and however triumphant parts of it are - for example, the exceptionally wonderfully vivid passages of the crucifixion, and the harrowing of Hell.[1] In *Piers Plowman*, which looks as if it was the production of a whole lifetime that revised it and rethought it, strenuous textual efforts are made to discover how the soul may be saved. That drive, which looks positive, turns the poem inwards, and makes it autobiographical, so that 'William Langland' names a problem. Questioning the nature of the subject who speaks - and *why* he must speak is also a question - emphasises a negativity expressed in several moments of the poem, and whose various effects are the substance of this chapter.

In the poem's several versions and rewritings, each says more, and less, and each needs the other. Material discarded, redistributed or reassigned makes all modern commentary work on a plural text never available at the time of writing. Though cutting it, the third version, the C text, cannot repress the memory of Piers tearing the Pardon in the second version, the B text.[2] Successive lengthenings from A to B to C, assuming that that is the right order, indicate an authorial obsessiveness only partially readable, and each version has moments of violent interruption of passages of painstaking detail. In the last

---

[1] In the B text, Passus XVIII, in the C text, Passus XX.

[2] Quotations come from A.V.C.Schmidt, *William Langland, Piers Plowman: A Parallel-text Edition of the A, B,C and Z Versions* (London: Longman, 1995). Where I have not specified otherwise, I use the C text. I also take B from the edition of A.V.C. Schmidt (London: Dent, 1987) and to the C text edited by Derek Pearsall (Exeter: University of Exeter Press, 1994), cited here as Pearsall. I have also used W.W. Skeat, *The Vision of William Concerning Piers the Plowman* (Oxford: Clarendon Press, 1886) 2 vols, and the editions of a A text (by George Kane) the B (George Kane and E.T. Donaldson) and the C (George Russell and George Kane (London: Athlone, 1988-1997). On the texts, including the Z text, which was brought out by A.G. Rugg and Charlotte Brewer (Toronto: Pontifical Institute, 1983), see Kathryn Kerby-Fulton, "*Piers Plowman*" in David Wallace, ed., *The Cambridge History of Medieval English Literature* (Cambridge: Cambridge University Press, 1999), pp. 513-538.

Joseph S. Wittig, *William Langland Revisited* (Boston: Twayne, 1997) dates the A text between 1370 and 1375 and the B, twice as long as the A, between 1377 and 1380 and the C, which revises all of B with the exception of the last two Passus, (and includes revisions of B's revisions of A) between 1380 and 1388. The earliest surviving text is 1400, and 50 manuscript copies survive. For guides to the poem see: Malcolm Godden, *The Making of Piers Plowman* (London: Longman, 1990), James Simpson, *Piers Plowman: An Introduction to the B Text* (London: Longman, 1990), Ralph Hanna III, *William Langland: Authors of the Middle Ages 3* (Aldershot: Ashgate 1993).

line of B and C, the sleeper wakes from a crisis-situation, which is that of the chaos of the then present-day church, but his state of living on allows him to wake neither from allegory, nor from his waking melancholia.[3] Calling this chapter 'triumphs of allegory' evokes Derrida's essay 'Living On: Border Lines', a piece simultaneously discussing Shelley and Maurice Blanchot.[4] One of Derrida's arguments, concentrating on the meaning of 'of', implies that this chapter's title could be 'triumphs of allegory' or 'triumphs over allegory' - as in the text's interruptions of its various forms of

---

[3] The text as part of a crisis of the fourteenth century is discussed by Charles Muscatine, *Poetry and Crisis in the Age of Chaucer* (Notre Dame: University of Notre Dame Press, 1972) pp. 71-110. He cites the view of Jeffrey Burton Russell, 'the period from 1349 to 1470 was a Golden Age only for bacteria' (p.148). On the enabling power of the text, e.g. its relationship with Lollardy see David .A. Lawton, 'Lollardy and the 'Piers Plowman Tradition', *Modern Language Review* 76 (1981), 780-793. On the use of *Piers Plowman* for the rising of 1381, see Steven Justice, *Writing and Rebellion: England in 1381* (Berkeley: University of California Press, 1994), pp. 102-139, arguing that the poem offered a 'language that could be formed ad hoc out of the common tongue to serve particular interests and to be mobilized against others' (p. 137). See also David Aers, informed by empirical historical study of England after the Pestilence, and attempting to rescue a medieval community, 'to discover where people spoke from, to whom they spoke, and in response to what questions ... [for]... nothing could be more mistaken than to abstract the unitary ambitions of certain discourses propagated by social elites and use these ... as adequate descriptions of medieval cultures' (Introduction to *Culture and History 1350-1600: Essays on English Communities and Writing*, ed. by Aers, (London: Harvester, 1992), p. 2). Here, Langland's imaginative insights dissolve received oppressive and 'inherited' (not unconscious) 'ideologies'. See also Aers' *Chaucer, Langland and the Creative Imagination* (London: Routledge and Kegan Paul, 1980), pp 1-37; his *Medieval Literature: Criticism, Ideology and History* (New York: St Martin's Press, 1986), pp. 58-73, on the dissolving of allegory's spiritualizations, and his *Community, Gender and Individual Identity: English Writing 1360-1430* (London: Routledge, 1988), pp. 20-72, which is Bakhtinian, and discussing the significance of a loss of community and fraternity. In David Aers and Lynn Staley, *The Powers of the Holy: Religion, Politics and Gender in Late Medieval English Culture* (Pennsylvania: Pennsylvania State University Press, 1996), pp. 15-76, Aers rejects the ascetic and abject images of Jesus that he sees Caroline Walker Bynum's work (*Jesus as Mother; Studies in the Spirituality of the High Middle Ages* and *Holy Feast and Holy Fast* (both Berkeleley: University of California Press, 1982 and 1987) promoting, in its stress on feminization. He takes Lollard iconoclasm to be against an official stress on the passive sufferings of Christ and reads Christ's body in *Piers Plowman* for its humanity and promotion of freedom. And indeed, Christ's body, that of the individual and unfeminized male, unconstrained ideologically, is an allegory of what Aers's work contends for, in its assertion of the 'real' world and author's 'intentions'.

[4] Derrida's essay appears in Harold Bloom, ed., *Deconstruction and Criticism* (London: Routledge, 1979), pp. 75-176.

allegory: for example, by waking from sleep. The 'living on', the *survivre* within this text, comes from a dogged continuation of different allegorical methods, each of which, however, is also marked by negativity.

Allegory is a form of cognition, and one cognition enforced in the poem is knowledge of the self. Cognition in *Piers Plowman* is allegorical, and that means that it is therefore indirect and deferred: Lacanian *méconnaissance*:[5]

> Clerkes kenne me that Crist is in alle places;
> Ac I seigh hym neuere soothly but as myself in a mirour.
> *Hic in enigmate, tunc facie ad faciem.* (B.XV. 161-3)

The 'I', whom Thought calls Will (X.71), addresses Anima, the soul. Searching for Charity, the search is like that for Christ, who can only be seen 'as myself in a mirror', which is followed by citation of I Corinthians 13.12: 'Videmus nunc per speculum in aenigmate' - now we see through a glass, in an enigma. Jerome's Latin Bible transliterated the Greek 'enigma'. The word 'per' means 'in', 'through', or 'by': looking through a mirror at an enigma, or looking from within an enigma.[6] God spoke to Moses plainly, and not *per aenigmata et figuras* (Numbers 12.6). Augustine (*De Trinitate* XV.ix.15) said an enigma was an obscure allegory.[7] The enigma, allegory and the mirror all work together, then.

Anima says that no-one can know Charity without help of Piers Plowman, who alone knows the will, and 'Petrus, id est Christus' (B.XV.212). I Corinthians 10.6: 'that rock was Christ' as a formula which is recollected in those words, connects Charity, Christ and Piers Plowman. But these figures are not separate from the self, who looks in the mirror. Knowledge of identity or knowledge of another is allegorical, *per speculum*, and exists in the condition of the dream. So we can start with the dream, as I will in the following section, but this is also a synonym for the enigma, and for allegory and the mirror. Further, the dream is the inside and outside state of a subject which, though it weeps 'for wo and for wrathe' because Scripture has

---

5   Lacan, 'The mirror stage' in *Écrits*, trans. by Alan Sheridan (London: Tavistock, 1977), p.6. *Mèconnaisance* means failure to recognize, and in Lacan knowledge (*connaisance*) is inseparable from *mèconnaisance*.

6   The point is made by Edward Peter Nolan, *Now Through a Glass Darkly: Specular Images of Being and Knowing from Virgil to Chaucer* (Ann Arbor: University of Michigan Press, 1990), p. 2.

7   On allegory see: Lavinia Griffiths, *Personification in Piers Plowman* (Cambridge: D.S. Brewer, 1986); Stephen A. Barney, "Allegorical Visions," in John A. Alford ,ed., *A Companion to Piers Plowman* (Berkeley: University of California Press, 1988) pp. 117-134; James J. Paxson, *The Poetics of Personification* (Cambridge: Cambridge University Press, 1994) pp. 114-139.

reproached it by saying 'Multi multa sciunt and et sepisos nesciunt' [Many know many things yet do not know themselves], knows also that such self-cognition will never emerge from any of these synonymous terms.

I - DREAM

The mirror first appears in the search for Do-bet, when the dreamer's melancholic anger at the words of Scripture produces a further sleep, dream in a dream, narrative inside narrative, where Fortune brings him to 'the land of longyng and loue' for, 'in a myrrour that highte Myddelerd she made me to loke' (C.XI.165-170).[8]

The irrationality of dreaming is recognised in Chaucer's dream-poem *The House of Fame*, roughly contemporary with the B and C texts.[9] This record of a dream has a confusion and disorder so intense that like some other Chaucer dream poems, it is unfinished. Part of its subject is the impossibility, through the disturbing instrumentality of Fame and Rumour, of transmitting any single message: this being a condition of life, not something that could be remedied. It makes interpretation impossible, requiring instead an 'apocalyptic tone' - Derrida's expression[10]- that the 'man of gret auctorite' of the last line never gets to use. But if he could, apocalyptic discourse, different from chatter, still cannot escape what 'Living On: Border Lines' calls the characteristic of the apocalypse, a "superimprinting of texts." That plurality is a virtual description of *Piers Plowman*.[11] Langland's dream within a dream, evoking increased irrationality, implies an irreducible plurality of voices.[12] It gives to an other state a further other state. But it will appear that being awake is also, for this dreamer, an other state.

---

[8] Pearsall reads "alone" where Schmidt reads "and loue", XI.169. "Alone" may be another pun with Langland, pointing to an introspective subject.

[9] A.J. Minnis, *Oxford Guides to Chaucer: The Shorter Poems* (Oxford: Clarendon Press, 1995) p. 167 dates the poem to 1379-1380.

[10] Jacques Derrida, *Of an Apocalyptic Tone Recently Adopted in Philosophy*, trans. by John Leavey, jr, *Oxford Literary Review* 6 (1984) 3-37. A revised version with Kant's essay, 'On a Newly Arisen Superior Tone in Philosophy', to which Derrida's was a response, appears in *Raising the Tone of Philosophy: Late Essays by Immanuel Kant, Transformative Critique by Jacques Derrida*, ed. by Peter Fenves (Baltimore: Johns Hopkins University Press, 1993).

[11] See Morton W. Bloomfield, *Piers Plowman and a Fourteenth-Century Apocalypse* (New Brunswick: Rutgers University Press, 1961). For the Derrida quotation, see 'Living On' p. 137. For *Piers Plowman* in terms of earlier apocalyptic (Joachite) texts (and interesting on the dreamer), see Kathryn Kerby-Fulton, *Reformist Apocalypticism and Piers Plowman* (Cambridge: Cambridge University Press, 1990).

[12] It includes the Latin quotations which mark the text: see John A. Alford, 'The Role of the Quotations in *Piers Plowman*', *Speculum* 52 (1977), 80-99.

The uncertainty about the origin and status of dreams that opens *The House of Fame* - which makes it, perhaps, in its scepticism which disallows authority the first modern poem in English - is also present in *Piers Plowman*, especially after the second dream, which ended not with resolution or single meaning, but with the priest and Piers jangling:

> And y thorw here wordes awoke, and waytede aboute,
> And seyh the sonne in the southe sitte that tyme.
> Meteles and moneyles on Maluerne Hulles,
> Musyng on this meteles a myle way I yede.
> Mony time this meteles hath maked me to studie
> Of al that I seyh slepynge - if hit so be myhte;
> And of Peres the plouhman fol pencif in herte [...](IX.293-299)

Beggary, solitariness, and melancholic contemplation are all increased by the dream, whose ambiguous ending increases the contentiousness implicit in asking whether there can be *Traumdeutung*, interpretation of dreams (sowngewarie):

> Ac men setteth nat by sowngewarie, for me seth hith often fayle;
> Caton counteth hit at nauht and canonistres at lasse.
> Ac the boek Bible bereth witnesse [...]
> Al this maketh me on meteles to studie [...] (IX.302-317)[13]

Dream-interpretation necessitates interpreting texts, and moving from one allegorical mode to another. For Hayden White, irony, defined as 'illusion', 'presupposes a fundamental contrast between things or qualities conventionally supposed to be affined or similar'. He adds, 'if Freud is right in his general analysis of the nature and function of dreams, then all dreams are ironical - saying one thing but meaning another, in the way that poetic allegories are ironical'.[14] White interconnects dream, dream-interpretation, and allegory, and allies all three with irony. The 'I' of the poem emerges from dream-allegory to another form of allegory, but this implies the difficulty of taking over one system of thought into another, which is itself a sufficient cause of melancholia.

In the inner dream, the land of desire is unrealised, and, as in Lacan on desire, unrealisable. The dream gives the whole of human life, for the dreamer appears young at first and can see 'murthes ful monye' in the mirror (180,182). And mirths (the point will return) encourage the dreamer towards total inertia. Warned by Elde (189),

---

[13] The equivalent passage in B reads 303 differently and adds a further line omitted in C: 'Caton and canonistres counseillen vs to leue / To sette sadnesse in songewareie - for *sompnia ne cures*'. C gives more place to dreams, perhaps fitting its emphasis on the intuitionalism of God's minstrels.

[14] Hayden White, *Figural Realism: Studies in the Mimesis Effect* (Baltimore: Johns Hopkins University Press, 1999), pp. 104, 107.

he continues for 'fourty wynter and a fifte moore' in this dream-state (B.XI.47). This is *La vida es sueno* indeed, or the *Trauerspiel* theme; illusion is folded inside a dream, another allegory. He is conducted by Fortune, a figure of deceptiveness, and of a certain otherness within the poem, since she is hardly otherwise represented in it.[15] Her two handmaids are *Concupiscencia Carnis* and 'Coueytise of Yes' - the lust of the flesh, who is named in Latin, and the other, the covetousness of the eyes. And the lady of the vernacular may be the more dangerous since she connects to the mirror, and to the deceptiveness of specularity.[16] 'Pruyde of Parfit Lyuynge' is a third figure of temptation, and the four women altogether richly figure the doubleness of utterance, the primacy of untruth in the land of longing.[17] The double language of the names, Latin and English, it may be noted, is one of many examples of catachresis in this poem, language shifting, like the people in the 'fair feld ful of folk', where 'some potte them to the plogh' while 'summe putte hem to pruyde' (Prologue 22, 25), the concrete term and the abstract being paired as though there were no difference between them. The double language increases ambiguity, and the difficulty which is posed by the land of longing - a name implying his own name, and so his own desire for identity - to any dream of possessing truth.

In C, Rechelesnesse dominates this inner dream, standing forth in Lollard-like 'ragged clothes' to interrupt ('"Ye? reche the never [...]"') as the poem's most compulsive talker, with, as Donaldson notes, a concentration of quotations on apostolic poverty in his speech.[18] CXI.198 adds that 'Sir Wanhope was sib [kin] to hym, as som men me tolde'. Despair, as part of Rechelesnesse, is one association: another is with 'me' (XII.3,4). Is Sir Wanhope also his sib? When does Rechelesnesse stop talking and does his speech voice a single position? Is there a single talker in what follows?

---

[15] Tristram, p. 141.

[16] On this, see Donald R. Howard, *The Three Temptations: Medieval Man in Search of the World* (Princeton: Princeton University Press, 1966), pp. 41-75, 161-214.

[17] Derrida, *Spurs: Nietzsche's Styles*, trans. by Barbara Harlow (Chicago: University of Chicago Press, 1981) is the classic statement illuminating Nietzsche on "truth as a woman."

[18] E.T. Donaldson, *Piers Plowman: The C-Text and its Poet* (New Haven: Yale University Press, 1949), p. 171. On Rechelesse, see Lawrence M. Clopper, *'Songs of Rechelesnesse': Langland and the Franciscans* (Ann Arbor: University of Michigan Press, 1997). Clopper aligns Langland to the poverty of the Franciscans, and sees Rechelenesse as a Franciscan friar. He argues that throughout, Langland identifies with the 'foles' of CIX, and with poverty, and sees Langland appearing under many different signatures in the poem; see pp. 299-323.

Rechelesnesse may speak throughout, as implied at XIII.128, though he does so at the same time as Loyalty (Leaute), who has been speaking from XII.90, also until XIII.128. And perhaps Leaute was speaking earlier, in XII.56-69, though he then gave way to three lines from Scripture, which were followed by the intervention of Trajan:

'Ye? bawe for bokes!' quod oen, was broken out of helle (XII.73)

Trajan interrupts in four senses. He cuts across Scripture; he interrupts books and their discourse, and he disrupts hell. If he has just broken out of hell, he interrupts chronology and spatial relationships. If he is dead, his talking is a further catachresis. Interruption repeats the pattern of a dream within a dream. Trajan's breaking in is an extraordinary arrest of thought, making interruption a trope running throughout the poem, analogous to the doubling effect of the Latin quotations with the English. A more forceful – indeed violent - comparison would be with the tearing of the pardon by Piers in the B version (B.VII.115), an interruption as vivid as the tearing of Jankyn's book by the Wife of Bath.[19]

Perhaps the tearing of the pardon was the refusal of the literal by the subject who sees it as oppressive and concealing, so that to tear up reveals that the order the priest maintains in the paper is exclusionary. But then, like Trajan, Piers is always a figure of interruption, when he appears at sudden points, as at his first entrance in C.VII.181. It might be said that this allegory was a figure of the unconscious, since Gayatri Spivak has characterized that as marked by 'discontinuous interruptions'.[20] Here the lines of connection between allegory and irony which Hayden White brought out, may be recalled, for irony, in Paul de Man, is awareness of the non-coincidence of meaning which comes when it is seen that a sequence of signifiers, because they are spatialized in a temporal pattern, can give nothing other than a deceptive appearance of consistency of meaning. Sanity exists, says de Man, because we function within the 'conventions of duplicity and dissimulation' which protect meaning; but irony means the end of the 'empirical self' which is based on a sense of its self-consistency of meaning. De Man compares irony to madness:

absolute irony is a consciousness of madness, itself the end of all consciousness, a reflection on madness from the inside of madness

---

[19] See Rosemary Woolf, 'The Tearing of the Pardon' in S.S. Hussey, *Piers Plowman: Critical Approaches* (London: Methuen, 1969), pp. 50-75. See also Simpson, pp. 71-85.

[20] Gayatri Chakravorty Spivak, *A Critique of Postcolonial Reason: Toward a History of the Vanishing Present* (Cambridge, Mass.: Harvard University Press, 1999), p. 208.

itself. But this reflection is made possible only by the double structure of ironic language: the ironist invents a form of himself that is 'mad' but that does not know its own madness; he then proceeds to reflect on his madness thus objectified.[21]

Consciousness of irony is not, then, an escape into lucidity. Irony is a 'permanent parabasis' or disruption: a definition de Man takes from Schlegel ("Rhetoric" 218). As with 'discontinuous interruptions', narrative coherence and systematicity are disrupted through the doubleness of a text whose madness is that it must say several things at the same moment, while in parabasis, allegory is revealed to be only allegory, i.e. the putting together of tropes, of figures.[22]

It seems as if each allegorical figure in the accumulating texts is unable to sustain a position, each contesting another in a recurring parabasis. And the interruptions may be set in relation to the madness of *Piers Plowman*, the catachreses being a minor example of this. Piers, Rechelesnesse and Trajan disrupt the allegory, implying a resistance to order, as at the end of the interrupted second dream, when the 'I' is left aware of a violent contesting of interpretations. By the end of the inner dream, the pairing of XIII.129 and XIII.134 makes it not only Leaute, but Rechelesnesse and also the 'I' who have been speaking, and by that stage it has become evident that it is impossible to assign a single speaker to a particular position, or, what is more puzzling in allegory, to link any single allegorical figure to a single subject-position. When Rechelesnesse is an allegory of the 'I', the 'I' is also allegorical. 'I' is at some moment 'Will', a name with allegorical force, as in the line 'wit shal turne to wrecchednesse for Wil hath al his wille' (XII.2). And that, it may be noted, has intensified the allegorical sense from the B text, where Elde and Holynesse complained 'that wit shal torne to wrecchednesse for wil to haue his likyng' (B.XI.45). 'Likyng' was what Concupiscencia Carnis had promised him (XI.182, see also B.XI.21). If Will has his will, 'I' is as allegorical as Rechelesnesse.

According to Bloomfield, personification allegory makes the speeches the predicates of the named speakers.[23] This is obviously the case and it would constrain, in the sentence that 'Wil hath al his

---

21   Paul de Man, 'The Rhetoric of Temporality' in *Blindness and Insight*, 2nd edition, ed. by Wlad Godzich (Minneapolis: University of Minnesota Press, 1983), p. 216.

22   Paul de Man, 'The Concept of Irony', in *Aesthetic Ideology*, ed. by Andrzej Warminski (Minneapolis: University of Minnesota Press, 1996) p. 179. The translator adds a footnote derived from de Man's notes: 'irony is (permanent) parabasis of allegory - intelligibility of (representational) narrative disrupted at all times'.

23   Bloomfield, *Essays and Explorations: Structure in Ideas, Language and Literature* (Cambridge, Mass.: Harvard University Press, 1970), p. 254.

wille', the second will to mean the same as the first, but Derrida's summary of the work of Levinas on the violence of discourse might be invoked here, because it makes that problematic. In this argument, 'nonviolent language would be a language which would do without the verb *to be*, that is, without predication. Predication is the first violence'.[24] Derrida questions whether such a language, free from all rhetoric, is possible, and perhaps it is not. But if an allegorical person speaks, then to take his speech as the extension of the character, or to say that what is said of the character is the same as his name, can only be possible by a violence of interpretation, which refuses the difference inherent in the speech, which makes different the 'I' in the speech from the 'I' who speaks. (If I say 'I am busy' - and 'busy' is ready to become a plausible allegorical name, 'Busy' - I am not just busy; the 'I' is more than, other than, 'busy' - and the 'I' who says 'I am busy' is also different from the 'I' of the sentence 'I am busy'.)[25] Personification allegory conceals, but by the same process reveals, the difficulty of thinking of the coincidence of the subject and the predicate; and that non-coincidence may be added to the non-coincidence of the subject who looks and the specular subject in the mirror.

II - MIRRORS

At XIII.129, Rechelesness has finished his 'rage' in which he has been speaking to Clergie, and the 'scorne' which he has shown Scripture. At that point, Kynde helps Clergie:

> And in the myrour of Mydelerthe made hym efte to loke
> To knowe by vch a creature Kynde to louye.

It is no longer Fortune who shows, and what is now seen seems different. As Rechelesnesse is the 'I', so is Clergie, for the grammar makes it him who looks in the mirror, though in the next line, it is the 'I' who does so. In B, Kynde took the 'I' - having named him by his name - and brought him to a mountain called Myddelerthe (B.XI.323). C, however, links still the dream and the mirror.[26]

In Lydgate's *The Daunce of Machabree*:

> In this myrour euery wight may fynde

---

[24] Derrida, *Writing and Difference*, trans. by Alan Bass (London: Routledge, 1978) p. 147.

[25] Benveniste, *Problems in General Linguistics* (Miami: University of Miami Press, 1971) pp. 223-230.

[26] See Steven F. Kruger, *Dreaming in the Middle Ages* (Cambridge: Cambridge University Press, 1992) pp. 136-139. See also Kruger's 'Mirrors and the Trajectory of Vision in *Piers Plowman*', *Speculum* 66 (1991), 74-95.

That him behoueth to gone upon this dance [...] (49-50)[27]

This trope of the poem as mirror, links with allegory and the dream. In the late medieval it seems a mirror could mean anything that showed anything to any other subject within a system which assumed that everything, including books, could be an image.[28] When Salisbury is called, in *1Henry VI* I.iv.76, "the mirror of all martial men," following a passage treating Salisbury in *The Mirror for Magistrates*, the image gives character to those people who looked at him: they become martial men; he became the mirror because they looked at him, for a mirror has no essential image. To give attention to anything would be to find it a mirror. The OED first cites Lydgate, c.1430, for 'reflection' as that which a mirror has, in that it shows a copy of the original. The mirror will reappear later in this book with both Hoccleve and Henryson, and in the latter it is linked with Cresseid's dream, in a double figuration of the poem. There is a partially discernible shift taking place during the period of the texts studied in this book making the beholder identify with the image in the mirror. That alteration of perception, fixing identity, a turning-point in the history of the subject, coincides with the moment when allegory ends as a mode of writing. But this, which successive chapters will mark, has not yet quite happened in *Piers Plowman*.

The mirror of Midelerthe shows all creation to be dominated by Reason, save humans, for 'out of reasoun they ryde and rechelesliche taken one' (XIII.153). Pearsall annotates this as 'they have intercourse at unnatural times and continue in it without restraint' (Pearsall 229), which is significant if only because Rechelesnesse reappears in a textually specular relationship with the viewer. The episode produces a further dialogue between the 'I' and Resoun, and the sleeper waking out of the inner dream:

> Tho cauhte y colour anoen and comesede to ben aschamed,
> And awakede therwith, Wo was me thenne
> That I ne hadde met more, so murye as I slepte,
> And saide anoen to mysulue, 'Sleeping hadde I grace
> To wyte what Dowel is, ac wakynge neuere!' (XIII.214-218)

But he has only wakened from inner to outer dream, where, as if that dream is allegorical of waking, he cannot interpret what he has

---

27   Lydgate, *The Fall of Princes* III. p.1026. The image appears earlier: the poem is 'that proud[e] folkes that bene stout and bolde / As in a mirrour toforne in her reason / Her ugly fine there clearely may biholde' (30-32).

28   Three examples: in B.XII.95, Ymaginatif tells the 'I' to love clergie and kynde wit for both 'as mirours ben to amende our defautes'. In XVII.277, St Thomas is described as a 'forbisene [example] to alle bisshopis and a briht myrrour'. In B.XVI.156, Jesus says that Judas will be a 'myrour to manye, men to deceyue', which may make the mirror feminine and deceptive.

learned. Yet the inner dream has caused a consciousness of self, here presented by blushing, shame and the personification of woe. A person blushing feels under surveillance; as if s/he is in the mirror. Lacan speaks of the 'pre-existence of a gaze' - saying, 'I see only from one point, but in my existence I am looked at from all sides'.[29] So, the dreamer's 'I said anon to myself' implies an 'I' which looks at the 'myself', but that 'I' is also split, because the 'I' who says 'I said to myself' is a narrating 'I' who constructs past experience in that way.

And in the inner dream he had already been impelled towards introspection, when Scripture preached:

> Al for tene of her tyxt tremblede myn herte,
> And in a wer [doubt] gan Y waxe, and with mysulue to despute
> Where Y were chose or nat chose [...] (XII. 51-53)

The allegorical mode which has enabled allegorical figures such as Rechelesnesse and Will to 'dispute' with themselves, is insufficient; a second, more intense allegory is needed, of the heart and of a state of doubt holding the subject. Are these two different co-existing allegorical discourses? Is the melancholia which arises from doubt of his own salvation insufficient to be addressed by personification allegory, so that it must give way to another allegory? In the duality of modes, doubling a division of the subject which they have created, may be seen the inability of this text to coincide with itself in its utterance.

III - DREAMING DEATH

Within the dialogue in the inner dream, Couetyse of Eyes addresses both 'Rechelesnesse' and 'me', in an episode which starts as a fold within the thought that runs through the dream within the dream (XII.3). In the following action, Fortune abandons the 'I' after he has passed though youth and come into 'elde'. Ambiguous and deceptive, Fortune's capricousness is part of an unfixing of gender which may be one reason why historically, she disappears as a figure with the ending of allegory which she figures. She contrasts with Elde, and the allegory contains two forms of thinking, since Elde, like Death, fixes identity.

This interpretation is enforced by Ymaginatif, a figure of the outer dream, who says:

> I haue folwed thee, in feith, thise fyue and fourty wynter,
> And manye tymes have meued thee to mynne on thyn ende,
> And how fele fernyeres [many past years] are faren and so

---

[29] Jacques Lacan, *The Four Fundamental Concepts of Psychoanalysis*, trans. by Alan Sheridan (Harmondsworth: Penguin, 1979), p. 72.

> Fewe to come;
> And of thi wilde wantownnesse tho thow yong were,
> To amende it in thi myddel age, lest myght the faille
> In thyn olde elde, [...]
> Amende thee while thow myght; thow hast ben warned ofte
> With poustees [violence] of pestilences, with pouerte and with
>   angres [...] (B.XII.3-11)

Ymaginatif alludes to the three ages of man, as though these were three allegorical veils that are moved through and that bring the subject to his end.[30] The inner dream is interpreted, necessitating the dreamer "amending" (the word is repeated, and puns on 'thyn ende'). Its supplements are inclinations towards melancholia and bitterness, as implied in 'angres' - which may be the objective, or subjective, feelings of an embittered subject, such as in Envy's line: 'For whoso hath moore than I, that angreth me soore' (B.V.116).

At the end of the outer dream (X. 68 to the end of XIV), including the inset dream:

> And I awakede therwith, witteles nerhande,
> And as a freke that fay were [doomed to die] forth can I
>   walken
> In manere of a mendenaunt mony yer aftur,
> And many tymes of this meteles [dream] mochte thoughte I
>   hadde:
> Furste how Fortune me faylede at my moste nede,
> And how Elde manaced me [...] (XV. 1-6)

He has moved towards a subjectivity that is also no subject-position, being witless; he has interiorized the idea of death as his own death, and that has been the effect of the inner dream. The dream as allegory and the allegory as dream have proved modes of bringing death into focus, as in Chaucer's *The Book of the Duchess* and in *Pearl*: as if only in the dream state can the limit of death be thought, because there, as with Trajan, it is possible to return from it. In the case of this dreamer, the thought of what he is moving towards, which is the subject of the last Passus, which also returns to the "pestilence," has inscribed him with two things: lack (he is like a mendicant), and the heaviness of thought. The latter works through the gravity of memory which fixes identity. Madness ('witteles') and melancholia have come together in this self, allegorically constructed as nothing, a beggar, outside the allegory of the dream.

---

[30] See John Burrow, 'Langland *Nel Mezzo del Cammin*' in P.L. Heyworth, ed., *Medieval Studies for J.A.W.Bennett* (Oxford: Clarendon Press, 1981), pp. 21-41, and *The Ages of Man: A Study in Medieval Writing and Thought* (Oxford: Clarendon, 1986), pp. 69-70.

The dream shows the earth as a sphere, like a mirror, and the mirror shows death. The complex of ideas continues into such a *memento mori* as Jacob de Gheyn's picture of 1603, *Vanitas*, of a skull in an architectural niche with a reflecting sphere above it, the whole painting as a mirror, where the skull gazes back at the spectator. Langland's imagery unconsciously prepares the ground for this baroque still life.[31]

IV - IDENTITY

For John Bowers, Langland has created 'a figure of indeterminate nature who metamorphoses even in the process of being described. ... The portrait of Will lacks mimetic unity; it is not meant to imitate any single person or even a particular type'.[32] In this argument, the name 'Will' in the text suggests that 'Will' can 'take upon himself the role of *Voluntas* at certain important moments' (p. 177), and it responds 'to what the poet knew about the theology of *voluntas*' (p. 183). Bowers comes between Robertson and Huppé 'who hold that Will is simply a personification of the human will' and those who propose a 'strictly biographical reading' of the text (p. 60).[33] He sees the text as the record of a certain form of madness, a vagrant text, nomadic, with the consistency of the dream, where figure shades into figure, and dream into dream.

But the 'I' that can blush is something else than the simply allegorical, non-individual figure of Bowers, because it is under surveillance. Because it is looked at, it has, in imaginary form, been given an identity and it falls short of it; it has seen itself in an imaginary mirror. We may recall Lacan: 'what determines me, at the most profound level, in the visible, is the gaze that is outside' (Lacan, p. 106). That being seen is one part of the text, demonstrating a constraint towards the self being marked off in single terms. Anne Middleton, who argues for a textual acceptance of the author's single identity, finds three different kinds of signature in it: an attribution to William de Langlond on the last leaf of a copy of the C text in 1400; internal signatures, such as 'I have lyued in londe, quod I, my name is Longe Wille' (B. XV.152, the passage is

---

[31] See Victor I. Stoichita, *The Self-Aware Image: An Insight into Early Modern Meta-Painting*, trans. by Anne-Marie Glasheen (Cambridge: Cambridge University Press, 1997), pp. 28-29.

[32] John Bowers, *The Crisis of Will in Piers Plowman* (Washington DC: The Catholic University of America Press, 1986) p. 170. A crucial essay for modern studies on Langland is David Lawton, 'The Subject of Piers Plowman', *The Yearbook of Langland Studies* 1 (1987), 1-30.

[33] Referring to D.W. Robertson and Bernard F. Huppé, *Piers Plowman and Scriptural Tradition* (Princeton: Princeton University Press, 1951).

not in C); and occulted signatures, such as the 'lond of longyng' (XI.169). Or V.24 which puns on being too 'long' to stoop, in order to do manual work, followed by 'thenne hastow londes to lyue by' (line 26), which clinches the name.[34]

The reader's recognition of the signature parallels, Middleton thinks, the ability to follow a 'sustained narration' (p. 42). She writes, using emphasis, that 'only to someone capable of reading the poem as a narrative with an immanent design ... will the signatures be systematically legible as such at all'. (p. 42). She sees something Augustinian in 'Langland's ... fully conscious acceptance ... of both the literary and social consequences of developing a philosophic and spiritual quest in the narrative form of an apparently historically specific life-story'. (p. 42). About the anagram in Passus B.XV.152, she says: 'Will's satiric critique of his world is now subsumed in a massive historical reclamation of the subject's life in the light of salvation history' and she finds the moment analogous to Dante's name being cited by Beatrice in *Purgatorio* XXX. The citations of the name stress the importance of self-representation, and they suggest the improvisatory possibilities open to the self, illustrating the text as the confrontation 'at once shameful and exhilarating, of "myself in a mirour"' (p. 79).

Middleton says Bowers neglects 'the intertextualities of the authorial surname' (p. 60n) in concentrating upon Will as allegorical. She sees the name in other associations: 'long launde' suggests the strip of land where the ploughman works (p. 50), so that Piers's identity and the Dreamer's merge temporarily, just as in the A version, when the pardon is produced, 'many wept for ioye, / And gaf wille for his writyng wollene clothis; / For he copiede thus here clause thei couden hym gret mede' (A.VIII.43,44), while in B and C, they praise Piers who purchased the bill. In the vision of Dowel, Thought is described as 'a muche [tall] man, as me thoghte, ylike to mysulue" who calls him by his "kynde name' (C.X.68, 69), and uses the name later ('here is Wil wolde wite if Wit koude teche hym' [BVIII.127]).[35] And Wit is called 'long and lene' (CX.116); while his wife, Studie, is also 'ful lene' (C.XI.2). The Dreamer shades off into these other figures. The similarity of Thought and Wit to the Dreamer makes Middleton say 'they resemble Will too much to do him any good'. (p. 39). Beyond the allegory comes individuality and personal character.

---

[34] 'William Langland's "Kynde Name": Authorial Signature and Social Identity in Late Fourtenth-Century England', *Literary Practice and Social Change in Britain, 1380-1530,* ed. by Lee Patterson, Berkeley: University of California Press, 1990, 15-82.

[35] CX.125 reads 'Here is oen wolde ywyte' ... instead.

Middleton makes assumption of identity more voluntaristic and narrative more consistent than I would like to argue for. Identity is a matter of representation, which occurs through plural allegorical modes. The 'I' as Will is not a whole identity, but part of an identity, and cannot be the inner truth or being of the subject. All identities which appear have no more existence than their differential relationship with other figures. As the names of qualities and faculties seem unbounded, there is neither a totality making up the subject, nor an entitlement to think one more significant than another. Yet, that account I have given is also insufficient, for these allegorical modes differ from the subject who can speak of 'myself', and that latter mode differs too from that in which the subject is described as moving towards Elde. And within these several modes, is yet another constraint, which increases from the B text to the C, to think confessionally.

V - CONFESSION

> Thus I awakede, woet God, whan I wonede in Cornehull,
> Kytte and I in a cote - yclothed as a lollare,
> And lytel ylet by, leueth me for sothe,
> Amonges lollares of Londone and lewede ermytes [...]
> For I made of tho men as resoun me tauhte. (CV.1-5)

All accounts of the C text agree in finding something new in the writing here. This waking description, coming after the first dream, implies that the poet may be a 'lollare', a word that enters for the first time in the C text. Perhaps the word associates with Lollards, apparently first so named in 1382.[36] As if it were a new word, its meaning is defined in IX.213-218. But the 'I' says he is not much liked by lollares and the hermits, for he 'made of them' (wrote about them), satirizing them. Writing attempts to establish limits and borders, particularly significant when the subject feels his own nearness to what he wishes to be separate from. But the text does *not* establish such borders. He writes as if awake, but he continues to allegorize, with the appearances of Reason and Conscience; it is as if waking or sleeping and dreaming are equivalent states, or as if the self in its melancholia cannot distinguish.

Further, his profession of separation from the lollares is already compromised by the low associations of the place where he lives (Cornhill) and the implications behind the name of his wife.[37] In

---

[36] On this see Wendy Scase, *Piers Plowman and the New Anticlericalism* (Cambridge: Cambridge University Press, 1989) pp. 149-157. She discusses the autobiographical section in chapter 5 (120-160).

[37] John Burrow, *Langland's Fictions* (Oxford: Clarendon Press, 1993) p. 86n also comments on the name of the daughter, XX.472.

Langland and Hoccleve, as for Chaucer in *The House of Fame*, city-space seems productive of an anomic subject. London, named in the fourth line, is liminal, seeming to lend itself to begging (V.90), as if producing an identity marked in every way by lack.[38] Further, what follows in this autobiographical section (CV.1-104), indicates how he is indeed not much more than a lollar. He is met by Reason in a 'hot hervest', as if emphasising that his life is marked out by the absence of work. He is rebuked by Reason, as he was 'romynge in remembraunce' (11), contemplative, like the melancholic of the *Trauerspiel*. Reason has stepped across from the dream to waking reality, and the allegory continues; it is another of those episodes which implies that there is something nomadic in the text, in its lack of being bounded spatially or temporally. Equally the waking actions of the 'I', in saying 'romynge in remembraunce' make no distinction between the concrete and abstract. Is he wandering literally or in an abstract sense? The text implies that there is no getting out of allegory. Reason may be both part of the subject, his reason, or may be an image of an other, an absolute figure, who can refer to 'my corn', and who accuses him of begging and of living a 'lollarne lyf' (29,31).

The accusation forces the 'I' further into a realist, confessional, or autobiographical mode, though even here he puns, as with his 'longe' clothes (V.41). He describes himself as singing for the dead, and reciting the penitential psalms, assisting with 'penaunce discrete' (84). He says his conscience justifies him (83), but Conscience refuses the justification and returns him to his begging (90), while it virtually accuses him of being, if not one of the 'lollares of London' then a 'lewede hermit' (V.4), a gyrovagus, since, for Conscience, it is better to be obedient to a prior or to a minister (91). The 'I' must acknowledge 'that I haue ytynt [wasted] tyme, and tyme myspened', but adds that yet, 'I hope' (93-94) repeating 'So hope I' at line 99. Reason and Conscience speak as others to the I, who speaks of another allegorical character, hope. The effect of the rebuke from Reason and Conscience is to send him to church which will produce more penitentialism, 'wepyng and waylyng til I was aslepe' (108), like a child. In that state he dreams again, which implies not a move towards greater clarification, but towards another form of allegory. But the penitentialism has driven him away from the allegorical towards the realist autobiographical: that is part of the history of the subject that is witnessed here. The

---

[38] On London, see Derek Pearsall, in Steven Justice and Kathryn Kerby-Fulton, *Written Work: Langland, Labor and Authorship* (Philadelphia: University of Pennsylvania Press, 1997).

'I' becomes the confessional self rebuked by its reason and conscience, those earlier forms of the Freudian superego.

Nonetheless, the confessional self is also a fiction, fragmented, dispersed, as much as the signatures, like the allegorical names, imply dispersal of the self throughout the poem. The self names itself only in fragments of allegory. To name the self as Will, whether this is literal or allegorical, misnames, because the self that names the self is outside that self, and therefore adds one extra piece to the self, it cancels its unity, illustrating that what had been thought of as the whole self is only an abstraction. The autobiographical mode, like the confessional mode, denies the possibility of ever something new happening to the subject, so that the subject which speaks, or writes autobiographically / confessionally, is mortified by that act. In the same way, elsewhere, the 'I' of the poem is brought to a position of penitence, or of a single-subject position through Elde.

It seems as though two contraries are working in the text, and that the discussion thus far may be summarized like this:

(a) The text recognises the constraint upon it to speak from a single-subject position, as epitomised in the "I" of the poem and it also resists this through a presentation of itself as heterogeneous.
(b) It also knows that there is no escape from allegory into a fuller mode of being, and
(c) this allegorical state is a form of resistance, while being also a kind of melancholy, dissolving or fragmenting the subject. Allegory relates to madness, as a heterogeneous, nomadic and melancholic state, because no allegory fits a single subject and no madness speaks other than allegorically.

When the self presents itself as mad, it becomes heterogeneous, a term which I take from Georges Bataille - who has in this the odd authority of a medievalist.[39]

VI - MADNESS

If the subject speaks of his clothes, as in V.2, then, as with his blushing, he knows he is being looked at. This constitution of the subject meets with resistance, for he speaks as or as like, a madman, or a fool, or a beggar, in a moment when vagrancy and was becoming a topic of new laws, and religious mendicancy a subject of

---

[39] As a medieval scholar, Georges Bataille edited *L'Ordre de Chevalerie*. On the heterogeneous, see 'The Notion of Expenditure' and 'The Psychological Basis of Fascism', *Visions of Excess: Selected Writings 1927-1939*, edited by Allan Stoekl, (Minneapolis: University of Minnesota Press, 1985).

heightened controversy.[40] As between the positions of being lay and fully in orders, truly marginal, on the borders, he appears from the beginning as impotent, as only imitating reality:

> Y shope me into shroudes as Y a shep were
> In abite as an heremite, unholy of werkes
> Wente forth in the world wondres to here [...] (Prologue, 2, 4)

A hermit, committed to a life of solitude, was particularly a figure prone to *acedia*, the 'demon of noontide', but a hermit who wandered about (as a gyrovagus), is neither solitary nor living the rule of a cenobite existence. John Bowers takes the reference to the habit of a hermit unholy of works to refer to *acedia*, saying that 'If Will were a hermit and unholy, he would most likely be slothful' (p. 99). He understands the clothing of the first Passus literally: the hermit's habit would have been normally gray or black wool, 'but some hermits, harkening back to Cassian's instructions on dress, sought to imitate the desert fathers by wearing the skins of goats or sheep' (p. 102). So the shrouds are those of a sheep, implying an apostolic character, sheep in the midst of wolves (Matthew 10.16). But the character of the hermit is equivocal, because unholy of works, and also because the hermit-dress was already imitated - and that by vagabonds (see Prologue 53-55). In short the 'I' has an ironic appearance: in every way he undoes what identity there is, and associates with what is heterogeneous. Yet the figure who attempts to stand outside events - indifferent observer of wonders rather than participant in them - feels his lack when Holy Churche speaks:

> Thenne Y knelede on my knees and criede here of grace,
> And preyede her pitously to preye for me to amende [...]
> [...] tel me this ilke -
> How I may sauen my soule that seint art yholden. (I.76-82)

The subject, penitential, melancholic, saves its soul through the poem, through dreaming, which performs a work of allegory, and by waking contemplation of the dream which has possessed it.

We have found several contradictory ways in which the self is constructed in the text; but, composed in allegorical fragments, (heterogeneous and yet confessing, melancholic and saving its soul through the allegorical work of the text), it has yet still another aspect. In contrast to the melancholia there is the madness of the lollar who appears in Passus IX. At that point of the poem, the subjects of the pardon have been described, and beggars and lollares

---

[40] Wendy Scase, *Piers Plowman and the New Anticlericalism* (Cambridge: Cambridge University Press, 1989) discusses this, see p. 72. She suggests that manuscript variants in *PP* 'often seem to have been generated by the volatility and sensitivity of the subject of poverty' (p. 75).

have been declared exempt from its value (61-104). But after that, the text, which is here unique to C, considers other forms of beggars, fools, (C. IX.105-138). These 'want wyt' (106), they are 'lunatyk lollares' (107) and 'lepares aboute' who 'madden as the mone sit, more other lasse' (108), 'meuynge aftur the mone' (110). Further, they have a 'good will' (111), which word implies the 'I' who is writing. The text identifies these poor fools with God's apostles:

> For hit aren merye-mouthed men, munstrals of heuene,
> And Godes boys, bourdyors [jesters] , as the Book telleth,
> *Si quis videtur sapiens, fiet stultus ut sit sapiens*
> [If anyone thinks he is wise, let him become a fool that he may be wise.] (C.IX.127-9a)

The theme returns, when the rich are told that they should:

> Welcomen and worschipen and with youre goed helpen
> Godes munstrals and his mesagers and his mery bordiours
> The whiche arn lunatyk lollares and lepares aboute [...] (IX.134-6)[41]

These figures are counterposed against the others: 'lollarne lyf and lewede ermytes' (IX.140). They are seen as fools because they go out like the apostles, 'seluerless in a somur garment' (119), abandoning rational identity, in a praise of folly, as Christianity, on the basis of the quotation already cited from I Corinthians 3.18, could have been a wonderfully affirmative *histoire de la folie*.[42] And if it had been, we would not have had the sad history that Foucault had to write in *Madness and Civilization*. Acting out the apostolic rules, these minstrels make themselves mad, leaping about.[43] The passage defines the subject who writes: a lunatic, a fool, one of God's minstrels; manic in his melancholia.

This can be traced further. In the apocalyptic moment of the end of the poem, Antichrist appears and everyone follows him

> saue onelich foles;
> The whiche foles were wel gladere to deye
> Then to lyue lenger, sethe Leautee was so rebuked. (XXII.61-63)

The context has already spoken of not being afraid to be needy, giving a hint that begging may be appropriate (C.XXII.48-50), so returning to the material of Passus IX. The 'foles' are again the mad, and there seems no need to read the description as ironic (as

---

41 Russell reads 'loreles' for 'lollares'.

42 Note the reversal of this statement in '*Sapienca huius mundi stulticia est apud Deum*' (XIV.83a) – 'the wisdom of this world is folly with God' - 1 Corinthians 1.19.

43 See Derek Pearsall, '"Lunatyk Lollares' in *Piers Plowman*" in Piero Boitani and Anna Torti, eds., *Religion in the Poetry and Drama of the Late Middle Ages in England* (Woodbridge: D.S. Brewer, 1990), pp. 163-178.

Pearsall does, on p.364). They include the 'I' of the text, who joins them a little later. Since the moment of Antichrist is both present and future, again the emphasis is on the utopian, which is where fools belong. Further, the reference to fools is continued by Conscience (XXII.74, 77). It is also clear that the word 'fool' is a term of reproach to the Christian: so it is used by the priest to Piers in the quarrel over the Pardon, in a moment in B.VII.135-6, not, of course, in the C text.

And the phrase 'Goddes munstrals' had appeared earlier, at VII.99, describing beggars, where it was placed in contrast to a phrase used four lines earlier, 'kynges munstrals'. (Both phrases appear also in the B text, XIII.437,440.) Donaldson (146), associates 'Goddes munstrals' with Franciscans who were called *Joculatores Domini*, where a 'joculator' is a minstrel. In AI.137-8, the 'I' is told to preche about love 'in thin harpe / Ther thou art mery at mete', which implies that he is a minstrel. The passage in CIX leaves it questionable whether it is describing existing people or is utopian, speaking for the importance of being mad, or being a fool in a situation where that is impossible. Certainly, there seems to be a desire to be thought of as mad. In the Prologue, a 'lunatik, a leene thyng withalle' cries out to the King (B.Prologue 123: C.Prologue 147 makes this Kynde Witt). The lunatic is a holy fool. Skeat thought it must be the poet, and Donaldson (151) agrees. Notably, the lunatic praises 'leaute' (B.Prologue 126, C.Prologue 149), which, to the fools' dismay, is traduced at the end. In B, the 'I' is the dreamer and the dreamed.

Yet it is a source of anxiety whether the subject *is* mad, and so genuine, because Passus IX later satirizes workmen who have set up as hermits to beg, and who are 'kyndeliche' called 'lollares' (IX.213). So is the poem mad enough? For Foucault, recording the non-utopian *histoire de la folie*, madness is the 'absence of work',[44] and the 'I' of the poem is in terms of productive labour (*travail*), idle, inert, *désoeuvre*, a word that also appears in the writings of Maurice Blanchot. *Le travail* and *l'oeuvre* are opposites, since, the first is opposed to inaction and passivity, while the second has to do with non-productive work, such as writing, in which 'impotence [is] endlessly affirmed'.[45] Blanchot's word *désoeuvrement* - worklessness - implies a state of inertia, which is analogous to the description of madness. I would like to suggest that it also, increasingly, describes

---

[44] Not in the English translation but in the Preface to *Folie et Déraison: Histoire de la Folie à l'Age Classique* (Paris: Librarie Plon, 1961) p. v.

[45] Quoted from Ann Stock's introduction to Maurice Blanchot, *The Space of Literature* (Lincoln: University of Nebraska Press, 1982), p. 13.

the wanderer in the poem, and perhaps accounts for the endless re-
writing of the poem, a labour perhaps only ended by death. In literal
terms, the absence of work of the 'I' and his association with the
fools, or mad, calls his existence into being: 'Foel, flaterere or
frentike peple!' is Dame Studie's estimate of him and his like (XI.6).
In the beginning of a long speech, the B text, (not C), makes
Ymaginatif accuse him of meddling with 'makynge' (B.XII.16-28), so
letting his life's three ages go by.

At the beginning of the poem's second part, before he dreams
again, and in language recalling the beginning, there comes a second
waking passage. The puzzlement felt after he had wakened from the
second dream continues:

> Thus yrobed in russet I romede aboute
> Alle a somur seson for to seke Dowel (C.X.1,2)

Being clothed in poor russet, different from the costume in the
Prologue, may have associations with Lollardy, which, therefore,
continues to bring out his heterogeneity.[46] 'Romede' recalls the word
of V.11; it indicates that at all times the activities of the subject are
questionable: and what, literally, would it mean, in the time-span of
the summer, which suggests realism, to roam around to seek Dowel?

The next passage which I quote, which is found only in B,
commences the Dobet section and, in B, the fifth dream. The fourth
dream was not consolatory: it has made him worse, and the waking
passage deepens the witlessness, which had become apparent before
the dream (the passage, from C.XV.1-6, was quoted earlier.) His
behaviour follows the moon and makes him deliberately anti-social,
going beyond all limits where, as it were, he would be able to blush.
It moves from 'fool', to its implications: 'folie':

> Ac after my wakynge it was wonder longe
> Er I koude kyndely knowe what was Dowel.
> And so my wit weex and wanyed til I a fool weere,
> And some lakkede my lif - allowed it fewe -
> And leten me for a lorel [wastrel] and looth to reuerencen
> Lordes or ladies [...]
>
> That folk helden me a fool; and in that folie I raued,
> Til Reson hadde ruthe on me and rokked me aslepe (B.XV.1-6, 10-11)

Bowers discusses the fool, referring to the Middle English senses of
the fool as a jester, a dazed man, or a sinner and he links the
Dreamer's lapse into folly in Passus BXV with melancholy and with
acedia. The two are not the same, but they are related: for Bowers
(149-153) argues that *acedia* could arise from melancholy. In this

---

[46] Compare XVI.342. See Pearsall, 178, and Scase, 168. See also Pearsall 203.

Passus, Anima calls Christians 'Goddes foweles' (B.XV.313).[47] In the B text, XVI.170, the "I" says he 'yede forth as an ydiot' (XVI.170). In the quotation that has just been given, it is emphasised that there can be no separation from what people say about him, and what is true – 'folk helden me a fool' - making him an heterogeneous object, a figure like the mad – 'and in that folic I raved' - which means that he is, in his own sense of himself, mad. Can the mad confess? Or give an autobiography? The last line of the quotation brings an allegorical character - Reson - to bear on the dreamer's waking experience - just as Reason will be used in C.V. Perhaps this implies a mental fight that is necessary to bring the dreamer back to dreaming, which will allow the work of allegory to take place. Reason taking pity on the dreamer by allowing him to sleep and to dream, permits a new triumph of allegory.

The next quotation, introducing the sixth vision, gives another waking section. The Samaritan of the previous vision has disappeared and the dreamer wakes. The sense is of an experience unfinished, interrupted, which produces in the next Passus an 'I' even more reduced to lack; dressed penitentially ('wollewaerd'), while poverty appears in the lack of shoes. As in the B passage, he is a 'lorel':

> Wollewaerd and watschoed wente I forth aftur
> As a recheles renk that reccheth nat of sorwe,
> And yede forth ylike a lorel al my lyf tyme
> Til I waxe wery of the world and wilnede eeft to slepe,
> And lened me to Lenten - and longe tyme I slepte [...] (C.XX.1-5)

Bowers finds Will at the opening of this Passus, (in the B text, XVIII), 'at the nadir of his decline' and draws a heavy lesson from the word 'lorel' - as 'a rogue, beggar, fool, or one of the damned', seeing him as at the point of despair (152,153). The repeated word 'recheles' picks up from the appearance of this character in C.XI.196, and it is ambiguous: the 'I' cares nothing for sorrow but then he waxes weary of the world, which implies melancholia, or a suicidal state, which perhaps means that caring nothing for sorrow is also melancholic indifference.

If so, the work of allegory that follows in the dream enacts a triumph, which culminates in a triumph over death and, significantly, over the macabre, over ghosts ('may no grisly ghost glyde ther hit [the cross] shaddeweth!' (CXX.478).[48] After it, the 'I' is a secular figure with wife and daughter, and the seventh vision opens:

---

[47] See Schmidt's reading in his edition of the B text as 'foles'.

[48] For the link between ghosts and the macabre, see Jean-Claude Schmitt, *Ghosts in the Middle Ages: The Living and the Dead in Medieval Society*, trans. by Teresa Lavender Fagan (Chicago: University of Chicago Press, 1998) pp. 212-

> Thus Y wakede and wrot what Y hadde ydremed
> And dihte me derely, and dede me to kyrke [...] (XXI.1-2)

It is a new start: writing, and dressed, no longer a wanderer. He writes again at the end of the seventh vision (XXI.284) but the last Passus begins with him 'heuy chered' and 'elyng in herte', and hungry, and then 'with Nede I mete'.

'My most nede' had been the topic of the inner dream (XV.5); now, he meets Need or dreams him, for 'mette' may mean both, so illustrating the loss of distinction between sleeping and waking.[49] Need can mean 'violence, force, constraint or compulsion' (OED). Since Nede 'afrounted me foule and faytour [knave] me calde' (XXII.5), the passage draws attention to violence, including the violent interruption of allegory, which seems to realise that it has no right to an existence, which it must assert over the 'I' who speaks. In forty-five lines, Nede mentions 'nede' some seventeen times. This figure of allegory asserts itself as claiming a place, its imperiousness implying necessity and the state of emergency. Whether justifying begging or not, this is virtually the text's last word, presenting the 'I' as in a state of conflict, justifying a heterogeneous and marginal position, which, if it must be thought of confessionally, still has a right to resistance, and demands the last dream, as out of need. Afterwards there is no comment.

VII - SLOTH

Before turning to the last dream, which shows another form of triumph, I would like to comment on the force of the oppositional force working within the dreamer. Bowers argues for the centrality of sloth to the poem, and it has been seen in melancholia and acedia and indifference. It is focused in B.XIII.221, when Patience and Conscience meet with the minstrel and waferer, who is named Actiua Vita and later Haukyn (273) and who is another avatar of the text's 'I', save that he says 'al ydel ich hatie' (B.XIII.226). The state of Haukyn's clothes is noted by the 'I' and by Conscience, who seems, then, to be like the superego, the gaze which constitutes the subject and judges it. Haukyn is marked by the seven deadly sins, and he dreads to die in a state of deadly sin. He falls into 'wanhope' 'and wende nought to be saued / The whiche is sleuthe, so slow that may

---

9. The medieval ghost, for Schmitt, appears as an interruption in the course of the rite of the passage of death and the funeral services (p. 6): it interrupts mourning.

[49] Penn R. Szittya, *The Antifraternal Tradition in Medieval Literature* (Princeton: Princeton University Press, 1986) p. 276 reads the hour of noon when Nede is met as the hour of death, so anticipating the events of the following dream.

no sleightes helpe it' (407,408). This introduces a section on sloth (410-457), which seems to be the liability of the active man.

In the C text, the state that Haukyn represents is transferred to the section describing the seven deadly sins, which came much earlier, in the second dream.[50] Reason and Conscience preach to the people, and the result is Will weeping (VI.2). So the sins allegorize the self, though in no single mode, for Purnele Proude-herte who comes first is an allegory of Pride, while Glotoun, whose vividness of description implies a resistance to confession, is a glutton, not abstract gluttony. But one point emerges: that everything tends towards sloth. Enuye's anger when he cannot have the mastery produces 'malencolie' (VI.77), When Glotoun has had his excess, 'he hadde an accidie' (C.VI.416). Sloth itself is placed at the end of the sins, because it leads to the end and to death. The last of the sins is melancholic because it cannot mourn.[51]

Sloth is 'whan a man moorneth noght for his mysdedes, ne maketh no sorwe' (B.XIII.411) because he thinks only of mirth (418, C.VII.77). It could be like a manic state. The passage, B.XIII.410-457, is transferred to the end of what Sloth says in his confession in C, as a commentary, as if delivered by Repentance. In B, it had been the voice of Will, who was offered mirth in the mirror of Myddelerd. What Haukyn represents is split into two in C, but in both B and C the passage on sloth turns to the resolution of identity that takes place in 'deeth deyinge' (B.XIII.426, C.VII. 85) and into criticism of minstrels, whose entertainments deceive.[52] In contrast are God's minstrels, who will give comfort at 'deeth dyinge' (451, C.VII.110). Haukyn's wanhope connects with Recchelesse, whose kin is Sir Wanhope; in Chaucer's *The Parson's Tale*, 'neclìgence, or recceleesnesse, that rekketh of no thyng' (X.710) is part of Accidia. All these connect with the poem's 'I', like the minstrels. Sloth, *accidia*, has a direct relationship to death, and the text's anxiety about its relation to sloth is its melancholia.

---

[50] See Morton Bloomfield, *The Seven Deadly Sins: An Introduction to the History of a Religious Concept: With Special Reference to Medieval English Literature* (East Lansing: Michigan State University Press, 1952) pp. 196-201. See the reading of the confessions (A and B versions) by Elizabeth D. Kirk, *The Dream Thought of Piers Plowman* (New Haven: Yale University Press, 1972) pp. 46-70.

[51] Compare the gluttonous in Passus II: 'they ben falle in Slewthe, / And awake with wanhope and no will to amende' (II.102,103).

[52] Compare Patience's reference to 'deeth day' in B.XIV.106 – 'the deeth' in C.XV.286. For discussion of the language of minstrels see Edwin D. Craun, *Lies, Slander and Obscenity in Medieval English Literature: Pastoral Rhetoric and the Deviant Speaker* (Cambridge: Cambridge University Press, 1997), pp. 157-186.

VIII - DEATH

> Ther cam a privee theef men clepeth Deeth
> That in this contree al the peple sleeth,
> And with his spere he smoot his herte atwo,
> And wente his weye withouten wordes mo.
> He hath a thousand slain this pestilence.[53]

> O Mors, era mors tua (B.XVII.112a, quoting Hosea 13:14: O death, I will be thy death)

> Then she turned slightly towards the nurse and said in a tranquil tone, 'Now then, take a good look at death', and pointed her finger at me.[54]

> Metaphor always carries its death within itself.[55]

Allegorization does not stabilize ever in this poem save in one allegorical figure, Death, the de-personifying figure who represents stabilization itself. According to Faith, Death threatens 'a wol fordo and adown brynge / Alle that lyueth or loketh a londe or a watre' (XX.29, 30) but he is opposed in this by 'Lyf'.[56] That triumph, and challenge of death leads in to the accounts of the crucifixion and the harrowing of hell, which gives the triumph of life. But the text does not rest there; its movement is not towards triumph in the last two Passus; and the presentation of Need to begin the last Passus and introduce the last dream implies things are worse than they have ever been before. In the dream, Antichrist appears (XXII.53) and Conscience is heard by Kynde, who brings plagues out of the planets, as souls call out 'Here cometh Kynde / And Deth that is dredful, to vndoen us alle' (XXII.88, 89). Elde and Kynde appear with pestilences, like that of 1348, and:

> Deth cam dryuyng aftur and al to duste paschte
> Kynges and knyhtes, caysers and popes.
> Lered ne lewed, he lefte no man stande
> That he hitte euene, that euere stured aftur.
> Many a louly lady and here lemmanes knyhtes
> Swowened and swelte for sorwe of Dethes duntes. (XXII.100-105)

The historical appearance of the plague may have engendered a new presentation of death in art, as here it produces the macabre vision.[57]

---

[53] Chaucer, *The Pardoner's Tale* C.675-9.
[54] Maurice Blanchot, *Death Sentence*, pp. 129-188.
[55] Derrida, *Margins of Philosophy*, trans. by Alan Bass (Brighton: Harvester, 1986), p. 271.
[56] In the comparable alliterative poem of the late fourteenth century, *Death and Life*, Death and Life are female. See Susanna Fein, 'The Poetic Art of *Death and Life*', *Yearbook of Langland Studies* 2 (1988), 103-123.
[57] Bloomfield, *Piers Plowman* p. 223 discusses the possibility that these lines are evidence for the Dance of the Dead motif in the fourteenth century. The classic text on a reaction in art brought about by the pestilence appears in

In this presentation of a history emerging around 1348, there is a new positioning of Death, for in the outbreak of the plague, he appears as an agent counteracting Antichrist, which makes him a figure of life. Lyf in contrast reverses into becoming a figure of death when he acquires a 'lemman' - Fortune - and they engender a child:

> Oen that moche wo wrouhte, Sleuthe was his name.
> Sleuthe wax wonder yerne, and sone was of age,
> And wedded oen Wanhope, a wenche of the stuyves. [...]
> This Sleuthe was sley of werre, and a slynge made,
> And threw drede of dispayr a doysayne myle aboute. (XXII.157-164)

Sloth can go fast as well as slow (V.XIII.408). Fear of despair, a form of melancholia, is differentiated from Wanhope who has now altered gender from when s/he was associated with Rechelesnesse. Her association with the stews, and so with mirth, links a manic and a melancholic state within melancholia, which may be symptomatic of the spirit of the dance of the dead.[58] The circulation of characters makes allegory temporary, provisional, but repeating obsessive topics, and focussed on sloth.

Millard Meiss, *Painting in Florence and Siena after the Black Death: The Arts, Religion and Society in the Mid-Fourteenth Century* (Princeton: Princeton University Press, 1951); for comments on this thesis see Samuel K. Cohn, jr, *The Cult of Remembrance and the Black Death* (Baltimore: Johns Hopkins University Press, 1992), pp. 272-8; for revision of Meiss' view of the Pisa Camposanto fresco of the Triumph of Death being post 1348, see Alastair Smart, *The Dawn of Italian Painting, 1250-1400* (London: Phaidon, 1978), pp. 107-108, 116-118.

Cohn returns to post-plague individualism and death as 'one's own death' - the view of Philippe Ariès in *The Hour of Our Death*, trans. by Helen Weaver (New York: Knopf,1980) - in discussing post-Huizinga historians: Jean Delumeau, Jacques Chiffoleau and Michel Lauwers, reading their different versions of individualism before and after the pestilence, and singling out Chiffoleau and J-P. Deregnaucourt for arguments on 'la grande mélancholie' 'where citizens faced death "uprooted" from former familial solidarities that had cushioned the blows of death in the feudal period' - Samuel K. Cohn, jr. 'The Place of the Dead in Flanders and Tuscany: Towards a Comparative History of the Black Death', in *The Place of the Dead: Death and Remembrance in Late Medieval and Early Modern Europe*, ed. by Bruce Gordon and Peter Marshall (Cambridge: Cambridge University Press, 2000), pp. 17-43.

[58] David Herlihy, *The Black Death and the Transformation of the West* (Cambridge, Mass.: Harvard University Press, 1997), pp. 63-64 discusses the merry-making in funerals. 'Few indeed were those to whom the lamentations and bitter tears of their relatives were accorded; on the contrary, more often that not bereavement was the signal for laughter and witticisms and general jollification - the art of which the women ... had learned to perfection' - Boccaccio, *Decameron*, trans. by G.H. McWilliam (Harmondsworth: Penguin, 1995) p. 10. Boccaccio also notes a new arrival: the gravedigger; whose career this book traces, from the pestilence to Hamlet's father's victory over Fortinbras.

But in contrast to the disavowal of death which the agents of Lyf practise here, and whose causes may have to do with increased horror at it, the text turns in another direction, towards mourning. For Elde is evoked by Conscience to fight against Wanhope, and against Lyf, and as part of that, the 'I' of the poem, who must therefore be a figure of Lyf, and indeed of Sloth and Wanhope, is assailed by age and rendered impotent sexually. This other form of *désoeuvrement* brings out what has always marked him: it is what he has always chosen; marginal in his life he is now marginal in sexuality, melancholic indeed. When he has become a figure of Elde, who approaches the state of death who is skeletal, deprived of sexual organs, then the 'I' becomes an allegorical figure of death in life.[59] At that point he needs help, and is brought into Unity, where Conscience had urged 'fools' to come (XXII.75, 213).[60]

To move from the triumph of Lyf, associated with sloth and despair and so with one form of melancholia, where there is no *Trauerarbeit*, to the triumph of Deeth, presaged by Elde, means moving into another form of allegory and another form of melancholia, which includes mourning. Derrida draws attention to Freud's use of the concept of the triumph in 'Mourning and Melancholia' ("Living On Border Lines", pp.108-109). As Freud speaks of mourning being overcome, so he also sees a manic state as having mastered the ego's sense of defeat, so that mania is a triumph over melancholy.[61] It was so with Lyf's son, Sleuthe. The end of *Piers Plowman* gives a similar triumph over one form of melancholia by another: this continues to the last line.

When the 'I' - Will - loses his (sexual) will, an allegorical figure who has associations with Sloth and Wanhope becomes himself doubly allegorical as a figure of death, or almost as a posthumous figure. No wonder his wife does not want to sleep with him. The

---

[59] Karl S. Guthke, *The Gender of Death: A Cultural History in Art and Literature* (Cambridge: Cambridge University Press, 1999) pp. 43-44, and 265-6 discusses the date for the iconography of death as a skeleton: by the fourteenth century, but particularly in the sixteenth.

[60] Two essays focus on the last Passus; James J. Paxson, 'Inventing the Subject and the Personification of Will in *Piers Plowman*: Rhetorical, Erotic and Ideological Origins and Limits in Langland's Allegorical Poetics' which gives a queer theory reading of the relations between Will and Elde in an attempt to 'remember the literal' reading; and Kathleen M. Hewett-Smith, '"Nede ne hath no lawe": Poverty and the de-stabilization of Allegory in the Final Versions of *Piers Plowman*', both in Kathleen M. Hewett-Smith, *William Langland's Piers Plowman: A Book of Essays* (New York: Routledge, 2001), pp. 195-232, 233-253. Hewett-Smith's essay discusses de Man's readings of allegory, and focuses on Nede. My reading of Elde's significance disagrees with Paxson's reading.

[61] Freud, 'Mourning and Melancholia', pp. 252, 254, 263, 264.

poem signals, in this, that it is approaching its end. Since Sloth and Wanhope and Will's will and Will's wife are aligned with Lyf rather than Death, allegorization is ambiguously linked to character. The Lyf / Death antithesis had worked in the favour of life in the scenes depicting the passion of Christ, but now it is the opposite. Life and Death are allegories (mirrors) of each other; dependent on the other for their own meaning. It is a state Derrida in a neologism calls 'life death' ('Living On' 165).[62] The triumph of life in Passus XX has turned, in Passus XXII, into the 'triumph over life' ('Living On' 80); the point being the mutuality of life and death.

Derrida's essay responds to Shelley's unfinished poem *The Triumph of Life* (1822): Shelley's title and the *terza rima* recall both Petrarch's *Trionfi*, including 'The Triumph of Death' (post 1348), and Dante. In Shelley, life becomes destructive, in that it annihilates individual lives in its own triumph. The poem becomes a vision - in that way like *Piers Plowman* - of a fair field full of folk, but it shows them borne down by a triumphal car, as so many souls are also borne down in *The House of Fame*. The 'I' who sees the vision comes across the figure of the dead Rousseau who then explains the vision of life he had had, an equally nihilistic one. At that point the poem finishes, but had it continued, its structure would have demanded Rousseau's finding another figure, historically upstream from him, who would have had the same vision, and so on in a pattern of repetition.

To read Shelley's *The Triumph of Life*, Derrida turns to two *récits* by Maurice Blanchot, *La folie du jour* (1949) and *Arrêt de mort* (1947) with its punning sense of 'death sentence' and the 'arrest of death' - a reprieve from death. *Arrêt de mort* is two separate narratives of two women, one of whom, J, dies; the other, Nathalie, lives, and it is a question how these two women figure each other. With J, 'her pulse, the nurse said, scattered like sand' (like the sand in the hour-glass) but she then revives when the narrator appears, and then dies again, so that her pulse again '"scattered like sand"' which leads Derrida to give a sense of death as 'the result of the dissemination of the rhythm of life with no finishing stroke [*coup d'arrêt*], unbordered and unbounded arrhythmy on a beach that is a continuation of the sea' ('Living On', 121).[63] In that the same thing

---

[62] See also his discussion of *Beyond the Pleasure Principle* in *The Post-card: From Socrates to Freud and Beyond*, trans. by Alan Bass (Chicago: University of Chicago Press, 1987) p. 277

[63] Derrida's sentence makes the sand that of the sea-shore, quoting Shelley to illuminate Blanchot: 'And suddenly my brain became as sand / Where the first wave had more than half erased / The track of deer on desert Labrador, / Whilst the fierce wolf from which they fled amazed / Leaves his stamp visibly

can be said about her twice, her death is as it were in quotation-marks; it is a repetition of what has happened, as though death was already contained within life.

Derrida and Blanchot are both fascinated by the relation of death to life: as is Langland. Death is the 'utterly *other*', ("Living On," 100) and speech may be said to include a 'reserve' in it that disallows its appearance within it. As Wittgenstein says, 'Death is not an event in life. We do not live to experience death'.[64] But Derrida implicitly goes beyond this Wittgensteinian view when he sees Hegelian philosophy practising a 'reserve' within language in order to keep death out, to maintain meaning and self-consciousness. He contrasts that with 'the heedless sacrifice of presence and meaning' associated with Bataille (Blanchot's friend). Derrida writes:

> The blind spot of Hegelianism *around* which can be organized the representation of meaning, is the *point* at which destruction, suppression, death and sacrifice constitute so irreversible an expenditure, so radical a negativity - here we would have to say an expenditure and a negativity *without reserve* - that they can no longer be determined as negativity in a process or a system.[65]

The breakthrough in language such as that of Bataille or Blanchot, is the possibility of seeing, and saying, 'life death'. This is allegorical thinking, and what Enlightenment thought - hence Hegel's relevance here - has repressed. The attempt in Blanchot may be thought of as to do again, in the conditions of modernity, what Langland could do.

In *Arrêt de mort*, the attachment to the two women, in two halves of a text separated by an

> *arête*' (ridge, fold) which 'signifies, desires, *arrête*, life death, the life the death of the other so that the other lives *and* dies, the other of the other - who *is* without being the *same*. For there is an other of the other, and it is not the same: this is what the order of the symbol seeks desperately to deny. ('Living On' 165-6)

This critique of the symbol - which would allow only the opposition of life and death - derives from Benjamin in the *Trauerspiel* study, where allegory contests symbolism which idealizes life, separating it from death. Allegory's fascination is with 'the other of the other'.

---

upon the shore / Until the second bursts' (*The Triumph of Life*, ed. by Donald H. Reiman (Urbana: University of Illinois Press, 1966) lines 405-9). The passage, rich in its implications of borders, and borders crossed, and of the trace, and erasure, illustrates Derrida's bringing a past text to bear on the present - in this he derives from Benjamin.

64   Ludwig Wittgenstein, *Tractatus Logico-Philosophicus*, trans. by Bertrand Russell (London: Routledge & Kegan Paul, 1971) p. 147, (6.4311).

65   Jacques Derrida, *Writing and Difference*, trans. by Alan Bass (London: Routledge, 1978), pp. 257, 259.

The symbol represses and excludes and its representation of death misrepresents. The 'other of the other' refuses to find death as the sole other. 'Living On', which also contains a supplementary essay called 'Border Lines', shows the impossibility of taking up a position outside the text. Nobody can talk about living, or on living, as though there was something that could be said about it: such talk can only be from inside life; there is no border-position possible. To talk about death, too, requires seeing that this is the other which is both inside and outside; inside as the blank or the stain within life, like the skull seen in Holbein's picture, *The Ambassadors*, which constitutes the border.

In *Piers Plowman*, denying an inside / outside distinction, Death is the allegorical figure inside the poem, because of its specular relation with life and because it points to allegory as catachrestic, being that and speaking of that which cannot be spoken of. For *Piers Plowman* to evoke Death as a figure that can be recognised is to assume a text which stands outside the outside. There is an interesting contrast here with Chaucer. In *The Pardoner's Tale*, after the rumour has been given about what Death is like, the wasters go out to destroy Death, but Death is not to be bidden; the Old Man who wants to die, prays 'Leeve mooder, let me in' (731) as though the earth was to be identified with Death, which would make Death feminine, but the Old Man is an allegory of the impossibility of including Death within representation, even though he tells the wasters that they shall find Death under the tree. By the end of *The Pardoner's Tale*, all three wasters are dead, and Death has not appeared, being rather inside the text, not as an hypostasised figure, but inside the characters and the tale's logic. Langland works in contrast with that astonishing *Tale*, which may be a critique of allegorizations of death, by, instead, bringing the utterly other into the text's 'other speaking'.

In doing so, *Piers Plowman* makes a stronger argument that everything in it is allegory, that it is like the dream, or the mirror. The text's melancholy can do no more - but no less than - circulate around that. Death is one character among many, whose textual existence *before* the end means the text cannot end, which is the exact counterpart to the last lines, when Conscience starts out again, and 'I gan awake' (XXII.387). The apocalyptic end is also delayed. Death destroys systems of representation, but putting death into representation subjects it to the differential system that marks all tropes, all figures; it puts this allegory beyond death. It is a strange triumph of the will's melancholia.

CHAPTER 2

The Knight Sets Forth: Chaucer, Chrétien and Dürer

I - HOLOCAUSTS

> Yet saugh I Woodnesse, laughynge in his rage,
> Armed Compleint, Outhees and fiers Outrage [...] (2011-2)

Madness, complaint and violence: these things are the substance of *The Knight's Tale* and so of this chapter. There are, however, three other contexts for the knight and *The Knight's Tale*: chronologically, first Chrétien de Troyes's poem *Yvain* (c.1170) and second, *The Monk's Tale*, which comes later in *The Canterbury Tales* and last an engraving by Dürer, *The Knight, Death and the Devil* (c1514). 'The Knight sets forth', my chapter-title, is also Auerbach's title in *Mimesis*, when he analyses Calogrenant's journey through the forest of Broceliande in *Yvain*. And even as early as *Yvain*, there is something anachronistic about knighthood[1] while in Chaucer, there seems to be a tendency for bourgeois knighthood to disavow its real conditions of existence. Peasants' uprisings, 'outhees', which marked the time of Chaucer and Dürer, 1381 and 1525, bring out class tensions only partially consciously registered in *The Knight's Tale*.

Though it appears to have had a prior existence in Chaucer as 'al the love of Palamon and Arcite / Of Thebes' (*LGW* F 420-1), and to belong initially to around 1386, *The Knight's Tale*, is importantly, the *knight's*.[2] It is a prior text which he must utter, challenging him and his class on certain points. The *General Prologue* to *The Canterbury Tales* idealized the knight. It made him a crusading

---

[1] 'The twelfth-century authors of the original chansons of the Carolingian cycle, were already writing about a period that was distant from their own and holding up its heroes as models of the true chivalry of antique times. The authors of the earliest Arthurian romances were looking back to a period even more remote. From the very first, it would seem, true chivalry was always presented in antique dress' - Maurice Keen, 'Huizinga, Kilgour and the Decline of Chivalry', *Medievalia et Humanistica* n.s. 8 (1977) 7. On knighthood in the fifteenth-century, see Larry D.Benson, *Malory's Morte Darthur* (Cambridge, Mass: Harvard University Press, 1976 section 3). See also on Huizinga, Malcolm Vale, *War and Chivalry: Warfare and Aristocratic Culture in England, France and Burgundy at the End of the Middle Ages* (Athens, GA.: University of Georgia Press, 1981), pp. 1-13.

[2] This agrees with H. Marshall Leicester, jr., *The Disenchanted Self: Representing the Subject in The Canterbury Tales* (Berkeley: University of California Press, 1990), pp. 221-382, whose 'voice-oriented reading' (p. 222), sees the Tale as demonstrating 'the knight's voice' (p. 380); however, I do not see the text as justifying knighthood by its negotiation of different textual positions, as Leicester does: I see it rather as bringing this to a crisis. The opposite point of view, that the tale and the teller are unrelated, is expressed by Helen Cooper, *Oxford Guides to Chaucer: The Canterbury Tales* (Oxford: Oxford University Press, 1989), pp. 61-91.

figure, going far afield but with no mention of the nearer to home Hundred Years' War. 'Worthy' appears five times, but knighthood becomes nostalgic, since its values are far back in the past – 'fro the tyme that he first began / To riden out'. They are not of the present.[3] As for as the knight's relationship to his tale, while recognizing the fitness of some formal details of the tale for a knight's telling - such as Theseus, the two knights, Emetreus and Lycurgus, the contest between Mars and Venus, and the investment made in order, the tale challenges the knight, making him speak and act differently from his prior existence in the *Prologue*. Both text and teller have had earlier existences, and take on new subject-positions here. And the possessive reads either way. Is this a tale a knight might tell? Is it a tale appropriate for a knight to listen to? Does it subvert the knight's identity?

'But of that storie list me not to write' (1201), and the references to 'enditing' (1209,1380,2741) relate the text to earlier writing, to 'Stace of Thebes and thise bookes olde' (2294), as with the epigraph which in some manuscripts opens the tale – 'Iamque domos patrias, Scithice post aspera gentis / Prelia, laurigero, etc.' – 'And now [Theseus approaching] his native land in his laurelled [chariot] after his fierce battles with the Scythians, etc.' (*Thebaid*. 12. 519-20). The knight could hardly have uttered that, or started that way; nor does the scholarship fit the first line's generalised reference to 'olde stories' (859). The lines point to writing, taking up Statius' *Thebaid* at the point of Theseus' entrance into the poem. They connect the opening with an earlier scene - the holocausts at Thebes arising from the rivalry of Polynices and Eteocles. We are not that far, thematically, from Oedipus, whose sons these are, and from history as a series of catastrophes - where, in *The Knight's Tale*, the rivalry of Arcite and Palamon will evoke the former mutual hatred of Oedipus' sons.[4] The knights are found within the piling up of ruin.

---

[3]   On the knight, see Michael A. Calabrese, in *Chaucer's Pilgrims: An Historical Guide to the Pilgrims in The Canterbury Tales*, ed. by Laura C. Lambdin and Robert T. Lambdin (Westport, Conn.: Greenwood Press, 1996), pp. 1-13; Jill Mann, *Chaucer and Medieval Estates Satire: The Literature of Social Classes and the General Prologue to The Canterbury Tales* (Cambridge: Cambridge University Press, 1973), pp. 106-115.

[4]   On the 'Theban genealogy in *The Knight's Tale*', see David Anderson, *Before The Knight's Tale: Imitation of Classical Epic in the Teseida* (Philadelphia: University of Pennsylvania Press, 1988). For the *Teseida*, see Piero Boitani, *Chaucer and Boccaccio* (Oxford: Society for the Study of Medieval language and Literature, 1977). Earlier criticism of the Tale used here includes classic discussions by Muscatine, E.Talbot Donaldson and Donald Howard: these are reprinted in Harold Bloom, ed., *Geoffrey Chaucer: The Knight's Tale* (New York: Chelsea House, 1988). The role of Saturn is played down by Lois Roney, *Chaucer's Knight's Tale and Theories of Scholastic Psychology* (Tampa:

Theseus has, like Saturn, destroyed Thebes, 'rente adoun bothe wall and sparre and rafter' (990) and the bodies have been burned:

> To ransake in the taas of bodyes dede,
> Hem for to strepe of harneys and of wede,
> The pilours diden bisynesse and cure
> After the bataille and disconfiture.
> And so bifel that in the taas they founde,
> Thurgh-girt with many a grevous blody wounde,
> Two yonge knyghtes liggynge by and by,
> Bothe in oon armes, wroght ful richely,
> Of which two Arcita highte that oon,
> And that oother knyght highte Palamon.
> Nat fully quyke, ne fully dede they were [...] (1005-15)

The history of Palamon and Arcite begins with ruin, a pile of dead bodies associated with the destruction of Thebes. The two are born out of the dead, as virtual twins ('bothe in oon armes') to recommence a cycle of violence, repeating something of the previous history of Thebes. This text cannot distantiate itself from the *Thebaid* narrative - which concludes with Theseus' killing of Creon (like Aeneas killing Turnus), and then moves to the funeral:

> Non ego, centena si quis mea pectora laxet
> voce deus, tot busta simul vulgique ducumque,
> tot pariter gemitus dignis conatibus aequem:
> turbine quo sese caris impleverit audax
> ignibus Euadne fulmenque in pectore magno
> quaesiverit; quo more iacens super oscula saevi
> corporis infelix excuset Tydea coniunx;
> ut saevos narret vigiles Argia sorori;
> Arcada quo planctu genetrix Erymanthia clamet,
> Arcada, consumpto servantem sanguine vultus,
> Arcada, quem geminae pariter flevere cohortes.

> [I could not, even if some god gave hundredfold utterance to my heart, recount in worthy strains so vast a funeral of chieftains alike and common folk, so many lamentations united: how fearless Evadne with impetuous bound had her fill of the fires she loved and sought the thunderbolt in that mighty breast, how as she lay and showered kisses on his terrible form his unhappy spouse made excuse for Tydeus; how Argia tells her sister the story of the cruel watchmen, with what lament the Erymanthian mother bewails the Arcadian, who keeps his beauty though all his blood be spent, the Arcadian, wept for by either host alike.][5]

University of South Florida Press, 1990); she notes that Saturn is Chaucer's addition to Boccaccio, but argues that Saturn is subordinated to the Prime Mover.

5   Statius, *Thebaid*, XII. 797-807, trans. by J.H.Mozley, (Loeb, Harvard University Press, 1929) II. pp.502-5. For these lines see Winthrop Wetherbee,

Declaring the impossibility of writing it adequately, Statius's text closes with the women mourning over the dead bodies of the men, where grandeur becomes elegiac as the solitary Arcadian, Parthenopeus, is spoken of, in a mourning which returns in *The Knight's Tale* with the broken body of Arcite, who does not, however, keep his beauty though his blood be spent, but instead lies 'as blak...as any cole or crowe' (2692). Nothing remains for Statius save his envoi, which had earlier, before the writing of *The Knight's Tale*, been drawn on in the closing down of the *Troilus* (V.1786-92). A pile of bodies for burning: a pile of bodies where the two knights are found. The first funeral displaces and defers a marriage, so does the second. Arcite's funeral connects to the *Thebaid* by echoing the final funerals there, though with the sense that the new details of Arcite's funeral, in which everything of value is thrown, and everything left desolate, cannot fit with the earlier model − hence the *occupatio* (2919-2966) where the narrator says what he does not intend to describe.

In the tale's third part, the lists mean that violence is given order and coherence in design and the aleatory − chance that decides combat − is raised to the level of a formal game. From this follows the description of the temples of Venus, Mars and Diana. But the effort to allegorize different modes of experience through the three Olympians collapses: arbitrary violence works equally with Venus, who catches people in her 'las / Til they for wo ful ofte seyde "allas"' (1951, 52), and with Mars and with Diana, whose hunting - also using a 'las' - emblematizes predatoriness. The temples imply a frenzy of destruction implicit in the rhetorical performance produced through the paintings and existent in their descriptions. The text draws attention to the 'soutil pencel' (2049) of the draftsman:

> Wel koude he peynten lifly that it wroghte,
> With many a floryn he the hewes boghte. (2087-8)

Realism (cp. 'lifly') is guaranteed in the material signifying practice which designs these gods, and the breakoff from the subject-matter to the curtness of the comment shows that a rhetorical choice has been made how to portray these gods. And if the knight - or the text - minimizes tragedy through playful or off-handed comments, there is also a stress on inclusiveness − 'the toun destroyed' in one line; in the next, the means of escape destroyed in: 'Yet saugh I brent the shippes hoppesteres' (2016-7) - which evokes a will to ruin:

> Depeynted was the slaughtre of Julius,
> Of grete Nero, and of Antonius;

'Romance and Epic in Chaucer's *Knight's Tale*', *Exemplaria* 2.1 (March 1990), 303-328.

> Al be that thilke tyme they were unborn,
> Yet was hir deth depeynted ther-biforn
> By manasynge of Mars, right by figure. (2031-5)

'Figure' evokes Auerbach's *figura*, but also the textual and allegorical character of the portraiture. Nero and Caesar re-appear in *The Monk's Tale* (2463-2550; 2671-2726), where they are destroyed by Fortune and not by Mars. Criticism can hardly differentiate Arcite and Palamon by relating them to either Mars or Venus, for the poem makes the values of the one the other's, so that the dispute between Arcite and Palamon, over Emelye, is actually motivated by fear of lack of difference. René Girard, who defines tragedy in terms of 'the opposition of symmetrical elements',[6] sees fraternal opposition, as here, in terms of an anxiety over a lack of separation, the need to enforce difference, related to the Oedipal struggle against the father. The temple-portraiture makes differentiation between the heroes impossible: the chivalric code which promotes hierarchical difference as the thing it lives by, disallows it. The textual drive occludes humanistic differences between characters. The suggestion of a will to destruction asks for a more complex reading of the text than can be given in even Muscatine's reading, when he takes the poem as 'the struggle between noble designs and chaos'.[7] This binary division invites deconstruction.[8] Noble designs and chaos are more intricately worked together in Theseus's and the knight's mind than appears; the noble design *is* chaos, and the text brings out the elements of *différance* within noble designs and chaos that make neither unitary concepts. That is part of the melancholy that reads allegorically: that sees them as non-unified. The discovery within fratricidal rivalry - these 'brothers' have fought up to their ankles in their blood - of the futility of efforts to set up a system of differences with positive terms points to a deeper ambiguity about the reasons for destructiveness in people so committed to order.

II - THE MADNESS OF THE TEXT

That the *Thebaid*, like the *Teseida*, underlies *The Knight's Tale* makes this text an unconscious other within the later text, a foreign

---

[6] René Girard, *Violence and the Sacred*, trans. by Patrick Gregory (Baltimore: John Hopkins University Press, 1972) p.44.

[7] Muscatine, quoted Lee Patterson, *Chaucer and the Subject of History* (London: Routledge, 1991), p.165.

[8] A recent attempt to affirm allegorical categories appears in Edward I. Condren, *Chaucer and the Energy of Creation* (Gainesville: University Press of Florida, 1999), pp. 28-51. I can accept little here, including his sense that the knight's allegorical distinctions make him 'wander closer to treatise than to literature' (p. 51).

body which continues to affect it.[9] Debra Hershkowitz, writing on the classical epic, shows that its motivating force always seems to be madness, and to require a like madness in its author. She makes three points whose significance should be drawn out. She calls the *Thebaid* 'an epic about madness, pervaded by madness, dependent upon madness'; she shows a link between madness and enervation, loss of energy, stagnation; so that excess of violence, immoderate anger, is followed by a weakening and loss of power which though she does not call it melancholy, could be seen as that. She links Theseus's acts within the poem (from the point which was quoted in *The Knight's Tale*'s epigraph) to the madness of Polynices and Eteocles, and finds the same violence and excess in him – including violence towards the Amazons he captures – so he is part of the text's 'overwhelming madness'.[10] Certainly the conquest Theseus carries out in *The Knight's Tale* which makes him a conqueror (981, 1027) is relativized by the sight of Conquest in the temple of Mars (2028-30); Theseus exists within a cycle of violence. Herschkowitz's examples are powerful enough to inflect the violence of *The Knight's Tale* with madness: at the beginning, in the portrayal of violence in the temples, and in the textual detachment or repression which separates itself from what violence has just been announced:

> With soutil pencel was depeynted this storie
> In redoutynge of Mars and of his glorie (2049-50)

or in the statement about Arcite, 'Fare wel phisik! Go ber the man to chirche!' (2760), said when the man is still alive. It is there too in the destruction of everything for Arcite's funeral, where the *occupatio* shows the wastefulness of the excess.

The detachment is melancholic, and it appears in *The Knight's Tale* when Arcite is love-sick. Sorrow takes hold of him so that he becomes 'as dry as is a shaft' and in appearance, 'pale as asshen colde' (1364). The adjective's significance develops through the *Tale*. In Mars's temple, 'the colde deeth' (2008) is personified. Saturn is 'colde' (2443), Arcite is 'overcome' as a knight by 'the coold of deeth' (2800), and ready for the 'colde grave', (2778),

---

[9] For the significance of Boccaccio's *Teseida* (c.1340-1341), in twelve books, as long as the *Aeneid*, see Piero Boitani, *Chaucer and Boccaccio* (Oxford: Society for the Study of Medieval Languages and Literature, 1977); see also Boitani in *Chaucer and the Italian Trecento* (Cambridge: Cambridge University Press, 1983), pp. 185-199. David Anderson, *Before The Knight's Tale*, p. 199 says that 'Chaucer follows Boccaccio in proposing an open imitation of the *Thebaid*'.

[10] Debra Hershkowitz, *The Madness of Epic: Reading Insanity from Homer to Statius* (Oxford: Clarendon Press, 1988), pp. 247-301, quotations pp. 248, 301.

ending by being 'brent to asshen colde' (2957). Death is in the body from the beginning, working like melancholy and madness:

> And in his geere for al the world he ferde
> Nat oonly like the loveris maladye
> Of Hereos, but rather lyk manye,
> Engendred of humour malencolik
> Biforen, in his celle fantastik. (1372-6)

The melancholic spirits, or liquid, have risen up in him and taken over the front ventricle of the brain, the 'celle fantastik', seat of the *vis imaginativa*, which retains images of sensory experience. This is the place for mania, as the middle venticle, the *vis estimativa*, where insensible intentions are apprehended, is the place of melancholia. The lover has been possessed by an image of the woman, by a phantasm, and this produces first melancholy and then madness. Arcite suffers from a melancholy called 'Hereos' – which name associates the condition with eros, with heroes and with knights – and also from mania.[11] Agamben, linking melancholia to erotic desire, writes: 'If the external world is in fact narcissistically denied to the melancholic as an object of love, the phantasm yet receives from this negation a reality principle and emerges from the mute interior crypt in order to enter into a new and fundamental dimension'. The melancholic acts like this because, Agamben says, the lesson of melancholy is that 'only what is ungraspable can be truly grasped'.[12] Melancholia is a relation to desire that collects substitute phantoms that it knows to be such: in doing so it makes a fetish of what it has lost. It cannot be said that Arcite recovers from this melancholia - except in death.

---

[11]   See Edward C.Schweitzer, 'Fate and Freedom in *The Knight's Tale*', *Studies in the Age of Chaucer 3* (1981) 13-45. For love-melancholy, discussed by Burton in *The Anatomy of Melancholy*, see Stanley W. Jackson, *Melancholia and Depression: From Hippocratic Times to Modern Times* (New Haven: Yale University Press, 1986), pp. 352-372. See also Mary Frances Wack, on the Arabic text translated by Constantine the African as the *Viaticum* in the eleventh century, *Lovesickness in the Middle Ages: The Viacticum and its Comentaries* (Philadelphia: University of Pennsylvania Press, 1990). See also the quotation from Arnaldus of Villanova in D.W. Robertson, jr. *A Preface to Chaucer; Studies in Medieval Perspectives* (Princeton: Princeton University Press, 1962), pp. 108-110.

[12]   Giorgio Agamben, *Stanzas: Word and Phantasm in Western Culture* trans. Ronald L.Martinez (Minneapolis: University of Minnesota Press, 1993), pp. 25, 26. See also p.117.

III – 'YVAIN FURIEUX'[13]

> First on the wal was peynted a forest,
> In which ther dwelleth neither man ne best,
> With knotty, knarry, bareyne trees olde,
> Of stubbes sharpe, and hidouse to biholde,
> In which ther ran a rumbel in a swough,
> As though a storm sholde bresten every bough,
> And dounward from an hille, under a bente,
> Ther stood the temple of Mars armypotente [...] (1975-1982)

Mars's and Arcite's temple includes within it a painting of a forest inside which is the temple of Mars in a *mise en abime* which frames the temple with the forest. The paintings inside the second temple also evoke the forest, as in such lines as 'The careyne in the busk, with throte ycorve' (2013). The forest is inside and outside, and it evokes a mad state.

In Chrétien, Yvain's madness, which drives him into the forests of Broceliande, compares with Arcite's love-melancholy. When Yvain stays away from his wife, Laudine, for more than the year he had promised, a messenger comes to him at Arthur's court to take back the ring she had given him, leaving him speechless, and wanting to flee away to a land so wild no one could follow him.

> He hated nothing so much as himself and did not know whom to turn to for comfort now that he was the cause of his own death. But he would rather lose his mind than fail to take revenge on himself, who had ruined his own happiness.[14]

The splitting, which relates to a contradiction between the masculinity of the court and the claims of the woman, which the romance cannot resolve, appears in this self-hatred. Yvain leaves the court, going far from the tents and pavilions.

> Then such a tempest ['torbeillons', 2804] arose in his mind that he went mad; he ripped and tore at his clothing and fled across fields and plains.

'Torbeillons' is different from the word 'tempest' ('tanpeste', 431) which appears when Calogrenant pours the water from the spring onto the stone and raises the storm at the bidding of the wild man of the forest, but the sense is similar. Calogrenant's act was like splitting

---

[13] Frappier's title, on the analogy of *Orlando Furioso*, for the scene of Yvain's madness: see Jacques Le Goff and Pierre Vidal-Naquet, 'Lévi-Strauss en Broceliande', *Critique* 30 (1974), 541-571 (p. 544).

[14] Chrétien de Troyes, *Arthurian Romances*, trans. by William W. Kibler and Carleton Carroll (Harmondsworth: Penguin, 1991) pp. 330-333. See also the translation by D.D.R. Owen (London: Everyman, 1987). French edition of *Yvain* edited Jan Nelson, Carleton W. Carroll and Douglas Kelly (New York: Appleton-Century, 1968).

reality at its very heart; it is contact with the real. This Lacanian term, 'the real', what is outside symbolization, helps with understanding what Calogrenant and then Yvain risk at the place where the tree of life and the spring which is boiling yet cold come together. The potential of madness is, however, unlike Arcite, manic, not depressive; masculine, and violent.[15]

Yvain's people seek him among the knights' lodgings, and through the hedgerows and orchards, but he has gone beyond these zones:

> And he ran on, until, near a park, he encountered a youth, who had a bow and five barbed arrows, whose tips were broad and sharp. Yvain approached the youth and took from him the bows and arrows he was holding; yet afterwards he did not remember anything he had done. He stalked wild animals in the forest and killed them and ate their raw flesh.
>
> He lived in the forest like a madman and a savage ['hon forsenez et sauvage', 2828], until one day he came upon a very small and cramped abode of a hermit. The hermit was clearing his land; when he saw the naked stranger he was certain beyond any doubt that the man had lost all his senses; of this he was absolutely sure. From the fright it gave him he rushed into his little hut. The good man in his charity took some bread and clear water and placed it outside his house upon a narrow window-ledge; and Yvain, who was eager for the bread, came up: he took it and bit into it. I don't believe he had ever tasted such hard and bitter bread ... and drank cold water from the pitcher.
>
> After he had eaten, he plunged again into the woods and hunted stags and does. And the good man in his hut, when he saw him leave, prayed to God to protect the stranger and keep him from ever returning this way. But no one, no matter how mad, would fail to return very gladly to a place where he had been kindly received. Not a day passed during Yvain's period of madness that he didn't bring to the hermit's door some wild game. This was the life he led from that day on; and the good man undertook to skin the game and put a sufficient amount of meat on to cook. The bread and the pitcher of water were always at the window to nourish the madman; thus, for food and drink her had venison without salt or pepper, and cool spring water. And the food man was at pains to sell the skins and purchase unleavened bread of barley and oats.

The description then passes to the time when Yvain is discovered sleeping in the forest by a lady and her two women. He is naked; to be known only by a mark on his body, the only sign that there is something to distinguish him from the animal, is that he has been touched by the signs of human conflict – a scar. His madness ('la rage et la tanpeste', 2950) is driven away by the woman rubbing his

---

[15] Anne Hunsaker Hawkins, 'Yvain's Madness', *Philological Quarterly* 71 (1992), 377-397 distinguishes between Yvain's mania, and lovesickness as in the case of Arcite; she sees Yvain's madness as produced by yellow bile affecting the anterior part of the brain. But there is a relation between yellow and black bile.

body with an ointment under the hot sun so that "she expelled the madness and melancholy ['la rage et la melencolie'] from his brain.

When does his madness begin? In losing the ring, he loses sense and power of speech: he is outside reason and discourse. He cannot go back to Laudine; hence his desire for madness, to get away from what he sees and hears; he wants a land so wild ('sauvage terre', 2785) that it would be as if he had gone to the abyss ('abisme', 2789), to the pit of Hell. Going out of his mind in self-hatred and the desire for self-destruction, and going far away seem analogous. Loss of sociability follows: he moves out, first beyond the tents and pavilions, second across the fields beyond the hedges and gardens, third beyond the park, an enclosed area for grazing, last, into the woodland. In the park he takes the bow and five arrows, where five might imply the five senses – all that he is left with. At his nadir he eats the raw flesh of the animals he has killed, becoming the nearest to a wild animal. The wood means what Vance refers to when quoting Bernard of Silvestris's *Cosmographia*: that *silva* is primary matter:

> *silva*: intractable, a formless chaos, hostile coalescence, the motley appearance of being, a mass discordant with itself, longs in her turbulence for a tempering power; in her crudity, for form; in her rankness, for cultivation. Yearning to emerge from her ancient confusion, she demands the shaping influence of number and the bonds of harmony'.[16]

Yvain has been in the wood before, where he saw the wild man who guarded the beasts of the woods; he has now become like him. The wood is only apparently the opposite of the character of the knight; Dodinel, one of the knights to whom Calogrenant tells the original story of his disgrace in the forest, is called 'the wild man' (*Erec* 1688).[17] The wood, Dante's *selva oscura* (*Inferno* 1.3), is the place of madness.

---

[16] See Eugene Vance, *From Topic to Tale: Logic and Narrativity in the Middle Ages* (Minneapolis: University of Minnesota Press, 1987), pp. 63-79 for the episode, p. 64 for the quotation.

[17] Richard Bernheimer, *Wild Men of the Middle Ages: A Study in Art, Sentiment and Demonology* (Cambridge, Mass.: Harvard University Press, 1952), p. 8 refers to 'Sir Dodinel le Sauvage', and discusses the relationship of knighthood with wildness, pp 8-15. In a footnote to p. 15 (pp. 191-192) he notes that wild men were often thought of as black; cp. Calogrenant's description of the giant who guards the beasts as like a Moor (Mor, line 286). For discussion of Bernheimer, see Hayden White in Edward Dudley and Maximilian Novak, eds., *The Wild Man Within: An Image in Western Thought from the Renaissance to Romanticism* (Pittsburgh: University of Pittsburgh Press, 1972), pp. 3-38.

The link between the wild man and insanity comes in Geoffrey of Monmouth (*Vita Merlini*, c1150),[18] as though the production of the subject in the twelfth century – as urban, outside feudal models – places the knightly class outside the urban, and makes it tendentially mad.[19] The point appears with the hermit, a figure between the wild wood and society, seen clearing the land round his hut, as the fields and plains are the cleared space around the court. The hermit, non-knightly, is not wild. If the turn to the woods is like desire for the womb, he acts like a mother, by providing bread and water in a pitcher.[20] He first lays out bread (however poor in quality, it is cooked), and responds to Yvain's dumb, animal-like gratitude when he skins and cooks meat, then sells the skins and buys better quality bread (barley and oats). Auerbach comments that

---

[18] See Geoffrey of Monmouth, *Life of Merlin* (*Vita Merlini*), ed. by Basil Clarke (Cardiff: University of Wales Press, 1973). It coincides with Stephen's reign (1135-1154) and the second crusade (1147-1149). Geoffrey of Monmouth wrote his *Historia Regum Britanniae* in 1136-8; this, however gives 'the madness of the bard of prophecy' (p. 53), when Merlin becomes *silvester homo* (line 80) – the man of the woods, in lamentation for the death of his companions. Merlin declares 'I was taken out of my true self' (line 1161). But in a speech of lines 1156-1178, addressing God, 'I was as a spirit and knew the history of people long past and could foretell the future'. See Timothy Husband, *The Wild Man: Medieval Myth and Symbolism* (New York: Metropolitan Museum, 1980), p. 61. For the wild man theme, in addition to Bernheimer and Husband, see Roger Bartra, *Wild Men in the Looking Glass: The Mythic Origins of European Otherness*, trans. by Carl T. Berrisford (Ann Arbor: University of Michigan Press, 1994); J.B. Friedman, *The Monstrous Races in Medieval Art and Thought* (Cambridge, Mass.: Harvard University Press, 1981) and Judith S. Neaman, *Suggestions of the Devil: Insanity in the Middle Ages and the Twentieth Century* (New York: Octagon Books, 1978).

[19] For Husband, the wild man becomes hairy in the twelfth century; shagginess being associated with the medieval maniac or melancholic (pp. 99-100). Perhaps Yvain's madness is associated with lycanthropy, for which see Charlotte F. Otten, *A Lycanthropy Reader: Werewolves in Western Culture* (New York: Syracuse University Press, 1986). Although 'lycanthropy' appears not until 1584, 'werewolf' is a word of c.11, and appears in Marie de France, 'The Lai of the Werewolf' (*Bisclavret*). The disease of *melencholia canina* was discussed in c7 Alexandria, by Paulus Aeginata, where 'the patient delights to wander among tombs, imitating the cries of dogs' (p. 13). That would be cynanthropy. See also Corinne J. Saunders, *The Forest of Medieval Romance: Avernus, Broceliande, Arden* (Woodbridge: Boydell and Brewer 1993) p. 51ff (and pp. 67-72, 115-122 and 158-160). On the forest in literature see also Robert Pogue Harrison, *Forests: The Shadow of Civilization* (Chicago: University of Chicago Press, 1992).

[20] Gaston Bachelard discusses the forest as always 'ancestral', never young, always 'before me, before us' in *The Poetics of Space*, trans. by Maria Jolas (Boston: Beacon Press, 1994) pp. 188-9. For a reading, in the tradition of D.W. Robertson, jr, see Tom Artin, *The Allegory of Adventure: Reading Chrétien's Erec and Yvain* (Lewisburg: Bucknell University Press, 1974), pp. 194-218.

74

Chrétien de Troyes, who lived first in Champagne, where ... the great
commercial fairs began to assume outstanding continental importance,
then in Flanders where the burghers attained economic and political
significance earlier than elsewhere north of the Alps, may well have
begun to sense that the feudal class was no longer the only class.

Auerbach senses a lack of realism: 'Courtly culture gives rise to the
idea ... that nobility, greatness and intrinsic values have nothing in
common with everyday reality'.[21] In Chrétien, everything works to
rescue the knight, for whom the wild wood is a 'natural' habitat, but
it should be added there is a double movement in the text; whch is
both on the side of madness and wildness, and on the side of
clearing,[22] which implies a removal of the excluded terrain which the
knight occupies. A history is at work which makes the knight's
existence physically unsustainable, while the text works to uphold
knighthood. A splitting in the text has as a symptom the splitting
within Yvain.

In Chrétien, the madness of Yvain is inseparable from the context
of the knight. In Chaucer, melancholy and madness stand as threats
to an order which they also destroy; hence the tale invokes madness
as an external threat. Arcite's melancholy associates with madness,
and is picked up in many other references. Palamon says 'I moot been
in prisoun through Saturne / And eek thurgh Juno, jalous and eek
wood' (1328-9). In the *Aeneid*, 10.760, Juno, whose anger drives the
epic on – 'flectere si nequeo superos, Acheronta movebo' (If I am
unable to bend the heavens, I shall move Acheron" [*Aeneid* 7.312])[23] -
is 'Saturnian Juno'. In Book 12.830-31, Jupiter says that she is the
second child of Saturn (he is the first) 'irarum tantos volis sub
pectore fluctus' [you roll such great waves of anger in your heart].
Anger, then, which is on the way to madness – the point is made by
Seneca: 'ut scias autem non esse sanos quos ira possedit, ipsum
illorum habitum intuere' [in order to know that they are not sane
whom anger possesses, look at their expression (*De ira* 1.1.3)],
emanates from melancholia. Juno's cruelty is the subject of Arcite's
complaint (1540-71) in the grove in the second part. Her Jealousy

---

[21] Erich Auerbach, *Mimesis: The Representation of Reality in Western Literature*
trans. Willard Trask (Princeton: Princeton University Press, 1953), pp.
138,139. On the role of Chrétien in giving prestige to knighthood in the twelfth
century, see Tony Hunt, 'The Emergence of the Knight in France and England
1000-1200', *Forum for Modern Language Studies* 17 (1981), 93 114 (pp. 98-
99).

[22] Le Goff and Vidal-Naquet, p. 571 refer to the clearings in which encounters
take place: lines 277, 308, 393, 3344, 4096, 4106. The knight who challenges
Calogrenant, also refers to the clearing which seems to be the effect of the
pouring of the water onto the stone: lines 497-501.

[23] See discussion of this in Herschowitz, pp. 97-100.

appears in Venus's temple (1929-30). Palamon in fighting is as a 'wood leon' (1656). The grove, part of the forest, produces men like 'wilde bores' (1658), in another reversal to wildness (the mad images are repeated in the jousting, at 2626-2634). Wildness and madness associate in 'Yet saugh I Woodnesse, laughynge in his rage' (2011), and 'The statue of Mars upon a carte stood / Armed, and looked grym as he were wood' (2041-2).

IV - SATURN

Madness and melancholy make Saturn, first mentioned by Arcite (1088) presiding planetary influence in *The Knight's Tale*. Saturn is an allegory of instability, contrasting with the First Mover, also identified with Jupiter. After the prayers of Arcite, Palamon and Emelye, 'Strif' begins in heaven, with Venus and Mars human-like, anxious to preserve their differences, as though the values of the one were not the values of the other. Jupiter, the patriarch can do nothing, so matters pass to Saturn, the ultimate patriarch, the *castrated* god, (the point is not made here, but is familiar, from *Le Roman de la Rose* 5534ff and it suggests lack of difference, which underlies the pretence at order).[24] Melancholia contaminates and relativises Theseus' attempts to make Jupiter central and overarching; it adds to the difficulties readers have had with this last speech.[25] Order has already been subverted, before the rationalizations begin.

> My cours, that hath so wyde for to turne,
> Hath moore power than woot any man.
> Myn is the drenchyng in the see so wan;
> Myn is the prison in the derke cote;
> Myn is the stranglyng and hangyng by the throte,
> The murmure and the cherles rebellyng,
> The groynynge, and the pryvee empoysonyng;
> I do vengeance and pleyn correccioun,
> Whil I dwelle in the signe of the leoun.
> Myn is the ruyne of the hye halles,
> The fallynge of the toures and of the walles
> Upon the mynour or the carpenter.
> I slow Sampsoun, shakynge the piler;
> And myne be the maladyes colde,

---

[24] For castration in Lacanian psychoanalysis as the marker of lack of difference, the erasure of the phallic signifier which acts diacritically to permit a system of signification, see Roland Barthes, *S/Z*, trans. by Richard Howard (New York: Hill and Wang, 1974).

[25] The classic statement of these difficulties remains that of Elizabeth Salter, who stresses non-unification of the text's elements: *The Knight's Tale and the Clerk's Tale* (London: Edward Arnold, 1962). The essay's fundamental influence on my interest in the Tale I am glad to acknowledge.

The derke tresons, and the castes olde;
My lookyng is the fader of pestilence.
(2454-2469)

Violence is differentiated in the symmetry of 'the see so wan' and 'the derke cote', and class is at work, for it is the common people who are hanged by the throat, not beheaded, hence the phrase 'the cherles rebellyng', perhaps alluding to the Peasants' Revolt of 1381.[26] Saturn claims generic responsibility for all such uprisings. The ruin of the 'hye halls' may well have a specific sense of class anarchy - perhaps the burning of John of Gaunt's Savoy palace. But such destruction also includes the common people; the miner and the carpenter; perhaps this includes the collapse of the barrel that contains John the carpenter in *The Miller's Tale*. The passage closes with Sampsoun, killed killing the Philistines. Who shook the pillar, Sampsoun or Saturn? Samson's own act of destruction, bringing down a 'temple of greet array' with 'thre thousand bodyes' (*The Monk's Tale* 2081, 2088) comes out of its context of individual heroism and becomes part of a violence which piles up catastrophe - while in contrast, in *The Monk's Tale* there is at least a causality implied, in Sampsoun's relations to women.[27] Chaos appears in reference to the plague - most recently, for this tale, present in England in 1379,[28]

---

[26] For the dating, see J.D. North, *Chaucer's Universe* (Oxford: Clarendon Press, 1988) - as also for material on Saturn. He quotes Johnstone Parr, 'The date and Revision of Chaucer's *The Knight's Tale*' *PMLA* 60 (1945) 307-24; see also Parr's dissent from the view that the Tale refers to the Peasants' Revolt, *Modern Language Notes* 69 (1954), 129-30. Parr's views were questioned by Walter E. Weese, 'Vengeance and Pleyn Correcioun', *Modern Language Notes* 63 (1948) 331-333. North dates the tournament as Tuesday, May 5, 1388 (p.417). For him, the poem was revised after the tournament held in London in 1390. Peter Brown and Andrew Butcher, *The Age of Saturn: Literature and History in The Canterbury Tales* (Oxford: Blackwell, 1991) ch.5 place the Tale within the 1390s, find analogues to the Tale's happenings between 1389 and 1397 and justify their title by reference to those of the Tales (*KT, MT, PT FrT*) which use Saturn in the text. Also on Saturn, reading him as the embodiment of intellect and prudence, see John P. McCall, *Chaucer Among the Gods* (Pennsylvania State University Press, 1979), p.84

[27] Saturn was thought to overturn order because of his associations with the Jews. In *The House of Fame*, 'The Ebraye Josephus the olde, / That of Jewes gestes tolde' is described as of the 'secte saturnyn' (1432). See Eric Zafran, 'Saturn and the Jews', *Journal of the Warburg and Courtauld Institutes* 42 (1979) 16-27.

[28] May McKisack, *The Fourteenth Century, 1307-1399* (Oxford: Clarendon Press, 1959) p.331. See also Robert Worth Frank jr. 'The Hungry Gap: Crop Failure and Famine: the Fourteenth Century Agricultural Crisis and *Piers Plowman*', *Yearbook of Langland Studies* 4 (1990) 87-104.

and not, as in *Piers Plowman* (B.V.13) seen as punishment for 'pure synne'. Nonetheless *Piers Plowman* is also aware of Saturn:

> Ac I warne you werkmen - wynneth whil ye mowe,
> For Hunger hiderward hasteth hym faste!
> He shal awake [thorugh] water, wastours to chaste,
> Er fyve yer be fulfilled swich famyn shal aryse:
> Thorogh flodes and thorogh foule wedres, fruytes shul faille -
> And so seith Saturne and sente yow to warne... (B. VI.320-250

Earthly patriarchy, like Saturn, endorses the sense of ruin, contemplated and wished for:

> Right as ther dyed nevere man, 'quod he,
> 'That he ne lyvede in erthe in some degree,
> Right so ther lyvede never man', he seyde,
> 'In al this world, that som tyme he ne deyde.
> This world nys but a thurghfare ful of wo
> And we been pilgrymes, passynge to and fro.
> Deeth is an ende of every worldly soore'.
> (2843-49)

F.N. Robinson dubs this 'platitudinous' and Philippa Tristram sees in it 'senile tautologies [...] [an] [...] impotent and querelous submission characteristic of Elde'[29] and it confirms nothing save the uselessness of 'degree' as a defence, and perhaps the comparative futility of the pentitential gesture of pilgrimage. This parodic Egeus, parody of Saturn, gives parodic advice. But the rhetoric also promotes the sense that a knightly class can do nothing for itself. On J.D. North's reading the text (a) supports a strong sense of determinism, a refusal to consider human freedom, but (b) has been staged by reference to astrology, in an act of textual freedom, to make only a deterministic reading possible. And that is not all, for the text shows both nostalgic melancholy, and the destructive spirit that evokes Saturn.[30]

---

[29] Philippa Tristram, *Figures of Life and Death in Medieval Literature* (London: Paul Elek, 1976), p.89.

[30] If destabilization was attributed to Jewish influences, this concealed the economic and industrial features that produce gunpowder and cannon, the immediate sources of the decline of the knightly order, but also the pillars of Mars' temple, each one 'tonne-greet, of iren bright and shene' (1994). Walter Benjamin, 'The Ring of Saturn, or Some Remarks on Iron Construction' quotes from Grandville's *Another World* (1844) on iron bridges, for the dominance on Saturn in the nineteenth century, giving the conceit that the ring around Saturn is an iron balcony where the inhabitants of Saturn stroll in the evening: *The Arcades Project* trans. Howard Eiland and Kevin McLaughlin (Cambridge, Mass.: Harvard University University Press, 1999), p. 885.

V – THE MONK'S TALE

If the miller had not been drunk and intervened with his 'cherles tale' (3169) to 'quite' the knight's tale (3127) - the monk would have told his tale next.[31] *The Monk's Tale* critiques the knight's, who interrupts it. Gratian said that monks should not preach but should lament the misery and iniquity of the human condition in this contemptible world.[32] The monk, who says he will 'biwaille, in manere of tragedie / The harm of hem that stoode in heigh degree (1991-2) – the *Trauerspiel* theme - harps on catastrophic events, including modern instances, hitting, consistently, the ruling classes.[33] Their relation to the knight is unsubtle.

The first 'instance' is Pedro I of Castile and Leon (2375-2390), killed in 1369 by his half-brother Don Enrique of Trastamare, son of his father's mistress, aided by Bertrand du Guesclin, Oliver de Mauny and others.

> O noble, O worthy Petro, glorie of Spayne,
> Whom Fortune heeld so hye in magestee,

---

[31] See R.E Kaske, 'The Knight's Interruption of *The Monk's Tale*', *ELH* 25 (1957) 249-268. On the Monk 'quitting' the knight through his modern instances, see Terry Jones, *Chaucer's Knight: The Portrait of a Medieval Mercenary* (London: Metheun, 1980), pp.218-223 on the 'modern instances'. I agree with Jones on the Knight, though not that the portrait is meant satirically. See on Jones Maurice Keen, *History 66* (1981) 501-2; John H. Pratt, 'Was Chaucer's knight really a Mercenary?' *Chaucer Review 22* (1987) 8-27. On aspects of the fourteenth-century knight, see Richard Barber, *The Knight and Chivalry* (London: Longman, 1970) - including his poverty, p.18. See also Maurice Keen, *Chivalry*, (New Haven: Yale University Press, 1984) pp.153-55. The economic conditions of knighthood, the ideology of seeking adventure as a weapon to use against the threat of the emergent bourgeoisie, and the decline of knighthood from the adventure cult to courtly life existent under an absolute monarchy are dealt with in Michael Nerlich, *The Ideology of Adventure. Studies in Modern Consciousness 1100-1750, vol.1* (Minneapolis: University of Minnesota Press, 1987) chs 1,3,5. A knightly class lives by fighting: for the oppositions to the peace negotiations with France (1389-94), on the grounds that knightly prosperity depended on the war, see Anthony Tuck, *Crown and Nobility 1272-1461* (Oxford: Blackwell, 1985), pp.201-2

[32] Quoted, G.J. Englehardt, 'The Ecclesiastical Pilgrims of the Canterbury Tales', *Medieval Studies*, (1975) 287-315 (pp.301-3). Renate Haas, 'Chaucer's use of the Lament for the Dead', *Chaucer in the Eighties*, ed. by Julian N.Wasserman and Robert J. Blanch, (New York: Syracuse University Press, 1986), beginning with *The Book of the Duchess* is suggestive for an approach to *The Monk's Tale* which might align it with *Trauerspiel*. On tragedy, see D.W. Robertson, Jr. 'Chaucerian Tragedy', *English Literary History* 19, (1952) 1-37; Paul G. Ruggiers, 'Notes towards a theory of tragedy in Chaucer', *Chaucer Review* 8 (1973) 89-99.

[33] On the modern instances, and *The Monk's Tale* generally, see David Wallace, *Chaucerian Polity: Absolutist Lineages and Associational Forms in England and Italy* (Stanford: Stanford University Press, 1997), pp. 299-336.

> Wel oghten men thy pitous deeth complayne!
> Out of thy land thy brother made thee flee,
> And after, at a seege, by subtiltee,
> Thou were bitraysed and lad unto his tente,
> Where as he with his owene hand slow thee,
> Succedynge in thy regne and in thy rente. (2375-82)

This fraternal conflict implicated Spain, France and England. The Black Prince had fought with Pedro against his brother in 1367 at Nàjera, and had captured the mercenary du Guesclin. Du Guesclin was to be ransomed. Charles V wanted Don Enrique as king to guarantee a Spanish ally, as did England, so that in 1371 Pedro's daughter, Constance, married John of Gaunt, which was the reason for his claim to the throne of Castile and for his military adventures there. The narrative pattern of a brother exiled by another, then of a siege, echoes the *Thebaid*. The second stanza plays on the associations of du Guesclin's coat of arms and on de Mauny's name, mocking the chivalric order via the *Chanson de Roland*, and that earlier treachery in Spain:

> The feeld of snow, with th'egle of blak therinne,
> Caught with the lymrod coloured as the gleede,
> He brew this cursednesse and al this synne.
> The wikked next was werker of this nede.
> Noght Charles Olyver that took ay heede
> Of trouthe and honour, but of Armorike
> Genylon-Olyver, corrupt for meede
> Broghte this worthy kyng in swich a brike. (2383-2390)

J.N. Hillgarth explains: 'In order to get du Guesclin's military help, Enrique agreed (20 November 1368), to commit Castilian naval strength permanently to France against England. The Black Prince did nothing to counter this. On 14 March 1369, Pedro I was defeated by Enrique and his French mercenaries at Montiel. On 23 March he was betrayed by du Guesclin who had promised to help him escape from Montiel castle and murdered by his half-brother, "knight and servant of Jesus Christ" as he now entitled himself'[34] The 'meede' means the money that mercenary knights worked for: du Guesclin indicates what knighthood customarily means.

The second 'modern instance' (2391-8) is the assassination - out of envy at his chivalry, the Monk says - of Pierre de Lusignan (1329-69), commanding the crusade that sacked Alexandria in 1365, subverting the implication of the *General Prologue* (65) that the

---

[34] J.N. Hillgarth, *The Spanish Kingdoms 1250-1516* vol.1 (Oxford: Clarendon Press, 1981), p.381.

victory was complete.[35] The third (2399-2406) is of Bernabò Visconti (1323-85). By the 1360s, the Viscontis were becoming a European power, through intermarriage with France, and with England (Bernabò's niece, Violanta married Lionel duke of Clarence, Chaucer's first patron). The equestrian statue of Bernabò Visconti stood before the high altar in San Gottardo, 'sculpted in marble, armed as if setting out for war, brandishing his baton of lordship. At its sides were two statues of virgins representing his justice and strength, "those virtues by which he acted"'.[36] This knight, employer of mercenaries, whose daughter Donnina married the mercenary Sir John Hawkwood, exemplifies cruelty. In *The Legend of Good Women*, Alceste tells the God of Love not to be 'lyk tirauntz of Lumbardye/ That han no reward but at tyrannye' (*LGW* F 374-5). Visconti's murderer was both his nephew and son in law. How Visconti died as his nephew's prisoner is unclear: perhaps he was poisoned; but the fourth, 'modern instance' (2407-2462) of Ugolino, starved to death in Pisa in 1289, focuses on the prison. It reverses the trend established by the other instances in emphasising both pity and innocence, but it makes this ruler fall through the agency of a Bishop playing on the citizens of Pisa: 'the peple gan on hym rise' – like the Peasants' Revolt. This fourth instance is the only one in *The Monk's Tale* called a 'tragedy'. It comes not from oral testimony, but from a text not following a *de casibus* model: Dante's *Inferno*.[37] Chaucer ignores the episodes's framing and the first person narrative, and gives a third-person narration.[38]

---

[35] It may be a place where Chaucer is influenced by Dante: compare *Legend of Good Women* F360 (G336) and *Inf.* 13.64-65. See also the reference to envy in *Troilus* V.1789.

[36] John Larner, *Culture and Society in Italy, 1290-1420* (London: Batsford, 1971), p. 138 and plate 16.

[37] The exception is Pierre de Lusignan, see Wallace, pp. 315-319, where Chaucer draws on Machaut, who called his death a martyrdom, a *Trauerspiel* theme; see Henry Ansgar Kelly, *Ideas and Forms of Tragedy from Aristotle to the Middle Ages* (Cambridge: Cambridge University Press, 1993), p. 1789; he also discusses Philippe de Mézières's 'matter of lamentation and tragedy' following the siege of Alexandria, pp. 179-181, in his Latin work, *A Tragedic or Declamatory Prayer on the Passion of Our Lord* (1389-90). Chaucer could have known the Ugolino episode also independently of Dante: (e.g. Boccaccio, *De Casibus* IX.20). See Piero Boitani, *The Tragic and the Sublime in Medieval Literature* (Cambridge: Cambridge University Press, 1989) pp. 20-55 and Helen Cooper, 'The Four Last Things in Dante and Chaucer: Ugolino in the House of Rumour', *New Medieval Literatures* 3, ed. by David Lawton, Wendy Scase and Rita Copeland (Oxford: Clarendon Press, 1999), pp. 39-66.

[38] I discuss Ugolino in my *Dante and Difference: Writing in the Commedia* (Cambridge: Cambridge University Press, 1988), pp. 79-87; 'Dante and Benjamin: Writing in the *Commedia*', *Exemplaria* 4 (1992), 341-63; 'Dante and Blake: Allegorizing the Event', in Nick Havely, ed., *Dante's Modern Afterlife:*

Dante passes judgements on his contemporary history, but if six hundred extant pages of Chaucerian life-records never suggest that he was a poet,[39] Chaucer's poetry is, apart from these modern instances virtually silent on any matter of then contemporary history: attributing Hugelyn's fate to Fortune denies historical processes. There is nothing of Saturn in Chaucer's Hugelyn; instead pathos accumulates in the text. Perhaps famine conditions were too close to Chaucer. This fourth instance could have followed the line of the other three, but the Monk feminizes and maternalizes Ugolino. He has 'langour' (2407), 'litel children thre' called 'briddes' (2414); his 'teeris', his 'barm' (2440), his 'lappe' (2454) and his affection for his children are all suggestive. The patriarch of *Inferno* becomes, in that text, harder and more like stone, but Hugelyn weeps and makes no gesture to prevent his children embracing him. The feminization brings the father into further contact with the children, and he is the first subject of the monk's tragedies to speak – '"Allas!" quod he', Allas, that I was wroght"' (2429). He breaks into an alliterative mode like a lullaby – '"Allas Fortune, and weylaway / Thy false wheel my wo al may I wyte"' (2445-6).

This differentiation from Dante goes in the reverse direction from that expressed at the end of the earlier *Troilus and Criseyde* V (1786-1792):

> Go, litel bok, go, litel myn tragedye,
> Ther God thi makere yet, er that he dye,
> So sende myght to make in som comedye! (1786-1789)

This envoi makes the *Troilus* tragedy, perhaps like much of Chaucer's previous work. There is a new desire to write 'in som comedye', but it seems that he could not (though he could write in comic mode).[40]

Reception and Response from Blake to Heaney (London: Macmillan, 1998), pp. 33-48. Benjamin refers to a late example of *Trauerspiel* (p. 121) in Heinrich von Gerstenberg (1737-1823), whose *Ugolino* (1769) dramatizes the prison scene over five acts, adding in the arrival of the coffins, of Ugolino's poisoned wife, and his son, Francesco, who attempted escape. See Werner P. Friedrich, *Dante's Fame Abroad, 1350-1850* (Roma: Edizioni di Storia e letteratura, 1950), p. 367.

39 The point is made by Charles Muscatine, *Poetry and Crisis in the Age of Chaucer* (Notre Dame: University of Notre Dame Press, 1972), p. 26.

40 I agree with Karla Taylor, *Chaucer Reads the Divine Comedy* (Stanford: Stanford University Press, 1989), p. 3 that Chaucer calls his work a tragedy to distinguish it from Dante's comedy. See also Donald Howard, *The Idea of The Canterbury Tales* (Berkeley: University of California Press, 1976), pp. 30-45, that only here does Chaucer use the word 'comedy'. Winthrop Wetherbee draws attention to the word 'poesie' – only here in Chaucer, and relates it to Dante's reference to 'poesi' in *Purg.* 1, 7: see 'Dante and the Poetics of *Troilus and Criseyde*', *Critical Essays on Geoffrey Chaucer* (New York: G.K. Hall, 1998), pp. 243-266. For tragedy in *Troilus*, see Barry Windeatt, *Oxford Guides to*

But if Chaucer could not follow Dante, there is still a new pathos at work in Hugelyn, and a new attention to femininity. Dante's narrative has been medievalized in the insistence on pathos, on Fortune and on a de-historicized situation. Chaucer could write tragedy as in the form of *Troilus and Criseyde*, or in the form of *The Knight's Tale*, though it is not called that, or tragedy in the form of *The Monk's Tale*: these approaches to tragedy, however, are more like *Trauerspiel*. The knight is not only mocked by the modern instances, but has mirrored for him that his own tale is complaint. He interrupts the tale, saying it is 'a greet disese'

> Whereas men hath been in greet welthe and ese
> To heeren of hire sodeyn fal, allas!
> And the contrarie is joye and greet solas,
> As whan a man hath been in povre estaat,
> And clymbeth up and wexeth fortunat,
> And there abideth in prosperitee.
> (2772-7)

The story he would like, of material prosperity, where Fortune allows someone to 'abide' in one place, makes him bourgeois. His own tale is outside that tradition: it belongs to his unconscious, which, split from his conscious desire as expressed here, sides with the ruin, and the knowledge of disaster, while disavowing that through the sense of the tale as an old romance, and with a happy ending. But before reaching the ending, I want to turn to Dürer's knight.

VI – *THE KNIGHT, DEATH AND THE DEVIL*

In *The Knight, Death and the Devil*, perhaps a companion to *Melencolia I* and *St. Jerome in his Study*, a knight rides through a deep wooded valley, a fixed expression on his face, his eyes looking straight ahead to focus on the hourglass that his squire holds out to him: the squire here being death, a decomposing body, partly revealing the skull, crowned and with snakes in his hair. His horse looks down at a skull at its feet. Behind the knight is the devil as a footman, swine-snouted, with goat's ears, the horns of a sheep, and holding a pickaxe. Beneath the knight goes his dog. A lizard moves in the contrary direction. A dominant element in the engraving is the Italianate horse, which seems to provide a formal reason for the

---

Chaucer: Troilus and Criseyde (Oxford: Clarendon Press, 1992), pp. 154-161. He brings Chaucer near to the *Trauerspiel* by commenting that 'the last two books of the *Troilus* are a study in the art of lamentation' (p. 159). The prominence of Dante in Chaucer is evidenced by how often he is referred to: *House of Fame* 450, *Legend of Good Women* F Prologue 360; *Monk's Tale* 2461, *Wife of Bath's Tale* 1126-7 and *Friar's Tale* 1520.

engraving in the first place.[41] The background is a wild, gnarled landscape – this, the antithesis of the urban, being the place of the knight, and a reminder of his association with wildness.

Wölfflin took the knight as the Christian for whom life is military service. Panofsky quotes from Erasmus' *Enchiridion militis Christiani* of 1501 - the handbook of the Christian soldier - and says that Dürer has made the soldier a knight. Yet nineteenth century interpretations, such as Heinrich Merz in 1878 had taken the knight differently: as a robber knight: 'The last knights regarded the traders and financiers of the cities with a bitter hatred, which was reciprocated. The "shopkeepers" who ruled the towns avenged themselves for the raids on their convoys of merchandise by hanging the knights, when they could lay hands on them, or by burning down their strongholds'.[42]

Death and the devil are the knight's companions, or his nemesis. Perhaps the knight represents that class who backed Luther and the Empire against the Papacy and then also stood against the changed economic conditions that were ending feudalism, rebelling in 1523. According to Scriber and Benecke, 'their aim was to annihilate the spiritual and secular power of the princes, to split Germany from Rome and to restore dominance of the nobility'.[43] They refused to accept that 'they were becoming citizens of a state rather than vassals of a lord'.[44] They were losing out to the rise of the bourgeoisie, whose goods they could only damage and confiscate in robber raids, rather than meet them in competition. Ulrich von Hutten (1488-1523) figures these knights. Intended for the church, he associated at Erfurt with Renaissance humanists, such as Willibald Pirckheimer (1470-1530), a friend of Dürer. A scholar attracted to Italy, and an anti-clerical figure who backed Luther, he stood close to the robber knights, who captured merchants and held them to

---

[41] José Antonio Maravall, *Utopia and Counterutopia in the 'Quixote'*, trans. by Robert W. Felkel (Detroit: Wayne State University Press, 1991) quotes from *Guillem de Vàroich, Tractats de cavalleria*: 'the horse' [not necessarily Dürer's, of course] symbolizes the people, whom the knight must uphold in peace and concord by maintaining justice [...]' (p. 163).

[42] Heinrich Wolfflin, *The Art of Albrecht Dürer* (1905, London: Phaidon, 1971), p.198; Erwin Panofsky, *The Life and Art of Albrecht Dürer* (New Jersey: Princeton University Press, 1971 ed.), pp.151-4; Wilhelm Waetzoldt, *Albrecht Dürer* (London: Phaidon, 1950), p.75 citing Merz.

[43] Bob Scriber and Gerhard Benecke, eds., *The German Peasant War of 1525: New Viewpoints* (London: Allen and Unwin, 1979), p.16. See also Peter Blickle, *The Revolution of 1525*, trans. by Thomas A Brady, jr and H.C. Erik Midelfort (Baltimore: Johns Hopkins University Press, 1981) for justification of the title 'the revolution of the common man'.

[44] Walter R.Hitchcock, *The Background of the Knights' Revolt* (Berkeley: University of California Press, 1958), p.10

ransom.[45] He joined with Franz von Sickengen, Rhenish knight and mercenary leader, loyal to Charles the Fifth, who joined campaigns: in France, (with Charles), and against towns such as Worms in 1513, and Mainz in 1518, in order to pay his troops. Engels called Ulrich of Hutten 'the theoretician of the German nobility', and Franz von Sickingen 'its military and diplomatic representative'. The knights wanted monarchy and power based on the continuance of serfdom. Engels completes the story of the revolt, starting with Hutten and Sickingen who:

> organised in Landau, in 1522, a union of the Rhenish, Swabian and Franconian nobility for the duration of six years, ostensibly for self-defence. Sickingen assembled an army, partly out of his own means and partly in combination with the neighbouring knights. He organised the recruiting of armies and reinforcements in Franconia, along with the lower Rhine, in the Netherlands and in Westphalia, and in September 1522, he opened hostilities by declaring a feud against the Elector-Archbishop of Trier. While he was stationed near Trier, his reinforcements were cut off by a quick intervention of the princes. The Landgrave of Hesse and the Elector of Palatine went to the aid of the Archbishop of Trier, and Sickingen was hastily compelled to retreat to his castle, Landstuhl. In spite of all the efforts of Hutten and the remainder of his friends, the united nobility, intimidated by the concentrated and quick action of the princes, left him in the lurch. Sickingen was mortally wounded, surrendered Landstuhl, and soon afterwards he died. Hutten was compelled to flee to Switzerland, where he died a few months later[...][46]

Hutten died on the island of Ufenau, on Lake Zürich. The revolt shows a contradiction between the knights' humanism and nationalism: between standing for a medieval unified Christendom, and national aspiration, of German freedom from Rome. Attachment to Lutheranism failed to shake their economic commitment to feudalism, which had produced the knightly class. So one Marxist interpretation of *The Knight, Death and the Devil* makes the print anticipatory, giving 'the ideology of Hutten and Franz von Sickingen, and express[ing] the abstract character of as well as the capitulation before the actual historical events which took place at Landstuhl in 1523'.[47]

---

[45] See A.G. Dickens, *The German Nation and Luther* (London: Arnold, 1974), p.47.

[46] Friedrich Engels, *The German Revolutions*, ed. by Leonard Krieger (Chicago: University of Chicago Press, 1967), pp.73-7 (earlier quotation p.71).

[47] Wolfgang Stechow, 'State of Research: Recent Dürer Studies', *Art Bulletin*, 56 (1974), 259-70, quoting Maurizio Bonicatti, p.263. For Dürer on the peasant, see Stephen Greenblatt, 'Murdering Peasants: Status, Genre and the Representation of Rebellion', *Representations* 1.1. (1983), 1-29.

The bourgeois Dürer stood in an ambiguous relationship to Maximilian (ruled 1493-1519). Maximilian created the Landsknechts at the beginning of the sixteenth century. Dürer's work points to the lack of future for the knightly class. Gombrich sees the engraving as a version of the *Totendanz*. The analogue is with Hans Baldung (c1484-1544), in 'Death and the Landsknecht',[48] or in the woodcut, 'Death Overtaking a Knight' (c.1510).[49] The knight on his journey does not actually *defy* death, as the first set of interpretations might imply; Gombrich argues that the good Christian does not defy death: for him death and the devil pose no threat.[50] But if this is the dance of the dead, death allegorizes the work of history; further, Sten Karling's view may be correct in pointing to the moral dubiety implied in the knight riding with a fox tail on his lance: the sign of the fox suggests the wiliness of the rider.

For Arcite, rebellion came from beneath, as the 'furie infernal' – feminine figure of madness - starts up from beneath the ground, making his horse rear. But no femininity intrudes on Dürer's iron-clad figure. The interpretations which imply the conflicts that work through the conscious and the unconscious of a knight, make his gaze melancholic,[51] but as part of paranoia. In the female figure in *Melencolia I*, attended by the *putto* whom Agamben reads as a little

---

[48]   For death and the knight, see the illustrations in J.R. Hale, *Arts and Warfare in the Renaissance* (New Haven: Yale University Press, 1990), p. 31. He reproduces the Baldung, as well as showing Baldung's drawing 'Death as a Standard Bearer' (1505-7) which shows how the soldier and death are mirrors of each other. In the Holbein Dance of Death, 'it is an aristocratic man-at-arms who is skewered with his own lance by a mocking death' (Hale, p. 31). Hale indicates the fascination for representations of knighthood between 1505-1515. In Holbein's woodcut, the sun is setting (as also for the Bishop and the Ploughman) and death is dressed in chain mail; the fight with the knight, complete with panache, has overturned the hourglass. The knight is stabbed in the back – fulfilling the paranoia of 'The Knight, Death and the Devil'. See *The Dance of Death: 41 Woodcuts by Hans Holbein the Younger* (New York: Dover Publications, 1971), p. 46.

[49]   Death attacks the knight from behind with a pitchfork: both are mounted on horses. See Joseph Leo Koerner, *The Moment of Self-Portraiture in German Renaissance Art* (Chicago: University of Chicago Press, 1993), p. 278. Koerner reads the figure of death here as deriving from the Death of Dürer's 'Four Horsemen of the Apocalypse' (pp. 284-5).

[50]   Gombrich's view is in Charles Singleton, ed., *Interpretation: Theory and Practice* (Baltimore: Johns Hopkins University Press, 1969). For other views, see Charles W. Talbot, ed., *Dürer in America: his Graphic Work* (National Gallery of Art, Washington, 1971) p.144; Henry Rox, 'On Dürer's "Knight, Death and the Devil"', *Art Bulletin* 30 (1948), 67-70; Peter Strieder. *Dürer*, (London, Francis Muller, 1982), pp.174-80.

[51]   On Jerome, see Eugene F.Rice, jr. *St.Jerome in the Renaissance* (Baltimore: Johns Hopkins University Press, 1985), pp. 11-112; 161-172.

spirit of love, there is no protection of the subject's boundaries or avoidance of the fragmentary and the allegorical vision. The knight's gaze is fixed in purpose because of the powers that encroach upon his borders to which he reacts with fear and nostalgia. The latter term came into currency later (1688, OED) to describe the homesickness of Swiss mercenaries. A military term sanctions one form of melancholy as inseparable from the cause of maintaining order. The anthropologist Renato Rosaldo, discussing 'imperialist nostalgia', 'where people mourn the passing of what they themselves have transformed' connects such nostalgia with guilt, concealing a complicity with their violence of domination; attempting to establish innocence about what has been destroyed.[52] The sense of repressed guilt in nostalgia comes out of a prior act of violence in which the nostalgic was complicit.

VII - CHILDREN OF SATURN

The paranoia comes from the forces acting on the knight from beneath, from the German peasants. The Bundschuh revolts, Bundschuh referring to the poor man's footwear, and to its leather straps and hence to the tying together of peasant groups, were active in 1502 and 1513 and 1517. That of 1513, led by Joss Fritz, took place around Lehen in Breisgau. 1514 saw the 'poor Konrad' rising, near Stuttgart. Peasant movements were accompanied by urban risings, culminating in the German Peasants' War, the Revolution of the Common Man, as Peter Blickle calls it (1524-5), where between 50,000 and 130,000 peasants died in an uprising the opposite to the knights. In the fourteenth century, Langland had imagined a unity between the knight and Piers, where latter will work for both:

> In couenaunt that thow kepe Holy Kirke and myselue
> From wasteours and fro wikked men that this world
>   destruyeth'.(B.VI. 27,28)

In 1381, John Ball cited Piers Plowman as a generic name for a militant peasant; bidding him 'go to his werk'.[53] In contrast, Chaucer's Plowman, is 'brother' to the poor parson, not conflicting with him, unlike Piers and the Priest in Passus VII.[54] But by the

---

[52] Renato Rosaldo, 'Imperialist Nostalgia', *Representations* 26 (Spring 1989), 107-122, quotation from p. 108.

[53] R.B. Dobson, *The Peasants' Revolt of 1381* (London: Macmillan, 1983), p.381

[54] References in Chaucer to the peasants and their uprising are negative. There is 'Jakke Strawe and his meynee' (*NPT*, 3394) involved in killing Flemings, the episode as 'blase of straw' (*TC* iv.184) and the man too, if the pun is admitted. The people are 'stormy...unsad and evere untrewe!' (*CLT* 995ff). Work on the peasant in the fourteenth-century would, however, now bring out not the poverty of the peasant, but the agrarian roots of European capitalism; see the

sixteenth century, separation between the knights and the peasants appeared in their separate revolts.

Saturn's signs were potent in 1523, as shown in the title-page of a prophecy concerning the expected Great Flood of February 1524, when Saturn and Jupiter were expected to be in conjunction.[55] At the top of the woodcut proclaiming this disaster is the sign of the fish, containing a corpse within it and the seven planets. From the belly of the fish a flood pours out onto a village. On the left side of the flood, at the picture's base, Saturn, crippled and holding a scythe, image both of time and of the labour of the peasants, leads the peasants, who follow his flag. Figures with pipes and drum stand behind him. On the right side of the flood stand the Emperor, the Pope, cardinals and bishops, 'children of Jupiter', looking on with fear. Above the peasants is a comet; Dürer had noted, in 1503, a comet and blood rain which fell on people, marking their clothes with the sign of the cross, and presaging the pestilence.[56] The conjunction of planets secures the 'cherles rebellynge'.

Norbert Elias adopts a different attitude to the 'children of Saturn' when discussing a sequence of drawings known as the Medieval House-Book, (*Hausbuch*)' 'from the late period of chivalry [1475-80], the time of Charles the Bold and Maximilian, the last knight'. For him, the artist 'must have been very familiar with the knightly life of his time...he must have seen the world with the eyes of a knight and largely identified with their social values'.[57] For Elias, the range of illustrations indicates the unrepressed and extended viewpoint of the life of a knight, including the absence of 'the nostalgic mood'. This certainly accords with the comedy Chaucer's knight permits himself, as in:

> No thyng ne knew he that it was Arcite;

---

essay by Lee Patterson, 'No Man His Reson Herde: Peasant Consciousness, Chaucer's Miller and the structure of the *Canterbury Tales, Literary Practice and Social Change in Britain 1380-1530*, ed. by Lee Patterson (Berkeley: University of California Press, 1990), pp. 113-155. Patterson makes *The Miller's Tale* a quitting of *The Knight's Tale,* but focuses on the economic conditions of the peasant class.

[55] Janos Bak, ed., *The German Peasant war of 1525* (London: Frank Cass, 1978), pp.42-43.

[56] Panofsky, p.90

[57] Norbert Elias, *The Civilizing Process: The History of Manners*, trans. by Edmund Jephcott (Oxford: Blackwell, 1978), p.208. Three pictures from the Medieval House-Book are reprinted in 'Scenes from the Life of a Knight', with comments on Elias by Richard Dunning in *Theory, Culture and Society 4* (1987) 363-374; others, including the children of Saturn, appear in V.A. Kolve, *Chaucer and the Imagery of Narrative* (Stanford University Press, 1984) pp.118-125. See also Chauncey Wood, *Chaucer and the Country of the Stars* (New Jersey: Princeton University Press, 1970) plates 13a and 13b.

God woot he wolde have trowed it ful lite.
But sooth is seyd, go sithen many yeres,
That 'feeld hath eyen and the wode hath eres'
It is ful fair a man to bere him evene,
For al day meeteth men at unset stevene.
(1519-24)[58]

Such casualness enables a reading of one illustration from the *Hausbuch*, where hows Saturn rides through the air, his children beneath him.

> In the foreground a poor fellow is disembowelling a dead horse or perhaps cutting off the usable meat. His trousers have slipped down somewhat as he bends; part of his posterior is visible, and a pig behind him is sniffing at it. A frail old woman, half in rags, limps by supported on a crutch. In a small cave beside the road sits a wretch with his hands and feet in the stocks and beside him a woman with one hand in the stocks, the other in fetters. A farm worker is toiling at a watercourse that vanishes between trees and hills. In the distance we see the farmer and his young son laboriously plowing the hilly field with a horse. Still further back a man in rags is led to the gallows, an armed man with a feather in his cap marching proudly beside him; at his other side a monk in his cowl holds out a large crucifix to him. Behind him ride the knight and two of his men. On the top of the hill stands the gallows with a body hanging from it, and wheel with a corpse on it. Dark birds fly around; one of them pecks at the corpse. The gallows is not in the least emphasized. [...] the symbol of the judicial knight's judicial power, is part of the background of his life. It may not be very important, but at any rate it is not a particularly painful sight. Sentence, execution, death - all these are immediately present [...].

The knightly standpoint enframes the several narratives of what happens to the 'children of Saturn', and docs not avert the gaze from peasant existence and the primacy of punishment. Elias's evidence may make the violence in *The Knight's Tale* is willed and the laughter at 'Venus folk' (1537) calculated, superior. But perhaps that needs supplementing by the alienating melancholy implied in Dürer, which means that melancholy was laughing at *another* form of melancholy, e.g. love-sickness. The casualness comes from a melancholic gaze.

VIII – THE DEATH OF A KNIGHT

Why grucchen we, why have we hevynesse,
That goode Arcite, of chivalrie flour,

---

[58] Richard Neuse refers to his 'unbuttoned mood' - see John Burrow, ed., *Geoffrey Chaucer* (Harmondsworth: Penguin, 1969), p.244.

> Departed is with duetee and honour
> Out of this foule prisoun of this lyf?'
> (3058-61)

The anxiety in Theseus' speech of attempted consolation, bringing the text to the end and to marriage between Palamon and Arcite, is of what would happen if no symbolic/ allegorical meaning such as the flower and the prison could be given to the events. Theseus does not allegorize in Benjamin's sense, where allegory precipitates ruin; but the text allows for that reading of Theseus's speech. The Boethian logic in Theseus's words allows no real religious consolation. As Palamon says:

> And whan a beest is deed he hath no peyne;
> But man after his deeth moot wepe and pleyne,
> Though in this world he have care and wo.
> Withouten doute it may stonden so.
> The answere of this lete I to dyvynys,
> But wel I woot that in this world greet pyne ys. (1319-24)

This agnosticism, heroic in its lack of consolation, as well as feminine ('man after his deeth moot wepe and pleyne': complaint continues after death) contrasts with the knightly class of Richard the Second's court, some known for Lollard sympathies.[59] Penitentialism and melancholy and fear of the other may relate to each other. That returns to how the text comments on the knight, and brings out a doubleness even in Saturn. His power and the fact of the 'cherless rebellynge' cannot be negated, even by embracing the order of a penitential, Lollard-like position. Lollardy cannot be separated

---

[59] Paul Strohm, *Social Chaucer* (New Jersey: Harvard University Press, 1989) chs.1 and 2. He points out the middle-strata rank of the knights, and through the names of those in the king's affinity: Simon Burley, John Beauchamp, John Salisbury and James Berners (condemned by the Lords Appellant in 1387-8) and John Clanvowe, William Nevill, Philip la Vache and Richard Stury (not condemned), emphasises Chaucer's part with that class. He establishes Chaucer's friendship with five of the ten or eleven chamber knights: Lewis Clifford, Stury, Clanvowe and la Vache, the first four of whom were cited by Walsingham as Lollard knights, and Nevill, another 'Lollard Knight'. Clanvowe's poetic work bears traces of *The Knight's Tale*. Chaucer's identification with Richard seems clear, as his resignation from his customs post at the end of 1386 and departure to Kent seems politic in the face of opposition to Richard's court. Lollardy was pervasive as when the Parson is blamed for it ('I smelle a Lollere in the wynd' - II.1173). The production of vernacular piety with a strong element of penitentialism in the period may extend to Chaucer himself, on the evidence of *The Parson's Tale* and the *Retraction*, though neither are Lollard texts. See the essays in *Social Unrest in the Middle Ages*, ed. by Francis X. Newman (Medieval and Renaissance texts and studies, Binghamton, New York 1986).

from the Peasants' revolt.[60] The knights are implicated in a radical movement indissociable from that which leads to their ruin. Is Lollardy linked to Saturn?

Refusal of religious consolation, desire to press towards destruction receives most haunting expression in the description of the death of Arcite (2742-2816). In the art of Mars' temple, the presence of death amongst personifications of 'Felonye', 'Ire', 'the pykepurs', 'the pale Drede', 'the smylere with the knyf under the cloke' 'the open were', 'Cotek', and 'Meschaunce', and many others (1995-2040) makes it no absolute, but an allegorical detail amongst many other allegories, as with Langland. But outside the art, death is not an allegorical figure, but something working in life; making life and death inseparable. Since 'man after his deeth moot wepe and pleyne', death alters nothing and corruption already works in the live body.

> Swelleth the brest of Arcite, and the soore
> Encreeseth at his herte moore and moore.
> The clothered blood, for any lechecraft,
> Corrupteth, and is in his bouk ylaft,
> That neither veyne-blood, ne ventusynge,
> Ne drynke of herbes may ben his helpynge.
> The vertu expulsif, or animal,
> Fro thilke vertu cleped natural
> Ne may the venym voyden ne expelle.
> The pipes of his longes gonne to swelle,
> And every lacerte in his brest adoun
> Is shent with venym and corrupcioun.
> Hym gayneth neither, for to gete his life,
> Vomyt upward, ne dounward laxatif.
> Al is tobrosten thilke regioun;
> Nature hath now no dominacioun.
> And certeinly, ther Nature wol nat wirche,
> Fare wel phisik! go ber the man to chirche!
> This al and som, that Arcita moot dye .[...]   (2743-2761)

The imagery suggests pestilence or the body as a battlefield or the site of a siege ('tobrosten' recalls the walls of Thebes), where Nature cannot maintain a position. 'Venym' (twice), 'corrupteth' 'corrupcioun', and 'Nature' show the body to be held by forces associated with what is beyond the grave. There is nothing to be done with Arcite except, in an ellipsis omitting dying, to bear him to the 'chirche' – a melancholic statement of forced carelessness or cynicism, crowning a flat detachment in recording or collecting the lacerations of the body. The division between life and death is

---

[60] See Rodney Hilton, *Bond Men made Free: Medieval Peasant Movements and the English Rising of 1381* (London: Methuen, 1973), pp.212-213 for the relationship between Lollardy and the Peasants' Revolt.

unclear. Arcite is 'yet in memorie and alyve' (2698) while a narrative drive pushes towards death in the question, if Nature will not preserve the knight, what use in medicine? The logic even *refuses* medicine as a supplement to nature; as though no compromise with Nature is admissable, and the knight must remain separate, 'allone'. Behind the description of the assault on the 'natural virtue' lies a melancholy wish to pre-empt a saving of the body. The flatness in this dismissal of Arcite after death expresses the materiality of the dead body -:

> His spirit chaunged hous and wente ther,
> As I cam nevere, I kan nat tellen wher.
> Therfore I stynte, I nam no divinistre;
> Of soules fynde I nat in this registre,
> Ne me ne list thilke opinions to telle
> Of hem, though that they writen wher they dwelle.
> Arcite is coold, ther Mars his soule gye! (2809-15)

The last line, as cold, or indifferent in feeling as what it describes, works with the other references to coldness, discussed earlier. The melancholic state and death are aligned; Arcite the knight has become what he was before, the figure of death.

Arcite's body, examined closely in its corruption, was pronounced not worth the attempt at physic. There is a melancholic heroism in unpicking so much of knightly idealism by attention to the rotten body. The gaze looks beyond surfaces to the body as other to the order that the rational mind can impose. The heroism of the melancholic gaze is double for there is also a continuation of the drive the text has had throughout, which re-surfaces in Theseus's reference to life to be a 'foule prisoun'. The prison is the body, as the 'hous' Arcite's spirit leaves. Michel Foucault refers to a discourse of subjection which operates by elevating the 'soul' to make it a dominant principle above the body. His formulation to describe the state the subjected person exists in has implications for the unconscious here:

> A "soul" inhabits him and brings him to existence, which is itself a factor in the mastery that power exercises over the body. The soul is the effect and instrument of a political anatomy; the soul is the prison of the body.[61]

The tale's drive has imprisoned the body, and discarded it in the vision of Arcite's sufferings. Death in Dürer's engraving externalises a threat: the knight rides on as if oblivious of what is other to him, though his melancholy countenance knows it and it may be he wishes

---

[61] Michel Foucault, *Discipline and Punish: The Birth of the Prison*, trans. by Alan Sheridan (Harmondsworth: Penguin, 1979), p. 30.

for it. Arcite's death, last scene in the life of a knight, allows for virtually no externality: not the peasants, nothing political and attendant on the condition of being a knight; death resides in the body.

CHAPTER 3

Allegory and the Madness of the Text: Hoccleve's *Complaint*

I – ALLEGORY

In *The Allegory of Love*, C. S. Lewis says about the opening stanzas of Thomas Hoccleve's *The Regement of Princes*, completed around 1411 for the future Henry V: 'here we have a description, much infected with allegory, but still unallegorical, of a sleepless night. [...] [Hoccleve] analyses the state of his emotions during the wakeful night, just as the love poets had analysed the state of the sleepless lover; and Thought personified [...] is recognised as the immediate enemy [...]'.[1] While Lewis is equivocal how far Hoccleve's text is allegorical, his description of the power of anxiety provokes a question about how three things connect: allegory, autobiography, madness. Like Langland, Hoccleve is an exemplary case for all three, for the text which brings them all together is his *Complaint*, a record of madness.[2]

Hoccleve (c.1367-1426) was employed from about 1387 in London, at Westminster, in the Office of the Privy Seal, so that he was a clerk, issuing documents authorized by the King's seal, as well as becoming, in the period after *The Regement of Princes*, a semi-official Lancastrian court-poet, his loyalty showing itself in *The Remonstrance Against Oldcastle* (August 1415). Pearsall notes a silence after that: 'for whatever reason, soon after 1415 and by 1419, Hoccleve was looking for a new patron'.[3] The dating is unclear, but it seems that ten years after *The Regement of Princes*, in November 1421, Hoccleve began his *Complaint* – which was to be the first poem

---

[1] C. S. Lewis, *The Allegory of Love* (Oxford: Oxford University Press, 1936), p. 238.

[2] Quotations from *Thomas Hoccleve's Complaint and Dialogue*, ed. by John Burrow (Oxford University Press for the Early English Texts Society, 1999). I quote from the 'Edited text' but omit the mid-line break which Burrow inserts, and have modernized archaic letters. The *Complaint* begins a sequence of linked texts known as the *Series*, beginning with a Prologue leading into a Complaint (both together may be called the *Complaint*). A Dialogue with a Friend follows, leading into the Tale of Jereslaus' Wife, a translation of a text 'Learn to Die' and the Tale of Jonathas. Quotations other than those for the *Complaint* and the *Dialogue* are taken from M.C. Seymour, *Selections from Hoccleve* (Oxford: Clarendon Press, 1981). Again, I have replaced the archaic letters. I have used the editorial matter of both, citing them as Burrow, Seymour plus page reference in the text.

[3] Derek Pearsall, 'Hoccleve's *Regement of Princes*: The Politics of Royal Self-Presentation', *Speculum* 69 (1994), 386-410 (p. 410).

in a proposed series whose intention was to produce a new patron, the Duke of Gloucester. The substance of the *Complaint* was Hoccleve commenting on a madness he had endured five years before.[4] Was Hoccleve ever mad or no? The question cannot be answered in that form, and not just since to 'define true madness, what is't but to nothing else but mad?'[5] nor because there is virtually no evidence on the point outside the text. What is entailed for a text to separate off a period and say that the subject was mad then? If the subject had been mad, how did it know? If the evidence that can be brought is the way the 'I' of the poem thinks that his contemporaries see him, in Westminster, Westminster Hall and walking the pavements of London (*Complaint* 72,73, 183-6) how that can be separated from a paranoia, possibly related to city-existence, as 'modern' paranoia seems to be city-induced?[6] This paranoia might be the very madness itself, though subsequent in date to the madness he thought he had endured. If the text could be taken as an objective account, there might be some point in finding a positivistic form of madness that could be described.[7] But no text, on account of its

---

[4] John Burrow argues for 1414 as the date of madness throughout his writings on Hoccleve; see 'Thomas Hoccleve: Some Redatings', *Review of English Studies* n.s. 46 (2995), 366-72. Seymour argues for 1416, as does Matthew Boyd Goldie, 'Psychosomatic Illness and Identity in London, 1416-1421: Hoccleve's *Complaint* and Dialogue with a Friend', *Exemplaria* 11 (1999), 23-52 (p. 25).

[5] *Hamlet* II. ii. 93-4. *Hamlet*, ed. by Harold Jenkins (London: Methuen, 1982)

[6] On paranoia and urban culture, see my 'We are Seven: Dante and the Serial Killer', *Paragraph* 22 (1999), 293-309.

[7] For accounts of Hoccleve's madness see Stephen Medcalf, *The Later Middle Ages* (London: Methuen, 1981), pp. 108-71; Gordon Claridge, Ruth Pryor and Gwen Watkins, *Sounds from the Bell-Jar: Ten Psychotic Authors* (London: Macmillan, 1990), pp. 49-70, 144-47; George MacLennan, *Lucid Interval: Subjective Writing and Madness in History* (Leicester: Leicester University Press, 1992), pp. 15-38. In the *Dialogue* the Friend says the madness was caused by study (*Dialogue* 302) - a Chaucerian note, reminiscent of the Eagle in *The House of Fame* (e.g. lines 655-8), but with implications for the dominance of the subject by thought - and the Hoccleve of the poem declares it was only sickness (*Dialogue* 426), which may ignore the text's penitential aspects. Neither view can be regarded as adequate.

In addition to other references to Hoccleve cited in the notes, see Jerome Mitchell, *Thomas Hoccleve: A Study in Early Fifteenth Century English Poetic* (Urbana: University of Illinois Press, 1968); David Lawton, 'Dullness and the Fifteenth-Century', *English LiteraryHistory* 54 (1987), 761-799. On the *Complaint*, see John Burrow, 'Hoccleve's *Series*: Experience and Books', *Fifteenth-Century Studies*, ed. by Robert Yeager (Hamden, Conn.: Archon Books, 1984), pp. 259-274 and Burrow, The Poet as Petitioner', *Studies in the Age of Chaucer* 3 (1981), 61-75; and 'The Poet and his Book', *Genres, Themes and Images in English Literature*, ed. by Piero Boitani and Anna Torti (Tübingen: Guater Narr Verlag, 1981); 'Hoccleve and Chaucer', *Chaucer Traditions*, ed. by Ruth Morse and Barry Windeatt (Cambridge: Cambridge

textuality, can be taken so objectively, and this one firmly draws attention to itself as a text, not least through its quasi-allegorical form, so that it confronts the reader with the madness of writing, which is the madness of thinking that a textual decision can be made between madness and reason. The evidence for the madness is in the writing, which is therefore the writing of madness. And that phrase brings together two positions which we might like to keep distinct: that of rational texts which describe madness from the outside, and texts whose being is mad, perhaps because their author is mad. Whether the distinction can be maintained, and which position corresponds to Hoccleve's text, or whether the *Complaint* makes for a confusion of both positions, is a question for this chapter.

For Lewis, the enemy seems to be 'thought'. So it is in Gower (c.1330-1408) in a passage in *Confessio Amantis* (c.1390) where Amans, the lover has to learn about anger, which his confessor, Genius, says has five servants, the principal one Malencolie, the name given here for an active and capricious state

> which in compaignie
> An hundred times in an houre
> Wol as an angrie beste loure.
> And noman wot the cause why. (28-31)[8]

The lover has to recognise himself in this state by confessing to the state of Melencolie, which comes out of a desire for love, producing a burning 'as doth a glede / For Wrathe that I mai noght spede' (39-40). At the end of the confession, it is a condition similar to Arcite's that is described: 'Malencolie / Which groweth of the fantasie / Of love' (125-7). Love and anger interrelate and both produce a self-division - already implicit in the demand to confess - which is caused by his 'thoght' and which is productive of further wrath:

> And thus ful ofte a day for noght
> Save onlich of myn oghne thoght
> I am so with miselves wroth,

University Press, 1990), pp. 54-61; *Thomas Hoccleve* (Authors of the Middle Ages; Aldershot: Variorum, 1994); see further Malcolm Richardson, 'Hoccleve in his Social Context', *Chaucer Review* 20 (1986), 313-22; Stephen Kohl, 'More than Virtues and Vices: Self-Analysis in Hoccleve's "Autobiographies"', *Fifteenth-Century Studies* 14 (1988), 115-127; D.C. Greetham, 'Self-Referential Artifacts: Hoccleve's Persona as a Literary Device', *Modern Philology* 86 (1989), 242-51; Anthony J. Hasler, 'Hoccleve's Unregimented Body', *Paragraph* 13 (1990), 164-83; Anna Torti, *The Glass of Form: Mirroring Structures From Chaucer to Skelton* (Cambridge: Cambridge University Press, 1991), pp. 87-106.

8 Quotations from Gower come from *The Complete Works of John Gower*, ed. by G.C.Macaulay (Oxford: Clarendon Press, 1901).

> That ho so that the game goth
> With othre men, I am noght glad;
> Bot I am wel the more unglad,
> For that is othre mennes game
> It torneth me to pure grame. [trouble]
> Thus am I with miself oppressed
> Of thoght, the which I have impressed,
> That al wakende I dreme and meet
> That I with hire al one meete
> And preie hire of som good ansuere:
> Bot for she wol noght gladly swere
> Sche seith me nay withouten oth
> And thus wexe I withinne wroth
> That outward I am al affraied,
> And so distempred and esmaied. (3:41-58)

In this fascinating confession of divided subjectivity, (running through lines 34-129), wrath (43,56,124) as both noun and verb, anger (77,92,102), despair (74), melancholy (87,125) circulate as synonyms, while thought (42,50,106) seems to dominate in intensifying negativity, as in the passage quoted. All these stand in relation to the 'I' whose subjectivity is that of a lover; an already divided state. In line with Gower's reading of a divided subject, Hoccleve's *The Regement of Princes* also opens autobiographically, with the subject of the poem musing on the world's 'restless business':

> As I lay in my bedde upon a nyght
> Thoght me berefte of slepe the force and myght. (6, 7)[9]

The power of thought is associated with death, and perhaps with a death-wish: 'to the deth he wel ny hath me feyntyd' (14). Thought has 'vexed' his 'poore goost' (9) before, so that the text makes two allegorizations, with himself objectified as his spirit, and with a double sense in 'poore' - i.e. in poverty, and an object of pity, the subject for a complaint. Thought has made him consider the lack of surety of anyone living, and he enumerates the dangers of poverty, before returning to the actual night:

> Thus ylke nyght I walwed to and fro
> Sekyng reste, but certeynly sche
> Appeeryd nought, for thoght, my cruel fo,
> Chaced hadde hyre and sleepe away fro me.
> And for I scholde not alone be
> Ageyn my lust, wach profrid hys seruyse

---

[9] The connection between Gower's "thoght" (in an example taken from VI. 907-918) with Hoccleve is made by James Simpson, *Sciences and the Self in Medieval Poetry: Alan of Lille's Anitclaudianus and John Gower's Confessio amantis* (Cambridge: Cambridge University Press, 1995), p. 208. See also p. 146 and Simpson's discussion of Book III, pp. 167-197.

> And I adytted hym in heuy wyse.
>
> So long a nyght ne felte I neuer non
> As was that same to my iugement.
> Who so that thoughtys ys, ys woe begon.
> The thoughtful wyght ys vessel of turment.
> Ther nys no gref to hym equypolent
>   He graueth deppest of seekenesse alle
> Ful wo ys hym that in swyche thought ys falle.   (71-84)

When Lewis calls this writing unallegorical, he means that it is realist description, the account of someone rendered sleepless by worry, worry about poverty. When saying it is 'infected with allegory', meaning that the realism is so inflected, he implicitly makes allegory a sickness, a contagious disease. The point, which is loaded for a poet whose work was written under the shadow of madness, is also present in Angus Fletcher, who takes allegory negatively when he refers to a relationship between contagion, sickness and allegory; the Latin *infectio* means a dyeing, or staining, just as allegory as a form of symbolic expression is a staining of the subject, while Fletcher quotes from Origen (*Contra Celsum* IV. xlviii) on making a connection between allegory and a fear of contagion.[10] But before we can take this as a general thought about allegory further, it should be noticed that 'Thought' as a particular instance of an allegorical conception and so an infection, is in this text already a form of sickness; since it is annotated by Seymour as 'anxiety' or 'worry' in a sense the OED dates from c.1220. So as soon as self-reflexiveness, self-consciousness, which may also be part of the meaning of 'Thought' enters into allegorical existence, it casts a staining or sickening quality upon the subject, in a way that Hamlet also records in like allegorical manner ('the native hue of resolution / Is sicklied o'er with the pale cast of thought' (*Hamlet* III.i. 83-4) so much so that it appears that modern self-awareness is inseparable from the history of allegorical writing, the allegory which is the subject of Lewis's text (*Le roman de la rose* dates from that same moment, soon after 1220). Here it seems worth quoting, as supplementary evidence, Louis Sass's comments on schizophrenia - which as a condition was first named as such by Bleuler, around 1910, which makes it, therefore, another aspect of a modernist condition. Sass, who is opposed to an 'anti-psychiatry' position which sees in schizophrenia an increased affectivity, finds in it 'not an overwhelming by but a detachment from normal forms of emotion and desire, not a loss but an exacerbation of various kinds of self-

---

[10]   Angus Fletcher, *Allegory: The Theory of a Symbolic Mode* (Ithaca: Cornell University Press, 1966), pp. 199-209.

conscious awareness'.[11] For Sass, schizophrenia is an overwhelming by thought; not a form of emotional hyper-activity but its opposite. If thought, then, is in Hoccleve inherently oppressive, that may in itself be a form of madness - where if madness is a state of alienation, thought is already alien, and the oppression itself. Or, thought may be a symptom of some other cause or problem, perhaps related to self-awareness. In which case, the desire to think allegorically may also be read as a retreat from such awareness, rather than as simply a development of it, since in allegory the subject moves back into abstractions, and sees its mental life in abstract, almost geometric forms. Allegory thus serves a double purpose; and it is not surprising that Lewis should see Hoccleve as allegorical and non-allegorical at once, also double.

Hoccleve's Thought, split off from himself, becomes his cruel foe. As masculine, it chases away the feminine rest and sleep.[12] Wakefulness as a substitute offers its services, and the subject is forced to take him 'in heavy wise' - in a melancholic spirit that recognises that there is no choice, as there is no resisting a disease. The thoughtful person is 'woebegone', a 'vessel of torment' (a vessel filled with torment, another form of possession by allegory).

This story of the night leads to reflection, which is not based on a specific occasion, and to a desire to be alone:

> What whyght that inly pensyf is, I trowe
> Hys most desyre ys to be solytarie.
> That thys is soth, in my persone I knowe,
> For euere whyl that fretynge aduersarie
> Myn herte made to hymn trybutarie
> In sowkynge of the fresshest of my blood,
> To sorwe soule me thought yt dede me good.

> For the nature of heuynesse ys thys.
> If yt habunde gretly in a wyth,
> The place eischewyt he where as ioye ys
> For ioye and he not mow acorde aryght.
> As discordant as day ys vnto nyght.
> And honure aduersarie is vnto schame,
> Is heuynes so to ioye and game.

> Whan to the thoughtful wyght ys tolde a tale,

---

[11] Louis Sass, *Paradoxes of Delusion: Wittgenstein, Schreber and the Schizophrenic Mind* (Ithaca: Cornell University Press, 1994), p. 12. Sass's discussion of schizophrenia as modernist appears in his *Madness and Modernism* (New York: Basic Books, 1992).

[12] Ruth Nissé, '"Our Fadres Olde and Modres": Gender, Heresy and Hoccleve's Literary Politics', *Studies in the Age of Chaucer* 21 (1999) in contrast reads the 'Thought' as feminine and feminizing. It seems to me that the 'force and myght' of Thought makes the subject feminized rather, by an act of violence.

> He herit yt as though he thennes were.
> Hys heuy thoughtys hym so plukke and hale
> Hydyr and thyder and hym greue and dere
> That hys eres avayle hym nat a pere.
> He understondeth nothyng what emn seye,
> So ben hys wytts fer gone hem to pleye.
>
> The smert of thought I by experience
> Knowe as wel as any man doth lyuynge.
> Hys frosty swoot and fyry hote feruence
> And troubly dremes, drempt al in wakynge,
> My mazyd hed slepless han of konnyng
> And wyt despoylyd, and so me be-iapyd
> That after deth ful often haue I gapyd.   (85-112)

Infection increases from the state of being inly pensive, as opposed to thinking outwardly, in a mode that directs attention away from the interior. Thought, a biting adversary, like a vampire, induces melancholia, called 'heaviness', which as a substantive becomes an allegorical force. Heaviness can be defined (92) and, conjoined with thought in the phrase 'heavy thoughts', has power to pull him about, so that he cannot be spoken to, for his wits have gone forth to play, - which when it returns as a phrase in the *Complaint* (50,51, to be discussed below), indicates madness. The last verse speaks of the smart of thought, its frosty sweat and fiery hot zeal, where the power of allegorization and the desire for it constructs thought in oppositional binary modes, and refers to troubling dreams, dreamed in a waking state, making sleep impossible.

In the *Complaint*, thought again assails him. The Prologue describes Autumn, where the seasonal change leads him into a depressive state where he returns to the topic of the *Regiment of Princes*:

> Sighynge sore as I in my bed lay
> For this and othir thoght which many a day
> Before I took sleep cam noon in myn ye,
> So vexid me the thoghtful maladie. (18-21)

In the last reference to thought in the *Complaint*, it is the 'thoughtful disease' (388).

Thought as 'anxiety' stains its other meanings, so that in the *Complaint* it cannot be taken other than as a malady, a cause of self-division - as in

> As that I ones fro Westmynstre cam
> Vexid ful greuously with thoghtful herte
>
> Thus thoghte I 'A greet fool I am [...]' (183-185)

- where thought possesses him, so that the thoughtful heart produces in the 'I' the activity of thinking, and where to think is to consider oneself a fool (afflicted with madness); followed by:

> And thanne thoghte I on that othir syde [...] (190)

- so that thought induces splitting and the divided self. Personifying thought, and its possession of him as melancholia go together. The man of the Prologue recalls his past, how he has been sourged with sickness, how 'the sonne abated and the dirk shour / Hildid doun right on me' (25-26), like Julia Kristeva's 'black sun' of melancholy.[13] In both Dürer and Hoccleve, melancholia and thinking interlink. And in Hoccleve thought is linked to memory, for now it is not his 'wits' which went out to play, as on holiday, in carnival excess, but everything of consciousness, including memory:

> But althogh the substance of my memorie
> Wente to pleye as for a certein space,
> Yit the lord of vertu the kyng of glorie,
> Of his hye might and benigne grace
> Made it for to retourne into the place
> Whens it cam which was at Alle Halwemesse,
> Was fiue yeer neither moore ne lesse.(50-56)

This 'nomadic' subject, whose memory seems to have gone out of his body, as with a loss of body-boundaries, may be compared with the subject in Deleuze and Guattari in *Anti-Oedipus: Capitalism and Schizophrenia*, as decentred and schizoid. However much Hoccleve despairs over his madness, the potentiality for a form of freedom in going forth to play also seems present. But Hoccleve's poetry shows no encouragement of going forth to play. The conservative remonstrating voice against Oldcastle accuses Lollards of asking such carnivalesque questions of the teaching of 'holy chirche' as:

> Why stant this word heere? and why this word there?
> Why spak God thus, and seith thus elleswhere? (*Remonstrance* 156-7)

The context is the influence on Oldcastle of women, 'lewed calates' (147), where the feminine is – as in Deleuze and Guattari – the agent of 'deterritorialization', wherein desire wanders off from fixed categories of perception and meaning. But as God's wits are not to be accused of having gone forth to play, the sacred text has no play within it.[14] Nomadism looks for 'lines of flight' which will bring

---

[13] Julia Kristeva, *Black Sun*, trans. by Leon S. Roudiez (New York: Columbia University Press, 1989), pp. 139-52. Kristeva quotes from de Nerval's 'El Desdichado', 'le soleil noir de la Mélancolie' which refers to Dürer's engraving of 'Melencolia I'.

[14] 'Play' is used here in Derrida's sense in 'Structure, Sign and Play in the Human Sciences', *Writing and Difference*, trans. by Alan Bass (London:

about its deterritorialization and so its freedom from the oppressive and paranoid dominant order, but in the *Remonstrance* and the *Complaint* it returns towards the imaginary centre, to speak its discourse more obediently.[15]

II - AUTOBIOGRAPHY

Hoccleve for Seymour is 'of course, a minor poet, whose closeness to Chaucer vividly illuminates the narrowness of his achievement' (Seymour, xxxiii), though he could not have anticipated the attention that has in the past twenty years undone that 'of course' by bringing out the extent of Hoccleve's interest. But to stay with Seymour: minor literature can also speak differently. One characteristic of a 'minor' literature for Deleuze and Guattari – an example is Kafka - is to exist as a deterritorializing space within a major literature, 'appropriate for strange and minor uses'. If Hoccleve may be read as minor in that other way, constituted by his madness as 'a stranger within his own language'[16] it would be because his melancholia made him transgressive within the discourse of the Lancastrian hegemony, where Chaucer was held as poetic father.[17] But the move towards *re*territorialization, re-incorporation within the dominant order is

Routledge and Kegan Paul, 1978), pp 278-93. Hoccleve's poetry attaches to the dream of 'full presence, the reassuring foundation, the origin and the end of play' (p. 292).

[15] For the nomadic subject, see Gilles Deleuze and Félix Guattari, *Thousand Plateaux*, trans. by Brian Masumi (Minneapolis: University of Minnesota Press, 1987), pp. 311-423 *passim*, but especially pp. 380-84.

[16] Gilles Deleuze and Felix Guattari, *Kafka: Towards a Minor Literature*, trans. by Dana Polan (Minneapolis: University of Minnesota Press, 1986), pp. 17, 26.

[17] For the relationship between Chaucer and his fifteenth-century 'official' status, the Lancastrian hegemony and the promotion of English as a way of promoting that, see John H. Fisher, 'A Language Policy for Lancastrian England',' *PMLA* 107 (1992), 1168-80. On the propagandist role of poets such as Hoccleve and Lydgate within the fifteenth-century formation, and under the dominance of Chaucer, see Richard Firth Green, *Poets and Princepleasers: Literature and the English Court in the Late Middle Ages* (Toronto: University of Toronto Press' 1980); and Paul Strohm, in *England's Empty Throne: Usurpation and the Language of Legitimation* (New Haven: Yale University Press' 1998) and his chapter, 'Hoccleve, Lydgate and the Lancastrian Court' in *The Cambridge History of Medieval English Literature*, ed. by David Wallace (Cambridge: Cambridge University Press, 1999), pp. 640-661. See Seth Lerer, *Chaucer and his Readers: Imagining the Author in Late Medieval England* (Princeton: Princeton University Press, 1993), pp. 87-88 on Chaucer as 'father'. But this does not discuss Hoccleve. See also Larry Scanlon, *Narrative, Authority and Power: The Medieval Exemplum and the Chaucerian Tradition* (Cambridge: Cambridge University Press, 1994), pp. 299-322, for Hoccleve's relation to the Lancastrian dynasty, and for his part in the canonization of Chaucer's authority.

present in Hoccleve. A desire towards an assertion of normality could account for the attitude taken up by the sane Hoccleve towards Lollardy. The discourse that judges the heretic also constructs the self as not heretical, not different. If Richard Green is to be followed, Hoccleve had so internalized a dislike of the Lollards that he went further than Henry V in his condemnation of them, and thought of Henry as too likely to fall into compromise with their error.[18]

This minor poet produces autobiographical poetry, and the problematics of autobiography are connected with his subject-matter: the madness endured five years previously, making him 'the first [...] to write at length and *in propria persona* of a madness that could be real'.[19] The earlier poem, *La Male Regle de T. Hoccleve* (1405) had invoked 'Helthe', speaking as being out of health both on account of his misrule (*La Male Regle* 56,90,290), and for his failure to adhere to 'reuled resoun' (70) or a 'mene reule' (352). Excess is both saturnalian carnival *and* melancholia, the anxieties of 'thought' *and* 'folie' (40). Since 'folie' includes madness, it seems impossible to put boundaries round the state of madness discussed in the *Complaint*, since:

> Excess of mete and drynke is glotonye;
> Glotonye awakith malencolie;
> Malencolie awakth werre and stryf
> Stryf causith mortel hurt thurgh hir folie [...]. (*La Male Regle* 300-303)

Penelope Doob reads this as what Deleuze and Guattari would call reterritorialization, the subject no longer nomadic, but returning to known and conventional ground; so she takes the madness of the *Complaint* as perhaps only a 'metaphor for the crippling state of sin which is the real subject of the poem'. In contrast John Burrow has concentrated on Hoccleve's newness in English as an autobiographical writer, while James Simpson finds innovation in his

---

[18] Richard Firth Green, pp. 183-6.

[19] Penelope Doob, *Nebuchadnezzar's Children: Conventions of Madness in Medieval English Literature* (New Haven: Yale University Press, 1974), p. 228. On this view see Seymour, p. 133. For an overview of medieval madness, see Muriel Laharie, *La folie au moyen age, xi-xiii siècles* (Paris: Le Leopard d'or, 1991), and more generally Liza Veith, *Hysteria: The History of a Disease* (Chicago: Chicago University Press, 1965); whose chapter 4 is on 'Hysteria in the Middle Ages' (possibly relevant for the *Complaint* 34-5), and citing Augustine, 'there are no diseases that do not arise from witchery and hence from the mind' (p. 55); Stanley Jackson, *Melancholia and Depression: From Hippocratic Times to Modern Times* (New Haven: Yale University Press, 1988). On Hoccleve's earlier autobiographical writing, see Ethan Knapp, 'Bureaucratic Identity and the Construction of the Self in Hoccleve's *Formulary* and *La male regle*', *Speculum* 74 (1999), 357-376.

writing, in contrast to the conservatism within his politics, so that the *Complaint* followed by the *Dialogue* is a 'critique of the premises of consolation literature . [...] it is deploying literary traditions to undercut the model of personality implicit in the consolatory tradition, and to create new models of personality, unauthorized by literary tradition'. Simpson thinks of the subject being differently created through different forms of writing. His Hoccleve is aware of 'the prison-house of language' - associated with forms of writing he must escape, and in this Simpson sees a tendential modernism, so if modernism is to be taken as a structural position, a recurrrent set or approach towards writing and the text (for example, associated with the foregrounding of the split between the signifier and the signified), then this modernism may perhaps be articulated with the modernism of schizophrenia as Louis Sass has argued.[20]

Nonetheless, Simpson believes it is Hoccleve the subject who changes those forms of writing. But there is a particular problem highlighted in poetry which is both assumed to be autobiographical *and* taken to be the record of madness. It is exacerbated if it is to be assumed that there is a normative subject about whom the term 'mad' can be used, or who initiates poetic changes or who works with a chronology that assumes the self-validating, continuously self-present subject. Simpson, discussing Hoccleve as someone who makes the rules for himself, puts the subject of autobiography outside the text. But autobiography, a nineteenth-century term, sets up the subject in a particular way and under certain constraints; it produces, in a pattern of blindness and insight, a certain form of subject, who is knowable in one way, and need not be known in another. As a compulsion, this splits the self, since it creates another self that must be known objectively and textually, and which may also be thought of as dead, as finished. While it may *seem* to be the expression of a full sensibility which is summed up in the proper name, which indeed Hoccleve uses of himself, in the subsequent words of the Friend (*Dialogue* 3), it compels a splitting off, which associates autobiography with two forms of splitting: madness and allegory. Schizophrenia implies the splitting of psychic functions in the individual, who in that state no longer operates as an integrated

---

[20] James Simpson, 'Madness and Texts: Hoccleve's *Series*' in Julia Boffey and Janet Cowen, eds., *Chaucer and Fifteenth-Century Poetry* (London: King's College London Centre for Late Antique and Medieval Studies, 1991) p. 26; see also James Simpson, 'Nobody's Man: Thomas Hoccleve's *Regiment of Princes*' in Julia Boffey and Pamela King, eds., *London and Europe in the Later Middle Ages* (London: Centre for Medieval and Renaissance Studies, Queen Mary and Westfield College, University of London, 1995), pp. 149-180; John Burrow, 'Autobiographical Poetry in the Middle Ages: The Case of Thomas Hoccleve', *Proceedings of the British Academy* 68 (1988), 115-127.

whole. What happens when the tools to describe a split state both replicate such splitting: autobiography and allegory?

Memory, in Hoccleve's case, has gone forth to play and by doing so it throws everything of the autobiographical possibility into jeopardy. What is an autobiography if it admits that its memory has disappeared? What good is it even if the subject says that its memory has come back? Can it remember not having a memory? To turn to an early autobiographical poet writing in English is to expect to find something of the history of the subject. Much of the recent turn to theory within medieval studies has been premised on the point that the 'early modernists' have neglected the bourgeois subject and its interiority within the fourteenth and fifteenth centuries. 'To write the history of the medieval subject is to write the history of medieval culture', as Lee Patterson has written.[21] It is baffling to turn to a text of autobiography, then, and find that in the place of evidence for the existence of the subject marked by interiority, a text marked by its absence, madness. Michel Foucault, so much of an inspiration to New Historicism, and to the project to think in terms of the 'early modern', begins the *Histoire de la folie* with the sixteenth-century, and with the possibility that madness could exist in a state governed by reason, that madness and reason could be in dialogue with each other, but here, a century earlier, madness seems to be a ground of exclusion, even from the subject's own speech. This exclusion means that Hoccleve's text disallows writing a history of the subject with the thought that here, the autobiographical desire is also a form of madness, since it cannot access the past, while to read it may also require the reader to listen to madness, in the sense that Shoshana Felman in *Writing and Madness: Literature, Philosophy, Psychoanalysis* means when she defines madness in the literary text

---

[21] See David Aers, *Culture and History, 1350-1600: Essays on English Communities, Identities and Writing* (London: Harvester, 1992), p. 182, quoting Lee Patterson, 'On the Margin: Postmodernism, Ironic History and Medieval Studies', *Speculum* 65 (1990), 87-108. (The volume was entitled 'The New Philology'.) See also Patterson's attack on adherents to New Historicism (including Francis Barker, Catherine Belsey, Jonathan Dollimore and Stephen Greenblatt) for an implicit denial of an earlier history of the subject in *Negotiating the Past: The Historical Understanding of Medieval Literature* (Madison: University of Wisconsin Press, 1987), chapter 2. For an overview of the interrelationships between critical theory and medieval literature, see Sarah Kay, 'Analytical Survey 3: The New Philology', *New Medieval Literatures* 3, ed. by David Lawton, Wendy Scase and Rita Copeland (Oxford: Oxford University Press, 1999), pp. 295-326, and in *New Medieval Literatures* 2 (1998), Louise O. Fradenburg, 'Psychoanalytic Medievalism', pp. 249-76. See also my 'Dante and the Modern Subject: Overcoming Anger in the *Purgatorio*', *New Literary History* 28 (1997), 401-20, for discussion of writing the history of the subject.

as an 'irreducible resistance to interpretation'.[22] The early text which might prove paradigmatic for understanding autobiography is indeed paradigmatic in one of two ways: either the subject says it cannot remember in a form of textual repression, which has willed its own forgetting, or, relatedly, in that its possibility of describing the self is inscribed by the impossibility of knowing whether it remembers or not. Its melancholy is that it cannot remember, and that it cannot remember the extent of its melancholy.

But the subject may be connected with another history. Paul Strohm finds in Hoccleve's poetry for the Lancastrian court 'less wholesome and inauthentic alternative[s]' – he lists 'heresy, effeminate fashion, female practices of reading and introspection, or false speech' regarded by Hoccleve as 'subversive of Lancastrian practice [which was] stabilized around ideas of the orthodox, the identity of inner and outer'. He adds that 'held at bay is the embarrassing fact of the Lancastrians as a usurping dynasty, and the extent to which issues of misrepresentation and false display reach a crisis-point during their regime. This is the unacknowledged issue around which Hoccleve's public poems revolve, never explicitly admitting the flawed nature of the Lancastrian title'.[23] The issues which mean that orthodoxy is the concealment of violence and at the centre of everything is a still 'empty' throne, disavowed as such, leads to the thought, then, that Hoccleve's madness, itself discursively constructed, articulates with a loss of memory, a loss of narrating ability, which is encouraged at the very centre of signification. The madness of Hoccleve, never described, about which hangs a silence, becomes another emptiness to add to the central emptiness of the throne itself.

That absence of memory tilts Hoccleve towards the modern state. Thought as a melancholic structure moves towards its breakdown, towards the Foucauldian 'absence of work'. Memory, in this paradigm of the modern subject, cannot be of a consistent, self-validating nature, but is overwhelming, threatening the subject with trauma. Perhaps that appears on the violence of the initial outburst of the *Complaint*, 'And for to preeue I cam of a womman / I brast out on the morwe and thus began' (34,35). That might mean 'to prove I was human' but the gender-reference makes the outburst feminine, aligning the subject with the feminine – though noticeably, the Friend will later say that he has offended women, (*Dialogue* 667-700) which would imply a normative anti-feminism, but would also imply

---

22 Shoshana Felman, *Writing and Madness: Literature, Philosophy, Psychoanalysis*, trans. by Martha Noel Evans and the author with the assistance of Brian Massumi (Ithaca: Cornell University Press, 1985), p. 254
23 Strohm, *England's Empty Throne* p. 185.

another registering of a splitting, as though this implied masculinism was another form of his alienation and a reason for his exclusion. The passage could also mean that his outburst proved, analeptically, that there was a woman in him, or that he felt it identified him with the mother: that was how he read his own outburst, in yet another splitting. The resultant outburst proved the sickness to be that of the presence of the feminine. At such a moment, on this reading, the subject speaks his own self-hatred. Memory of madness, of trauma, is read as memory of an excess which has momentarily split gender-difference.

The melancholic subject could not write autobiography: no self-consistent history of subjectivity could emerge from it. Writing, deferral, allegory and madness all connect. Allegory ends thought as self-consistent, complete and knowing itself; it undoes the power of Thought as a dominating agency, in its tendency towards fragmentation, associated with, and partly concealed by, the act of naming. When Hoccleve makes the Friend give him his proper name, this demonstrates not the end of personification-allegory and the beginning of a new, more immediate attention to the subject, but rather an allegorical mode continued in another form of naming, where both forms - whether referring to Thought, or Reason, or a Friend, or Thomas, or Hoccleve, or the name of the text as the *Complaint* (by calling it that, its other qualities are occluded) - are attempts to delineate and to fix. A double movement works within the text: the desire to affirm a substantial unity, which includes an assertion of normality, which the community would accept, and which would make them accept him, and a contrary movement towards the splitting of the subject, which makes the act of writing a form of madness, Blanchot's *désoeuvrement* - worklessness.[24] It is a state ironically split off from the conditions of clerkly work in which Hoccleve laboured for so long. Writing is allegorical, which means it fragments in two different ways. Thought, which in post-Cartesian terms splits the subject into a duality, does so in the medieval text by forcing aspects of the subject into isolation and treating them as

---

[24] Maurice Blanchot, 'The Essential Solitude' in *The Space of Literature*, trans. by Ann Smock (Lincoln: University of Nebraska Press, 1982), p. 23; see also translator's introduction p. 13. This sense of disappearance within the text needs to be placed against Simpson's contrasted, other emphasis in 'Madness and Texts' on the Series as 'a work peculiarly concerned with the story of its own composition' (p. 18). Robert J. Meyer-Lee, 'Hoccleve and the Apprehension of Money', *Exemplaria* 13 (2001), 173-214, which, exploring the pathology of his thought, takes Hoccleve's 'anxiety' to be related to the instability of money as a representational system (p. 210). If that sense could be generalised from, it could be said that *désoeuvrement* is writing in the absence of a sense of writing's representational power.

wholes. This splitting is part of a constraint on the self to speak itself, as though the one thing the self cannot do is to describe itself, to bring itself out into the open - it being, from the standpoint of normality, an act of folly to describe a state of madness. But it fragments too in that it prevents clear utterance, prevents the self from speaking itself.

Shoshana Felman discusses 'mad writing', whose resistance to interpretation is the text's resistance to reading. Perhaps the *Complaint* illustrates that. She also discusses that form of writing which Foucault in *Histoire de la folie* could not get beyond, according to Derrida's critique: writing about madness.[25] About this she says two things: that to write about madness - as Hoccleve seems to do, whether or not he can say anything about it - is to deny it. 'However one represents madness to oneself or others, to represent madness is always, consciously or unconsciously, to play out the scene of the denial of one's own madness'. That applies, whether the person is sane and writing about the mad, or, like Hoccleve, attempting to put madness into the past. It works by assuming that madness and reason can be seen as binary opposites - a tendency which exists in allegorical thought. Yet Felman adds that 'there still exists in these texts a madness that speaks, a madness that is acted out in language, but whose speaking role no subject can assume. It is this movement of non-totalizable, ungovernable linguistic play, through which meaning misfires and the text's statement is estranged from its performance, that I call ... the madness of rhetoric'.[26] Perhaps such a moment of linguistic play appears in the excess which Hoccleve himself notes when he bursts forth; perhaps such a play may also be noted in describing his memory – or his wits, which are certainly feminine - going out to play.[27] Autobiographical yet attended by memory-loss, Hoccleve's writing defeats a chronology which would provide an etiology of the madness and make it complete.

III - MADNESS

---

[25] For Derrida's critique of Foucault, see 'Cogito and the History of Madness', in Jacques Derrida, *Writing and Difference*, trans. by Alan Bass (London: Routledge, 1978), pp. 31-63, and Foucault's response to Derrida, 'My Body, this Paper, this Fire', *Oxford Literary Review* 4 (1979), 9-28. On the debate see John Frow, *Marxism and Literary Theory* (Oxford: Blackwell, 1986), pp. 207-35, and Felman, pp. 33-55.

[26] Shoshana Felman, p. 252. I have dropped the author's use of italics, and her use of quotation marks.

[27] Compare: 'Whan reuled wit and manly hardiness / Ben knitte to-gidre, as yok of mariage / Ther floweth of victorie the sweetnesse' – *The Regement of Princes*, 3991-3.

Even if something within the text defeats the oppression within the madness, yet Hoccleve's madness and the recourse to allegory still bear the marks of a damaged subject. The *Complaint* opens with a Prologue whose autumnal meditation on decay follows on from the opening of the General Prologue to *The Canterbury Tales*, as though writing had to preserve its normalizing quality by staying inside the terms set down by the poet whose status, the more it was elevated in Lancastrian circles, would keep Hoccleve as a 'minor' poet. Burrow comments that Hoccleve 'lacked his master Chaucer's ability to speak in voices other than his own'[28] but he is compelled by his minor status and by his madness to speak at all times in a voice which is 'other' to him – in a Chaucerian voice, including dialogue, the use of the Chaucerian persona, and the notion of linking narratives - which is another way of saying that in one sense he is always compelled to speak allegorically. But at the same time, something within his work makes him speak differently.[29] At the end of this November, he speaks of his melancholia, but this state, with its uncertainty, disconfirms the narrative that puts the madness away from him by five years, and means rather that nothing has changed.

He is in a state of 'languor' (implying *acedia*). Recollection of his grief leads him into the *Complaint*, which opens with the confession – and that means that the text has on it the marks of being forced to acknowledge a position in relation to normality - of 'the wylde infirmitee / Which that I hadde as many a man wel kneew /And which me out of myself caste and threew' (40-42). The *Complaint* acknowledges what he has been, but it emphasises that he has recovered his normality. The 'me' of line 42 seems to be identified with the 'substaunce of my memorie'; as he speaks of 'my wit' having come home again (64). It is self-deprecatory; as though continuing with the mock self-deprecations which are common to Chaucer in his personae, so that it complicates the sense that Hoccleve can be speaking in his 'own' voice, rather than that of another, more powerful predecessor, whose very power, as now made an aspect of Lancastrian ideology, may even be a source of madness. This description of having gone out and come back returns in the image of a drunk person about whom after his drunkeness 'he ... cometh to hymsilfe agein' (229-30). Hoccleve asserts that his wits

---

28 Burrow (note 15), p. 402.

29 A.C. Spearing writes, with reference to Langland, Margery Kempe and Hoccleve, that 'those who were driven to find ways of writing their individual life-histories tended to the eccentric, even the unbalanced, who felt their inner selves to be different from those of their neighbours'. He also finds in Hoccleve a 'persistent use of small-scale personification' which he calls non-Chaucerian. See *Medieval to Renaissance in English Poetry* (Cambridge: Cambridge University Press, 1985), pp. 113,119.

have come back again, and so has the 'substance of his memorie', so that he can say the 'soothe' (the truth):

> The soothe is this swich conceit as I hadde
> And vndirstondyng, al were it but smal,
> Before that my wittis weren vnsadde,
> Thankid be oure lord Ihesu Crist of al,
> Such haue I nowe but blowe is ny oueral
> The reuers wherethurgh moche is my mournynge,
> Which causith me thus sighe in compleynynge (253-59)

The first five lines, to the caesura ('nowe'), assert his normality, that his wits are no longer 'unsadde' - light, or unsteady, or unsettled; but the last two and a half lines reveal an anxiety that his normality will not be validated by the community. Instead, his madness is 'blown' as if by Fame or Rumour's trumpet, in a passage recalling Chaucer's *The House of Fame*.[30] The result is a mourning to supplement his melancholia and his 'compleynynge' - both title and substance of his text. A complaint is produced by an anxious melancholia; it declares that he does not have what he says he has: i.e. his normality. Autobiography then, is not the statement of a position but the desire for a position; that is the constraint upon it, that it is not written from where one would wish to be. It produces a subject outside the circle - of his wits, and of his friends, and of those who would give him social validation.

The drive towards asserting present normality is both repressive and an impossibility. Using the phrase that a drunk comes to himself again:

> Righte so thogh that my wit were a pilgrym
> And wente fer from hoom he cam agayn (232-3)

he makes himself like the prodigal son of the Bible who came to himself (Luke 15.17) and returned to his father. This might align Hoccleve's text with the progress of Augustinian confession. But the figure of returning in a circle is what the philosopher Levinas criticizes in Christianity as opposed to Judaism, in which he argues that the prototypical figure is Abraham who went out he knew not whither. The belief in return forms the basis of what Derrida would see as a logocentrism which is anxious to protect the word, - and Derrida opposes to what he sees as its presence in Lacan the concept

---

[30] The connection between the two texts is made by David Mills, 'The Voices of Thomas Hoccleve', in *Essays on Thomas Hoccleve*, ed. by Catherine Batt (London: Centre for Medieval and Renaissance Studies, Queen Mary and Westfield College, University of London, 1996), p. 107. He quotes *Dialogue* 477-9 as like the timbre of much of *The House of Fame* (e.g. line 1878).

of 'dissemination', where there can be no return.[31] The pilgrim, 'peregrinos' in Latin, is a stranger, an exile, an alien, and in Hoccleve seeing his wits as pilgrim, there is an obvious allegorization, which again goes further than the accidental, for if allegory is a figure of speaking other, of alien speech, it also associates itself with the figure of the pilgrim. Yet the pilgrim hopes to return home. Hoccleve anxiously fixes the identity of the place where 'the substance of his memorie' came back to, and above all the time - five years ago exactly, November the first, All Hallows' Day. Returning home denies any value in the experience of madness, in which sense it is potentially repressive; so that the text indeed plays out the scene of denial of the subject's madness by repressing it from memory.

The text, though trying to close the wound, or *béance* opened by madness, cannot do so, and into that gap, which is the place of trauma, an excess of signification appears to try and show that the subject can indeed think autobiographically, in terms of past and present. The formal elements of allegory - personification - repeat an allegory already in the text, and the text is constructed by a madness, that is, a split state, inseparable from the madness it describes. Hoccleve has described a condition of ecstasy, of his 'me' being outside the 'self'. The allegorical thinking which imported Thought as an outsider, in the *Regiment*, has thrown the 'me' of the 'myself' out, but now claims that these two things, aspects of an allegorical language, have come together again. Like saying that his memory has returned, it is impossible - and it will be noted too that, for whatever reason, he says nothing about the state that he was in when he was mad, as though that memory was gone for good. The anxiety in the text is that the friends who made him an object of their scrutiny cannot confirm that he was as he was. But no more can he.

The *Complaint* describes sitting alone in his chamber at home, and nervily jumping up to look at himself:

> I streighte vnto my mirour and my glas
> To looke how that me of my cheere thoghte,
> If any othir were it than it oghte;
> For fayn wolde I if it had nat been right,
> Amendid it to my konnynge and might.
>
> Many a saut made I to this mirour
> Thynkynge 'if that I looke in this maneere
> Among folk as I now do noon errour
> Of suspect look may in my face appeere.

---

[31] See on Levinas's article 'The Trace of the Other' Jill Robbins, *Prodigal Son, Elder Brother: Interpretation and Alterity in Augustine, Petrarch, Kafka, Levinas* (Chicago: University of Chicago Press' 1991)' pp. 106-110.

> This contenance I am seur and this cheere
> If I foorth use is no thyng repreeuable
> To hem that han conceits resonable.'
>
> And therewithal I thoughte thus anoon:
> 'Men in her owne case bene blinde al day [...].'   (157-170)

The dominance of the intrusive thought now becomes something to judge another allegorical quality: his 'cheere' - which Burrow annotates as 'face' or 'expression'. Hoccleve's face is the index to how far he may be thought to be out of a state of melancholia. Further, since he thinks of himself as containing more than his thought, he records what his thought thought, in a soliloquy (163-168), which is, implicitly, a further fragmentation. This soliloquy is followed by another, which begins at line 169, where his thought has itself split, thought against thought, in a process continued by his thought that the subject is blind, unknowing, about himself. But these forms of splitting are minor in comparison to the major form: of measuring his being by what he sees in the mirror. The skill he wants is to be like the 'they' of Shakespeare's Sonnet 94, who are 'the lords and owners of their faces'. But since the mirror may not be able to tell him what he wants to know about his face, since 'men in hire owne case been blynde alday', the mirror which tells will be the people whose look will confirm or disconfirm his state. Identity is fashioned not in a void but under paranoid constraints, not to be 'other' than expected.

In Lacan's essay on the mirror-stage, invoked here for comparison, the mirror gives an image which confirms a narcissistic sense for the subject whereby it may feel complete and secure. Narcissism is dependent on seeing the self as not split, as not the *corps morcelé*, the body in pieces, which is the other fantasy against which the mirror-stage works.[32] The image must come from the other, from the outside world which acts as a mirror to the subject telling him what he is. It is evident that no such narcissistic identification can be made by the subject, and the writing follows the problem this evokes.

A textual aporia about the timing of this repeated episode of going to the mirror repeats the aporia about the timing of the Prologue; how, chronologically, does the episode relate to his madness, and has he recovered or not? The ambiguity is repeated by another: silence about what he sees in the mirror. It may tell the subject what he is like inside — where, as Strohm suggested, inner and outer representations were supposed to correspond. He refers to the 'wylde

---

[32] Jacques Lacan, 'The Mirror Stage as Formative of the Function of the I as Revealed in Psychoanlytical Experience', *Ècrits: A Selection*, trans. by Alan Sheridan (London: Tavistock, 1977), p.4.

infirmitee' (40) and the 'wyldenesse' (107) caused by a grievous venom 'that had infectid and wyldid my brayn' (235), just as he is compared to a 'wylde steer' in a series of animal or monstrous images evoking him as a wilde man in his 'seeknesse sauage' (86). He fears that he may have become monstrous: but actually the monstrosity that he fears is worse than that: it is the state of not being able to fit his face (index to his cheer, his non-madness) into the social order, the social body.[33] The face is to be read allegorically, for an allegorical madness. To be different risks having the face read unfavourably.[34]

It will be recalled how Arcite's melancholy in *The Knight's Tale* changed him so completely so that he could return to Athens. Hoccleve's desire is to live in Athens - the modern Athens, London - unknown, unremarked, uncommented on, like Arcite; but Chaucer's text is different from Hoccleve's in that Arcite's face has changed; it has lost its figure. Hoccleve's face may express nothing exceptional (164-5), beyond the distortions coming from a convex mirror, which make all reflection monstrous. The face conveys nothing of what he has been going through. The aporia is in the absence of description. If the face appears normal, that would imply a further monstrosity; the face *not* marked, the wildness within unrepresented, perhaps unrepresentable, just as the madness is also unrepresented in the text. Autobiography, which continues the narrative of not knowing what to think of his cheer, his face, is the production of the monstrous.

We would like to know what Hoccleve thought his face looked like. He had a regard for Chaucer's face and kept a copy of it, as he tells the Old Man in *The Regiment of Princes*: 'the resemblaunce / Of hym hath in me so fresch lyflynesses / That, to put other men in remembraunce / Of hys persone, I haue heere hys lykeness / Don

---

[33] Compare for its suggestiveness Diderot's definition of a monster, 'a being whose survival is incompatible with the social order', *Elements de physiologie*, quoted by Michael André Berstein, *Bitter Carnival: Ressentiment and the Abject Hero* (Princeton: Princeton University Press, 1992), p. 24.

[34] To make a modern comparison, illustrating the power of national paranoia, Russell Berman refers to the fascist Ernest Jünger, who shows his dislike of others by showing he does not like their faces, because he does not like faces, i.e. the face as the index of an individual personality: Jünger wrote of Weimar artists; 'in Germany one meets this art world ... in close connection with all those forces on whom a hidden or overt treasonous character is written right across their faces' - quoted, Russell Berman, *Modern Culture and Critical Theory: Art, Policy and the Legacy of the Frankfurt School* (Madison: University of Wisconsin Press, 1989), p. 100. Meditation on the face should include reference to Levinas on the face of the other as the original site of the sensible: see Sean Hand, ed., *The Levinas Reader* (Oxford: Blackwell, 1989), pp. 82ff.

made' (4992-6).[35] The face, belonging to a man ten years dead, seems as important as the poetry: for, as Alberti puts it, 'through painting, the faces of the dead go on living for a long time'.[36] The face gives the illusion of a speaking voice within Chaucer's poetry; it puts a face on it. Chaucer's poetry accords with Chaucer's face.. And that suggests the aporia here in discussing Hoccleve's text as autobiography. The restraints on behaviour that Hoccleve exercised, alluded to, for instance, in lines 176-182, imply that his whole existence since his sickness has been assuming a mask; and that this is continued in the autobiography of the *Complaint*; preparing a face. The face that should look out on him ideally would be that of a normal man, which would be an allegorical image. Desire to have an identity confirmed in the mirror would meet the insuperable obstacle of a face expected to look in one particular way. Can there be a face outside the mask?

It is as though the face in the fifteenth century is being pushed into further visibility - further than *The Knight's Tale* could go. This move is resisted by the text's silence. Discussing a politics of 'faciality', where the body is being brought into a 'molar', single, disciplined form, Deleuze and Guattari say that 'the head, even the human head, is not necessarily a face. The face is produced only when the head ceases to be a part of the body, when it ceases to be coded by the body, when it ceases to have a multi-dimensional, polyvocal corporeal code - when the body, head included, has been decoded, and has to be *overcoded* by something we shall call the Face. This amounts to saying that the head, all the volume-cavity elements of the head, have to be facialized'.[37] The emergence of portraiture, by the end of the fourteenth-century may imply a new reading of the subject in terms of 'facializing', making the body more abstract and machine-like and producing the face as the index of individuality, and of the subject's place within sociality. But the face, particularized, must look like every other face. Hoccleve's fear and melancholy take two forms, both implicit: a face that is the same denies him as a subject while it also threatens him with the thought

---

[35] See Jeanne E. Krochalis, 'Hoccleve's Chaucer Portrait', *Chaucer Review* 21 (1986), 234-45, discussing late fourteenth-century realism in portraiture. Andrew Martindale, *Heroes, Ancestors, Relatives and the Birth of the Portrait* (The Hague: Gary Schwarz, SDU Publishers, 1988) p. 8, says that 'the first recorded portrait of in our modern sense - a painted or drawn life-like representation of a face -was produced by Simone Martini in 1336'. Martindale distinguishes between the work as *portraire* (representation) and *contrefais als vif*, a phrase dating from 1220: an imitation of living reality.
[36] Quoted, Andrew Martindale, *Simone Martini* (Oxford: Phaidon, 1988), p. 50.
[37] Gilles Deleuze and Félix Guattari, *A Thousand Plateaux*, p. 170.

that his experience as mad or as sane and trying to demonstrate this, has gone outside the representable.

Madness as the 'absence of work' is the loss of the subject's sense of self-presence. Near the end of the *Complaint* occurs a *mise en abime*, when Hoccleve turns from himself to describe another complainant, a mirror of himself:

> This othir day a lamentacioun
> Of a woful man in a book I sy
> To whom wordes of consolacioun
> Resoun yaf spekynge effectuelly (309-312)

The *mise en abime* is a reminder of Derrida, for whom the abyss represents the impossibility of the text establishing the subject's presence to himself. In the *mise en abime* appears a 'repetition and the splitting of the self. Representation in the abyss of presence is not an accident of presence; the desire of presence is, on the contrary, born from the abyss (the indefinite multiplication) of representation, from the representation of representation, etc'.[38] The desire is to replicate the self, to give the subject full presence, by doubling its presence by this further example of the mournful man - who is, however, by being mournful, already a shadow, only a figure, as much as he is also only textual. It is as though Hoccleve has taken the Chaucerian persona of *The Parliament of Fowls* who knows not Love indeed, but reads about him in books,[39] and applied it non-ironically; as though denying his own experience and shifting it to that of the woeful man in books. The particular book, identified as Isidore of Seville's *Synonyma* or *Soliloquia*,[40] speaks of the 'heuy man woful and angwisshous' who 'compleyned' (316-317) of - as Seymour explains it – 'the general willingness to accept rumour without proof and of the need to keep silent in the face of provocation' (Seymour, 135). Like Hoccleve, the woeful man speaks in allegorizations: 'Vexacioun of spirit and torment / Lakke I right noon I haue of hem plentee' (323-4); 'Sorwes so many in me multiplie' (332). Resoun, whose rule appears in *La Male Regle*, responds consolingly over six stanzas in dialogue with him, and gives a clue how the persona can escape his melancholia: 'Wrastle [...] ageyn heuynesses / Of the world troubles, suffrynge and duresses'

---

[38] Jacques Derrida, *Of Grammatology*, trans. by Gayatri Chakravorty Spivak (Baltimore: Johns Hopkins University Press, 1977), p. 163.

[39] Chaucer, *The Parliament of Fowls* 8-11.

[40] See A.G. Rigg, 'Hoccleve's *Complaint* and Isidore of Seville', *Speculum* 45 (1970), 564-74. See, for the extent of Hoccleve's reading of this, see A.G. Rigg, 'Hoccleve's *Complaint* and Isidore of Seville', *Speculum* 45 (1970), 564-74.

(342-3). But his speech is distanced from the Hocclevian persona by being framed within a book, and ceasing abruptly:

> Lenger I thoghte red haue in this book
> But so it shoop that I ne mighte naght;
> He that it oghte ageyn it to him took,
> Me of his haaste vnwaar. Yit haue I caght
> Sum of the doctrine by Resoun taght
> To the man as aboue haue I said,
> Whereof I holde me ful wel apaid.
>
> For euere sythen set haue I the lesse
> By the peples ymaginacioun [...] (372-80)

The reading is broken, a fragment of a consolation, and Hoccleve speaks of this breaking off as though he were the victim of an unconscious violence, since he says that the book's owner took the book away in haste. Burrow takes this to be a fiction to cover the point that he has got to the end of the anthology in which these extracts were contained. It is an instance of where the text's unconscious may speak: the fiction covers a sense that he is a victim of violence – that meted out to the subject who in some way is different. Nonetheless, Hoccleve tries to use the words between Reason and the woeful man as a consolation, stitching it into his own discourse, as in the phrase 'as aboue haue I said', and he then attempts to give to his text closure by taking what Reason says and applying it: 'He [God] yaf me wit and he took it away / Whan that he sy that I it mis despente / And yaf ageyn [...]' (400-402).

But the comparison cannot hold, for while the oppressed man in the book can be spoken to by Reason, Reason has for Hoccleve another valency in comparison to madness, in relation to which it may not be the healthy opposite, but the enemy - that which judges the state of 'madness' as mad; which victimizes it with its own violence, which by using the language of 'monstrosity' even associates Hoccleve, ironically if implicitly, with heretic Lollards. Thought was the oppressive force at the beginning; while now it seems that Reason has become accessible as another imposing force, discretely separate from the subject (there is no dialogue between reason and unreason here). But for Hoccleve to differentiate these two aspects of thinking, which have been so neatly discriminated between as allegorical figures, is not easy. Indeed, the allegory of Reason looks like a poetic closure, where one aspect of melancholic thought has been split off and declared to be sane and with power to impose itself on the subject. Hoccleve attempts to unite the experience of the man in the book with his own in the autobiographical relation he gives about his 'wit' (400-403), which makes for an implicit identification of melancholia with madness, or for an inability to separate the two. Further, as he attributes his madness to the judgment of God, it has entirely rational causes, questioning, indeed, whether the state can be called madness at all. This means that if Hoccleve did indeed suffer from a breakdown, his status as a 'minor' poet, with all that this implies in terms of the power of the Chaucerian / Lancastrian discourse that works in him, prevents him from reading his belief in a rationality that judges him as a form of oppression. He cannot read his own madness, nor see the potential for madness in the way he reads his situation after his recovery, in terms of its production of a further melancholia.

But what is that melancholia? It comes from the subject whose autobiography is also a confession, which works to strip the subject of any narcissism. We recall that Freud differentiates mourning from melancholia. Melancholia goes further than mourning in that it rests upon a failure of narcissism, so that Hoccleve's own crisis of narcissism, noticeable in his anxiety about his face, shows how thought has overthrown his subjectivity, not allowing the establishment of an ego, so that everything in and around the subject must be thought of as ruins - the very condition of melancholy in Benjamin, and the opposite of the stability invoked in poetry which would relate to the court. The subject in ruins cannot achieve the textual closure that is desired for and almost affirmed at the end of the *Complaint*. The text's chronology - its forwards and backwards rhythm, which cannot be assigned to a before and after - prevents the narrative from having such a force, and the text when finished is still called a Complaint in the first line of the *Dialogue*, in which text he declares to the Friend's horror his intention to publish it, so that it remains what it ever was: as much self-justificatory and not confessional as much as it is confessional autobiography. And something of the penitential continues in the *Dialogue* (215-6). In a sense, Hoccleve does not leave off the substance of the *Complaint*; this may explain why, as Burrow notes (Burrow 109), the *Dialogue* has exactly double the number of lines of the *Complaint*, as though he is continuing to argue and has split his identity between himself as the subject of the *Complaint* and a Friend.

Freud links melancholia to the word 'complaint': 'the woman who loudly pities her husband for being tied to such an incapable wife as herself is really accusing her *husband*' which leads him towards the aphorism that 'complaints are really "plaints" in the old sense of the word'. Freud is in part quoting from Nietzsche, who wrote 'all complaining is accusation' – 'Alles Klagen ist Anklagen'.[41] The

---

[41] Freud, 'Mourning and Melancholia', p. 257; Nietzsche, *Human, All Too Human: A Book for Free Spirits*, trans. by R.J. Hollingdale (Cambridge: Cambridge University Press, 1996), p. 230.

Complaint of Thomas Hoccleve, which incorporates into it the lamentation of another figure who must be instructed by Reason, may also be taken as an accusation, and hence as a record of suffering, which is the trace that madness leaves within the text. This means that it comes from somebody who finds what is around him to be the record of the untimely and sorrowful, and is determined to resist that; so the record of madness is not separable from the sense of his own oppression. The text's two opposing forces mean it cannot be interpreted singly; and since the Friend wishes the *Complaint* to be cancelled altogether, there is clearly an element in Hoccleve that wished to exclude all thought of his suffering, but its very repression about a madness it can only speak of indirectly and will not enlarge on, also implies a narrative that belongs within a history which is not just that of the subject, but of the production of the subject. Hoccleve as the mad subject is a casualty of unacknowledged usurpation, replicating in his own absence of work an emptiness elsewhere. It is indeed strange that writing the subject's autobiography in Langland and Hoccleve should produce such different allegorical inscriptions of madness and melancholia.

CHAPTER 4

Collecting Princes: Reading Lydgate

I - COLLECTING DEATHS

> He hes done petuously devour,
> The noble Chaucer, of makaris flour,
> The Monk of Bery, and Gower, all thre,
> *Timor mortis conturbat me.*[1]

In Dunbar's poem, (c.1500), Death is 'taking' 'all estatis' (17), as a collector, as well as a devourer. This elegy, naming those poets who have died, begins by singling out different groups who are on their way to death, with 'knychtis' given a stanza to themselves (21-24), but it opens with 'I', as though it was autobiographically justifying a sickness which he felt, whose cause might be from melancholia, because the sickness is actually fear of what death does to poets:

> I that in heill wes and gladnes
> Am trublit now with gret seiknes
> And feblit with infermite:
> *Timor mortis conturbat me.*

Writing poetry may be a form of collecting, and a poem which recalls those who have died an act of recollection (the sense of 'recollect' as 'to remember' is first cited in 1559 (OED)). Recollected names begin with Chaucer (c.1340-1400); Gower (c.1330-1408) and the 'Monk of Bury', John Lydgate (c.1370-c.1449). And then a line of twenty-one Scottish poets: many only names, though some the text distinguishes – for example, for being 'gude' (53), or 'for balat making and trigide' (59. Another has gone 'that maid the anteris [adventutres] of Gawane' (66). Another was 'quyk, of sentence hie' (75); another 'gentill' (86). Death has whispered - 'done roune' with Henryson, and 'embraced' Sir John the Ross (81-84). The last names are Quintyne Schaw – 'of quham all wichtis has pete' [all men have pity]' (87) and now 'Gud Maister Walter Kennedy', the subject of 'The Flyting of Dunbar' is dying.[2] This imminent death makes Kennedy a figure of the poet and circles back to the beginning as a justification for the thought that he will die next. The melancholia is a mourning for himself.

---

1 William Dunbar, *The Poems of William Dunbar*, ed. by James Kinsley (Oxford: Clarendon Press, 1979), p. 179.
2 For these poets, see Priscilla Bawcutt, *Dunbar the Makar* (Oxford: Clarendon Press, 1992), p. 26, and pp. 153-8. See also Bawcutt's edition, *The Poems of William Dunbar* 2 vols (Glasgow: Association for Scottish Literary Studies, 1998); she dates the poem c. 1505 on the basis of the reference to Stobo (John Reid), line 86, who died in 1505 (II. p. 333).

The list is selective; the poets are collector's items. Walter Kennedy is collected for the poem before he is collected for the grave. Poets who write about death, like Lydgate, or Patrik Johnnestoun, possible author of 'The Three Deid Pollis', or Henryson, to be spoken of in the next chapter, become figures of what their poetry signifies. The attempt to speak of death leads to a further taking away - of the poet - which produces a further attempt to speak, in an attempt to recollect what has been taken.

It seems that there can be no other topic for writing than death, and that writing may be inherently possessed by mourning, by absence and by desire.[3] Dunbar, a Scottish Chaucerian, begins the collection with the figure who has enabled his own poetry, Chaucer, so that not only does his own death creep up on him, his own silence, the moment when he will be collected himself, but the very basis on which he can write has also been taken away. Only writing out the line of poets is inseparable from seeing that the continuity is fragmenting as it is composed.

This chapter looks at collecting, remembering for comparison Walter Benjamin's discussion of the collector as a nineteenth-century social type, as in his essay 'Unpacking my Library' which is subtitled 'A Talk about Book Collecting', – the form of collecting that I concentrate on here.[4] If collecting is brought into play by modernity, as a form of consumption, it is also an effort to salvage its ruins, and it also has a prior existence, which Benjamin articulates:

> Perhaps the most deeply hidden motive of the person who collects can be described this way: he takes up the struggle against dispersion. Right from the start, the great collector is struck by the confusion, by the scatter, in which the things of the world are found. It is the same spectacle that so preoccupied the men of the baroque: in particular, the world image of the allegorist cannot be explained apart from the passionate, distraught concern with this spectacle. The allegorist is, as it were, the polar opposite of the collector. He has given up the attempt to elucidate things through research into their properties and relations. He dislodges things from their context and from the outset relies on his profundity to illuminate their meaning. The collector, by contrast, brings together what belongs together; by keeping in mind their affinities and their succession in time, he can eventually furnish information about his objects. Nevertheless – and this is more important than all the differences which exist between them – in every collector hides an allegorist, and in every allegorist a collector. As far as the collector is concerned, his collection is never complete, for let him

---

[3] The point is implicit in Lacan, 'Function and Field of Speech and Language', *Ècrits*, trans. by Alan Sheridan (London: Tavistock, 1977), p. 104.

[4] Walter Benjamin, *Illuminations* (London, Jonathan Cape, 1979), pp. 59-67.

discover just a single piece missing, and everything he's collected remains a patchwork, which is what things are for allegory from the beginning. On the other hand, the allegorist – for whom objects represent only keywords in a secret dictionary, which will make known their meanings to the initiated – precisely the allegorist can never have enough of things. With him, one thing is so little capable of taking the place of another that no possible reflection suffices to foresee what meaning his profundity might lay claim to for each one of them.[5]

In Dunbar, it might be said that Death may act as a collector but can never complete the series. It seems, from Benjamin, that collecting may be secretly allegorical, partly because the values the collector attributes to objects are only meaningful to him, not to anyone not collecting, but also because of the awareness that no complete order can emerge. In allegory, there seems the desire to collect in the attempt to gather a meaning from the objects which are found, but such meaning is always partial, fragmented. Baudrillard also discusses the collector, as interested in the whole series, but which cannot be possessed.[6] If Dunbar's conceit of death as devouring, or consuming also figures the collector, this is allegorical of collecting as a loss of meaning, just as Baudrillard insists, from a psychoanalytic standpoint, on the collector's impoverishment and infantility, which tries to authorize his or her being through a collection.

Death taking away for a collection links also with the trope of time, as in the *ubi sunt* motif, derivative from the apocryphal Baruch 3.6: 'Ubi sunt principes gentium' – 'where are the princes of the nations?'[7] Time devours, takes away (as if collecting). Baudrillard writes of the collector gathering things as if mourning his own death, 'outliving himself through his collection, which, originating within this life, recapitulates him indefinitely beyond the point of death, *by absorbing death into the series and the cycle*' (17, Baudrillard's emphasis). Death and time take away, leaving ruins behind them which the collector gathers. The collector incorporates, or 'absorbs' (the images of consumption are striking) loss of meaning (his own death) into his collection, as if acknowledging that the collection cannot be completed, but must be attended by a loss of meaning, and the pastime of collecting, as a way of taking up, or devouring time, dallies with lack of meaning, with blankness, while picking out

---

[5]   Walter Benjamin, *Arcades*, p. 211.

[6]   Jean Baudrillard, 'The System of Collecting' in John Elsner and Roger Cardinal, *The Cultures of Collecting* (London: Reaktion Books, 1994), pp. 7-24.

[7]   Rosemary Woolf, *The English Religious Lyric in the Middle Ages* (Oxford: Clarendon Press, 1968) p. 96.

objects for their singular value. If Dunbar comes close towards acknowledging death as a collector, and poetry as collecting, then that is also tending towards making collecting a form of death, and the key to collecting the killing of time while knowing that time is exactly the subject of fascination for the collector. For time, that allegorical conception, is the motivator of collecting. Thus, in this chapter, which concentrates on Lydgate, I am interested in collecting people who almost literally collect time – not just Dunbar, but Jean, Duc de Berry in his Books of Hours where I single out the *Très Riches Heures*, and Humphrey, Duke of Gloucester who both collected books and, in *The Fall of Princes* which he commissioned, a series of tragedies which would preserve a complete archive of those who had died. The poet Lydgate, author of *The Fall of Princes*, whose writing thus buys time, is the fourth collector.

Referring to the 'archive' recalls Derrida's *Archive Fever*, the English translation of *Mal d'archive: une impression freudienne*. The 'mal' of the archive includes the desire for the archive, meaning for a source (the 'arckhe') and for a traditional, founding and single commanding historical authority. Recalling the gendered and controlling nature of the authority that is wished for, Derrida's neologism for it is the 'patriarchive'.[8] The desire to produce an archive is traced, in Derrida's discussion of Freud, to the death drive, which, mute:

> never leaves any archives of its own. It destroys in advance its own archive, as if that were in truth the very motivation of its most proper movement. It works *to destroy the archive: on the condition of effacing* but also *with a view to effacing* its own 'proper' traces - which consequently cannot properly be called 'proper'. This drive, from then on, seems not only to be anarchic, anarchontic [against the archons] [...] the death drive is above all *anarchivic* [...] or *archiviolithic*. It will always have been archive-destroying [...].(10: Derrida's emphases)

The desire for authority and tradition finds that all that it might resort to rendered a fiction by the power of the death-drive which erodes the archive. *The Fall of Princes* comprises 36,365 lines in nine books, written between 1430 and 1436, collecting what Lydgate deems to be every tragedy of every prince since Adam and Eve, and lamenting the fate of princes.[9] Lydgate's reliance is upon prior books out of which he is translating, so that there is virtually no appeal to

---

[8] Jacques Derrida, *Archive Fever: A Freudian Impression*, trans. by Eric Prenowitz (Chicago: University of Chicago Press, 1996), p. 4.

[9] The discussion of collecting and of the Duc de Berry owes much to Michael Camille, '"For our Objects and Pleasure": The Sexual Objects of Jean, duc de Berry', *Art History* 24 (2001), 169-194.

experience or to thought outside the archive that it works from, so that he works out of past time to memorialize time past. There is no equivalent in Lydgate of the 'modern instances' of *The Monk's Tale*-those which do not fit into an archive. As Derrida's *Archive Fever*, with new technology in mind, discusses how 'the technical structure of the *archiving* archive also determines the structure of the *archivable* content' so that 'the archivization produces as much as it records the event' (17, Derrida's emphases), so it may be noted how Lydgate's working on the book which would contain the whole archive in itself suffers the decay that the death-drive brings about, for his patient copying would soon be replaced by type-setting and multiple copies, by the work of art in the taking on another form in the age of mechanical reproduction brought about by Gutenberg. And something of that lamentation for the form of the archive may work in Lydgate; not only the archive but its form are of the past. That brings the text towards the mode of the *Trauerspiel*; Lydgate's sphere, unlike Chaucer working on the modern instances, is the library. *The Fall of Princes* gives the lives of princes in brief, and then disperses them, just as what is collected by the verse has been dispersed by death. This dispersal is repeated in the text, as if the princes it gathers before it are all seen as inadequate to sustain any meaning in themselves.

These fifteenth century collectors – Jean Duc de Berry, who had working for him the Limbourg brothers; Humphrey of Gloucester and Lydgate, working for Gloucester but a collector as well - do not, then, collect substitutes for time, like watches, as the modern consumer who is also a collector does; they virtually collect the thing itself. The watch separates time from any personal application, arresting it, but the Book of Hours moves from January to December, in a cycle of birth and death, and is a reminder of the fleeting nature of time. In the same way, the collection *The Fall of Princes* is minatory, and it is, further, addressed to a prince. If Lydgate is indeed what Derek Pearsall said, 'a comprehensive definition of the Middle Ages',[10] then those Middle Ages may be a way of looking at what modernity has displaced, not replaced. What deadens Lydgate's poetry is not an inherent problem with its lack of range, about which it is easy to be cheap,[11] but the point that built into its own collecting

---

[10]   Derek Pearsall, *John Lydgate* (London: Routledge and Kegan Paul, 1970), p. 4.

[11]   Consideration of Lydgate would also have to review the components of the national ideology, and here a start might be made by considering the conventionality of Edward III's court and that of Richard II, according to V.J. Scattergood and J.W. Sherborne in *English Court Culture in the Later Middle Ages* (London: Duckworth, 1983); see Sherborne, pp. 67; see Scattergood, pp. 29-43 on the myth that Richard II was an assiduous book-collector; see J.J. G.

of material is something else: an accumulation of examples. Collecting responds to singularity, or tries to construct it. Accumulation, which is the opposite because it is not interested in the individual example, means only a slow loss of distinction and individual meaning, replicating the work of death which both collects and accumulates. Lydgate's poetry writes its own death.

II - CONTEXTS FOR COLLECTORS

Like Hoccleve, Lydgate began writing poetry at the beginning of the fifteenth century, a moment marked by the Lancastrian usurpation and Richard's abdication (30 September 1399), Henry IV's coronation (13 October 1399), the murder or suicide of Richard II at Pontefract (mid-January 1400), and the death of Chaucer (February 1400). For Henry V (1387-1422) then Prince of Wales, Lydgate wrote the *Troy Book* (1412-20) as Hoccleve wrote *The Regement of Princes*. Other court commissions followed: *The Pilgrimage of the Life of Man*, taken from Deguileville, was made for Thomas Montagu, the Earl of Salisbury (1388-1428) in 1427. In the 1430s Lydgate translated the 'Dance of Death' verses as *The Daunce of Machabree* for St Paul's, perhaps after a visit made to Paris in 1424, when he saw the Cimitière des Innocents, with its murals and its verses which had perhaps been written by Jean Gerson, the Chancellor of the Sorbonne.[12]

The Fall of Princes is addressed to Humphrey, Duke of Gloucester (1391-1447), whom Hoccleve wanted for patron. Gloucester, the 'good duke Humphrey' whose death forms the centre of *2 Henry VI*, was the youngest brother of Henry V, and the uncle and the named Protector (1427-9) of the infant Henry VI (1421-1471), who became king at nine months. As appears in Shakespeare, *Henry VI* parts 1 and 2, Humphrey's constant foe was his uncle Henry Beaufort, who died in 1447, the second illegitimate son of John of Gaunt. Beaufort became Bishop of Winchester and was made Cardinal by Pope Martin V in 1426. Humphrey both collected books and caused them to be

---

Alexander, pp. 141-162 on the paucity of books in the English court as compared with France and Burgundy and Italian courts; 'no English King; not even Henry VI, seems to have had the interest in books and learning of Charles V' (p. 161). The presence of the court and the University together in Paris made a difference.

12 The murals were destroyed in 1669, but Guyot Marchant made a woodcut copy in 1485. See Michael Neill, *Issues of Death: Mortality and Identity in English Renaissance Tragedy* (Oxford: Clarendon Press, 1997), pp. 51-53 (and see pp. 51-105 on the 'dance of death' motif. The cemetery was destroyed in 1786.

written.[13] *The Fall of Princes* comes from a tradition defined by Boethius's *Of the Consolation of Philosophy*, whose popularity Richard Firth Green indicates when he says that the Duc de Berry possessed four copies.[14] The tradition derived from re-readings of Boethius appears after Chaucer in Lydgate; it continues with the Burgundian Georges Chastellain, quoted so often by Huizinga, who wrote the *Temple of Bocace* for Margaret of Anjou. Since *The Fall of Princes* lives on in thirty-seven manuscripts, Lydgate's impact may be considered enduring also, however much it may now have fallen victim to archive-fever. It links with Shakespeare, through *The Mirror for Magistrates*, whose authors, William Baldwin and George Ferrers, continued both Lydgate and Boccaccio, treating 'chiefly of suche as Fortune had dalyed with heeere in this ylande: which mighr bc as a myrrour for al men as well noble as others, to shewe the slyppery deceytes of the waueryng lady, and the due rewarde of all kinde of vices'.[15]

Philip II of Spain owned five manuscripts of one of the texts which derived from Boethius, Boccaccio's *De casibus virorum illustrium*.[16] Drawing on Petrarch's *De viris illustribus*, written throughout his life to glorify great Romans who had achieved glory and virtue, Boccaccio, writing in 1356, and revising in 1373, planned his work as a vision or triumph, where dead famous figures of history moved before him and asked him to hear their sad stories. The pattern derives from Dante and the 'triumph', spoken of earlier in relation to Langland, from Petrarch. Between these autobiographies, other unhappy rulers' lives are summarized by the poet. In Book 8, Petrarch himself appears to exhort Boccaccio to finish, so that he may receive fame. Boccaccio's final narrative was of Jean le Bon (1350-1364), captured by the English at Poitiers, September 19 1356

---

[13]   For Humphrey's role as bibliophile and patron, see Roberto Weiss, *Humanism in England During the Fifteenth Century* (Oxford: Basil Blackwell, second edition, 1957), pp. 39-70.

[14]   Richard Firth Green, *Poets and Princepleasers: Literature and the English Court in the Late Middle Ages* (Toronto: University of Toronto Press, 1980), p. 145.

[15]   See Lily B. Campbell, ed., *The Mirror for Magistrates* (Cambridge: Cambridge University Press, 1938) p. 50. This collection of 19 tragedies, first issued in 1559 and added to in 1563, and in 1578 and again in 1587, joins the fifteenth-century to the sixteenth and connects, elliptically, Shakespeare's fifteenth century histories with his own sixteenth century. On *The Mirror for Magistrates* see Paul Budra, '"Exemplify my Frailty": Representing English Women in *De Casibus* tragedy', *Philological Quarterly* 74 (1995), 359-372.

[16]   See Thomas G. Bergin, *Boccaccio* (New York: Viking, 1981), p. 276; this account should be consulted for the translation of the story of Filippa of Catania, one of Bocaccio's modern instances.

and imprisoned for four years.[17] As the fiction is the possibility that the irretrievable past may be collected, the visions are therefore supplemented by authorial summaries.

The court of Charles V (1364-1380) translated Latin texts into French, and Laurens de Premierfait (Laurens Guillot, from Premierfait, in Troyes) followed this tradition in translating Boccaccio's Latin prose into French prose for Louis, Duke of Bourbon, in 1400, and so making Boccaccio popular for the French court. A second edition, *Des Cas des Nobles Hommes et Femmes* which Humphrey Duke of Gloucester acquired, followed in 1409 for Jean, Duc de Berry (1340-1413). It supplemented Boccaccio with moral details and interpolations, and it was this which Lydgate translated as *The Fall of Princes*. Premierfait died in 1418, 'année terrible de masssacres, d'epidémie et de misère' as Lydgate's editor Henry Bergen quotes from Paul Durrieu, and he was collected into the Cimitière des Innocents, charnel house of so many bones.[18]

Bergen finds both Jean de Berry and the much younger Humphrey of Gloucester equally 'egoistic, avaricious, untrustworthy, intriguing and dissolute' (p. xvi) - which makes it possible to compare the two collectors. It seems possible, then, to comment on their impulse to collect, to read the items of the collection in relation to each other, and to read these points allegorically.

III - JEAN DUC DE BERRY

The Duc de Berry was son of King Jean le Bon, and brother of King Charles V (1364-1380). Another, younger, brother was Philippe le Hardi, who died in 1404. Jean married twice, first Jeanne d'Armagnac in 1360, and then, after her death, Jeanne de Boulogne, when she was twelve and he 49. The events within and surrounding his life mark it off as like several moments in *de casibus* tragedy. His nephew, at the age of twelve, became Charles VI (1380-1422) and his insanity began to show itself on a military expedition on August 5 1392, and continued intermittently for the next thirty years.[19]

---

[17] An abridged version of Boccaccio appears as *The Fates of Illustrious Men* trans. Louis Brewer Hall (New York: Frederick Ungar, 1965). A selection from the text, with translations from Latin into Italian, appears in Pier Giorgio Ricci, *Giovanni Boccaccio: Opere in Versi* (Milano-Napoli: Riccardo Ricciardi), pp. 786-891.

[18] Henry Bergen, ed., *Lydgate's Fall of Princes* (Washington: Carnegie Institution of Washington, 1923) 4 vols. 1.p. xiii. Quotations from this edition are by line number, which continues over the four volumes.

[19] See R.C. Famiglietti, *Royal Intrigue: Crisis at the Court of Charles VI, 1392-1420* (New York: AMS Press, 1986), pp. 1-21 for a reading of the king's condition as 'schizophrenia'. For Froissart's account, see Froissart, *Chronicles*

Another nephew, Charles's brother, was Louis d'Orléans, leader of the anti-Burgundians (the Armagnacs). He was murdered in 1407 by his cousin Jeans sans Peur, the son of Philippe le Hardi. Jean sans Peur was murdered in his turn in 1419. Jean de Berry became identified with the Armagnacs when in 1410 he married his granddaughter to Charles d'Orléans, son of Louis d'Orléans. His last years in Paris, until his death on June 15 1416, saw him beleaguered in Paris. He lost many of his treasures when his château at Bicêtre in Paris was sacked by a crowd following Jean sans Peur's entry into Paris in 1411, as was the Hôtel de Nesle, where he died.

The *Belles Heures* and the *Très Riches Heures* were commissioned from the Limbourg brothers, Paul, Jean and Herman. The latter two had been apprenticed as goldsmiths, and all had worked for Philippe le Hardi. Jean de Berry was a builder, patron and collector of books. When he died, a post-mortem inventory named an incomplete Book of Hours. The collector and the fragment go together. The point that much seems to have been done after 1416, when all the brothers died, to bring the pictures to near-completion,[20] makes them also effectively a reading of the Duc de Berry, and adds to the sense that the pictures can neither be taken as a single work of art, nor as other than fragments of a design. The identification and naming of the illuminations as the *Très Riches Heures*, giving them a unity as a single work of art, did not come until 1881.[21]

---

[20] selected and translated by Geoffrey Brereton (Harmondsworth: Penguin, 1878), pp. 392-401.
The contribution of miniatures of Jean Colombe, working for the Duc de Savoie in the 1480s has long been known but Cazelles and Rathofer, pp. 217-8 accept also the arguments of Luciano Bellosi, put forward in 1975, that a third painter, coming in time between the Limbourg brothers and Colombe, and probably employed by the King, also worked on the *Très Riches Heures*.

[21] See Michael Camille, 'The *Très Riches Heures*: An Illuminated Manuscript in the Age of Mechanical Reproduction', *Critical Inquiry* 17 (1990), 72-107. I record my agreement with the critical positions advanced in that paper.

IV - *LES TRÈS RICHES HEURES*[22]

The title speaks of time. The calendrical part of the *Très Riches Heures* shows the passing of time, as with the signs of the zodiac, and with the labours of the months - as when sowing gives way to harvesting. The changes in nature can also be seen from month to month, and this topos invites a study of the representation of each particular month. Illuminations incomplete at the death of their patron, and whose illuminators all died the same year, and which memorialize the passing of the year and the passing of life become allegorical of themselves, especially when many of the châteaux they put on display have also gone. The seasons were commonly allegorized, as in *The Franklin's Tale* – 'Janus sit by the fyr, with double berd' (1252): in January of the *Très Riches Heures*, the Duc de Berry sits here (his wife is not represented), seated in front of a firescreen before a blazing fire, as an allegory of the opening year. Above the fireplace is a red canopy and tapestries. Knights are there: two, richly dressed, may be seen with spurs (and a battle, which is part of the siege of Troy, is depicted in the tapestry or wallpainting behind); behind the Duc a young man leans against his chair. The words 'Aproche, Aproche' are inscribed in the picture, as perhaps the words of the chamberlain, welcoming guests coming from behind to the feast, or to the year, as the viewer is led in from the front.

The picture evokes luxury, like the two dogs eating on the table from the dishes. Its interest in courtly existence threatens to exoticise the scenes of labour. And the *Très Riches Heures* are full of an exoticism, which is also part of a collecting taste. There are black Africans in the 'Martyrdom of Saint Mark', Africans and Asians in the 'Exaltation of the Cross' and especially evident in the 'Adoration of the Magi'. The attendants wear turbans, one of the Magi kisses the ground in worship, and there are leopards. A camel in the picture was based on an animal in Jean de Berry's possession. In 'The Temptation

---

[22] On the detail of these illuminations, see Jean Longnon and Raymond Cazelles, *The Très Riches Heures of Jean, Duke of Berry: Musée Condé, Chantilly* (New York: George Braziller, 1969) and Millard Meiss with Sharon off Dunlap Smith and Elizabeth Home Beatson, *French Painting in the Time of Jean de Berry: The Limbourgs and their Contemporaries* (London: Thames and Hudson, 1974), 2 vols. For Jean de Berry see Millard Meiss in *French Painting in the Time of Jean de Berry* (London: Phaidon, 1967), 2 vols; text volume pp. 30-35, and passim. The previous literature on the paintings is reviewed in Raymond Cazelles and Johannes Rathofer, *Illuminations of Heaven and Earth: The Glories of the Très Riches Heures du Duc de Berry* (1984; New York: Harry N. Abrams edition, 1988). See also Erwin Panofsky, *Early Netherlandish Painting: Its Origins and Character*, 2 vols (1953; New York: Icon Editions, 1971), vol 1, pp. 61-666, who reads the illuminations as 'mannerist' in quality (p. 64).

of Christ' a lion and a monkey 'evoke the wealth of Africa as part of
the riches of the earth'.[23] In the picture of the exorcism of a dumb
youth, the 'Healing of the Dumb-Possessed', turbaned, dark faces
look on in disbelief as Christ on the left blesses a possessed youth.
The boy is dressed in a tattered brown smock, with his right leg bare
and visible and his face ashen grey, his expression catatonic. He
twists and struggles in his mother's arms, while above his head flies
a miniature dark brown demon which has just left him, the
explanation for his madness.

Such exoticism centres the subject of the Duc, seen in 'January',
and the *Très Riches Heures*, in 'January', 'April', 'May' and
'August' show not the labours of the month, but the leisure activities
of the court, a further centring. To turn from January to 'February' is
to see a contrast with this aristocratic life. It is outside and winter,
with the "sheep that rouketh in the folde" and peasants sitting before
the fire on their farm. All life is not suspended, however, for a
peasant on the road travels with his donkey laden with wood, going
towards the village. 'March' shows farm work outside the Château de
Lusignan; a shepherd, four peasants pruning the vines, another with a
sack of grain and a ploughman in front, an old man with a white
beard. He is well dressed, but his clothes are tattered at the knees,
like the sower in 'October' and the huntsman in 'December'. He, the
plough and the oxen all cast shadows. I shall return to this figure,
but will notice here that he contrasts with another detail which
implies another world, distinct even from the château: the dragon
above the castle turret on the right (a representation of the dragon
appears on the tower on the left) is the fairy Mélusine. She was the
protectress of the château, who metamorphosed into a dragon on
Saturdays. The mortal Raimondin, whom she loved, disobeyed her
command not to see her on Saturdays, and she flew off from the
château, so withdrawing her protection. The fantasy has to do with
the castle; it is separate from the agricultural world taking place.

'April' shows a betrothal outside the chateau of Dourdan, which
became the Duc's property after 1400, and in the river Orge before
it, men in rowing boats are seen dragging nets.[24] One commentator
asks, 'does the artist wish to suggest that the search for human
happiness is ever a casting out of nets into the unplumbed depths of
destiny, and that the important event of a noble betrothal is a fit
occasion to point this moral?'[25] and however over-written, the remark

---

[23] Cazelles and Rathofer, p. 171.
[24] Cazelles and Rathofer p. 26 prefer to identify the château with Pierrefonds,
one of the residences of the Orléans family.
[25] Franz Hattinger, *The Duc de Berry's Book of Hours* (Berne: Hallwag, 1962);
text for plate IV (no page reference).

may point to the gap within the picture, which cannot be read in one way only. Nor could the beautifully attenuated figures in 'April', who stand on greensward that has the consistency of a carpet, their garments shining, chatoyant, ever be involved in the labour of 'February' or 'March'. 'May' shows figures dressed or garlanded in green, and the architecture behind has been identified as the Château de Riom, in the Auvergne, or, more likely, the Palais de la Cité in Paris, the then royal residence. The woman on the white horse may be Marie de Berry, Jean de Berry's daughter, whose third husband was Jean de Bourbon (Duke of Bourbon in 1410), for the horses bear emblems which seem identical with the badge of the Bourbons. There is again something dual in the picture; the courtiers on horseback with their dogs are decorous, and evoke the May spirit of *The Knight's Tale*, but the five musicians who lead them, blowing on trombones and pipes, are Dionysiac figures whose carnivalesque world is discontinuous with theirs. 'June' is harvest on the little Isle de Buci, later joined to the Ile de la Cité, whose walls behind an arm of the Seine are seen behind. The view, which follows on from 'May' gives the Palais de la Cité, the older palace of the kings of France before the construction of the Louvre, in detail; to the right is Sainte-Chapelle. It is seen from the Hôtel de Nesle, the Duc de Berry's Paris residence. It is as if the picture gives the aristocratic view from one palace window towards another, that of the patron's nephew, the King's palace, so that the peasants are in the space between two palaces.

'July' gives a scene of harvesting, using sickles; the peasants have straw hats and as nakedness appears with the peasants in the house in 'February' and the swimmers in 'August', so they are only partially dressed here. (The peasant in the white shirt and underwear is like the peasant seen scything in June.) Sheep-shearing takes place on the other side of the stream which feeds into the river, the Clain, in Poitiers, and the triangular-shaped building behind with three corner towers – which were built for Jean de Berry after the earlier château had been damaged by the English - is the Château de Clain. The Duc's architect was Guy de Dammartin. In 'July' the sheep-shearers are a possible reminder of death, as the sheep in 'February' were a sign of vulnerability. But the poppies in the field being cut are equally evocative.

'August' shows the Château d'Etampes, which the Duc de Berry acquired in 1400 and put at the disposal of Charles d'Orléans. Courtly figures on horseback, with falcons are at the front; in the middle distance are figures swimming in the river Juine and behind them peasants who have bound or are binding wheat into sheaves and putting it upon the cart. 'September' gives the grape harvest near the

Château de Saumur, near Angers, on the Loire. 'October', which shows tilling and sowing the land, is again viewed from the standpoint of the Hôtel de Nesle, but shows this time the Louvre, the royal residence, with the Seine between the Louvre and the fields. There is another duality, between the numbers of figures in motion, parodied by a scarecrow, and the massive keep of the Louvre, built by Philippe Auguste (reigned 1180-1223) and by Charles V, which rises in rhomboid form behind the enceinte. 'November' (the work of Jean Colombe) shows the acorn harvest, and 'December' gives the end of a wild boar hunt in the forest of Vincennes. The view is that of the Château of Vincennes, where Jean de Berry was born: its enclosure and nine towers, eight represented in the image, were built by Charles V. A hunter at the right of the picture blows the 'mort' on the horn. The place of birth and of death come together, and the image allegorizes the fall of another prince. Something of its ugliness as an event is conveyed in the face of the huntsman on the left; the lack of idealization showing in such details as the huntsman pulling on the ears of the hounds. The courtly world of 'January', if that is turned back to, is outside this world, which is also indifferent to princes. The prince who appeared in the first picture of the twelve may be the boar torn to pieces by hounds in the last. The boar hunt is 'a subject found nowhere else in calendars of Books of Hours of this period'.[26] Hattinger hints this is 'an artist's fitting image for the close of a self-willed patron's span of life'.

The Duc of 'January' is allegorized by his châteaux, which Panofsky calls 'architectural portraits'.[27] Metonymically, they are as his portraits. If a collector could collect châteaux, that would be true of the Duc: he had fourteen in all built or refurbished, not including those in which he lived without rebuilding.[28] Of the châteaux built or refurbished and appearing in the *Très Riches Heures*, only the great hall and the Maubergeon tower in the Poitiers castle, the Tour Guinette, in the Château d'Etampes remain; of the ones he did not build, only the château at Saumur and part of Vincennes remain. The Hôtel de Nesle, where he died, and which he had had extensively rebuilt, was sacked in 1411, as his château at Bicêtre, also in Paris was destroyed in the same year. But there are other castles and buildings represented, not made for him: Poitiers in the scene of the

---

26 Cazelles and Rathofer, p. 58.
27 Panofsky, p. 65.
28 Cazelles and Rathofer, pp. 201-202: they list Bourges, Riom, Poitiers, Mehun sur Yèvre, Concressault, Genouilly, Nonette, Usson, Gracay, Gien, Aubigny sur Nère, Lusignan, the Hôtel de Nesle and Bicêtre. See also the discussion on pp. 223-226.

'Annunciation to the Shepherds', Paris in the 'Meeting of the Magi', Bourges for the 'Adoration of the Magi', the Cathedral at Bourges for 'The Presentation of the Virgin', partly built for the Duc de Berry, and Mont Saint-Michel for the illustration of 'St Michael slaying the Dragon'. Architecture makes statements and legitimates forms of discourse, including through its mapping out of space. These châteaux are metonymies of princes and of kingship. In 'April', 'May' and 'August' they appear high on the horizon, diminished in size, but giving a finality to what is seen. There is a different visualization in 'March' (across the width of the picture), or in 'June', or 'July' - where the high angle of vision permits the eye to see inside the central courtyard. In 'September' and 'October' the building is the primary focus. These differences may be activated by distinctions in period, if it is accepted, that 'January', 'April', 'May' and 'August' are the earliest, and the work of the Limbourg brothers. 'January' already frames the viewer within architecture, within the interior of the Duc de Berry's château, but there is a château represented: Troy in the tapestry - which implies a narrative of the fall of princes.

These contrasted representations give contrasted senses, which build fragmentation into them already. In the 'Temptation of Christ', the Duc de Berry's château at Mehun sur Yèvre represents the riches of this world (following Matthew 4.8-9). The work of architecture is already doomed. The design of the raising of Lazarus, set in a cemetery, with Lazarus emerging from a tombstone placed over his body, shows a ruined church behind, the half-standing walls of the west and the north sides. Ruin and decay are associated in the same picture as Lazarus coming back to life - raised to die again - and they give a further ambiguity: Cazelles and Rathofer say that 'this appearance of a crumbling edifice ... appears to be unique in medieval iconography'.[29] It fits with the equivocalness of life and death seen in Lazarus' resurrection. In 'December', the towers of Vincennes go across the page, but this is ambiguous, for they are separated, not discernible as a unity, seen as though fragmented, placed behind the Bois de Boulogne which dominates, as though the wild wood occludes the power of this architecture to frame the subject. Fragmentation evokes the passing of time in the calendar. As the months are turned over, there is a sense of moving to the end, of each activity having its momentary place before it goes to be replaced by another. The pictures, like narrative, both defer, and hasten, the end.

---

[29] Cazelles and Rathofer, p. 178.

V - *DE CASIBUS* TRAGEDY AND LYDGATE

Boccaccio's work had as immediate successor Chaucer's *Monk's Tale*, discussed in chapter 2, which is headed in several manuscripts 'Heere bigynneth the Monkes Tale de casibus virorum illustrium'. The Monk opens:

> I wol biwaille, in manner of tragedie,
> The harm of hem that stode in heigh degree,
> And fillen so that ther nas no remedie
> To brynge hem out of hir adversitee.
> For certein, whan that Fortune list to flee,
> Ther may no man the cours of hire withholde.
> Lat no man trust on blynd Prosperitee;
> Be war by thise ensamples trewe and olde. (1991-8)

This turns Boccaccio's 'instances' of the fall of illustrious men – which Boccaccio sees as chronicles, as history, into tragedies. Such a move drives towards allegory. It perceives a pattern of rising and falling; detecting that, or imposing it upon historical events, remembering that in allegory, as has been quoted before, 'any person, any object, any relationship, can mean absolutely anything else' and that 'the detail is of no great importance' (*Origin* p. 175). There is marked loss of detail in the accumulation of the Monk's, and later, Lydgate's accounts of the fall of princes. Displacement of chronological time negates not history, but only history premised on development and progress. It lays different images alongside each other as if in a montage, and brings present and past into new and surprising conjunctions.[30]

Like a collector, or more, an accumulator, Chaucer's monk had a hundred tragedies in his cell (1972), of which he tells seventeen. The order is controversial, but perhaps they conclude with Croesus, succeeded by this conclusion:

> Tragedies noon oother maner thyng
> Ne kan in syngyng crie ne biwaille
> But that Fortune alwey wole assaille
> With unwar strook the regnes that been proude;
> For whan men trusteth hire, thanne wol she faille,
> And covere hire brighte face with a clowde. (2761-6).

Though the knight interrupts, it seems the monk has ended, and with tragedy as invoking the feminine. The change from history to tragedy, in a re-accentuation of the lives of the people who come lamenting and complaining before Boccaccio, who does not lament or

---

[30] I refer here to my own study of Benjamin on history, in *Becoming Posthumous: Life and Death in Literary and Cultural Studies* (Edinburgh: Edinburgh University Press, 2001), pp. 115-136.

complain himself - a contrast with Lydgate - makes tragedy, like *Trauerspiel*, and as discussed before, a defining term in Chaucer.[31] Unlike Boccaccio, the monk has no sense of a vision or dream-reality where the dead pass before him. He defines tragedy as:

> a certeyn storie
> As olde bookes maken us memorie,
> Of hym that stood in greet prosperitee,
> And is yfallen out of heigh degree
> Into myserie, and endeth wrecchedly. (1974-78)

This, unlike Boccaccio, makes him identify with those who have fallen. It follows Boethius's definition, which in Chaucer's translation, is followed by the gloss of the Dominican friar, Nicholas Trevet who wrote on Boethius (c.1304), and on Seneca's tragedies (c.1314-1317)[32]:

> What other thynge bewaylen the cryings of tragedyes but oonly the dede of Fortune, that with an unwar strook overturneth the realmes of greet nobleye? (Glose. Tragedye is to seyn a dite of a prosperite for a tyme, that enndeth in wrecchidnesse.) (II. pr. 2 67-72)

Lydgate also emphasises tragedy. Book V (mainly the history of Rome) ends with Jugurtha and the envoi pronounces:

> This may be weel callid a tragedie,
> Be discripcioun takyng auctorite;
> For tragedie, as poetes spesephie,
> Gynneth with ioie, eendith with aduersite. V.3118-21

There are several moods in *The Fall of Princes*, including the desire for death, ('Bet is to deie than lyue in wrecchidnesse' (I.3795), and the sense of prevalent ruin. The ending of Book II gives the founding of Rome (II.3963-4263) through the agency of Romulus, and the fate of Metius Suffetius, destroyed by the Romans, and Hostilius, first Roman king to wear purple, and this leads to the final Envoi of the Book, where, before the history of Rome is given (Books 3-7), its ruin is thought of in nineteen stanzas, each ending with the same refrain. The city has never been other than false; it is not associated with an originary wholeness, so that the *ubi sunt* motif asks where those things have gone which were actually only illusory:

> Wher be thyn Emperours, most souereyn off renoun?

---

[31] It appears in *The Monk's Tale* in 1971,1973, 1991,2458,2761; in *The Nun's Priest's Tale* 2783, and in *Boece*, in 2 prose 2, 68 and 70; in 3 prose 6, and *Troilus* 5.1786.

[32] On Nicholas Trevet, see Henry Ansgar Kelly, *Ideas and Forms of Tragedy from Aristotle to the Middle Ages* (Cambridge: Cambridge University Press, 1993), pp. 125-134.

Kynges exiled for outraious lyung?
Thi senatours, with worthi Scipioun?
Poetis olde thi tryumphes rehersyng,
Thi laurreat knyhtis, most statli ther ridyng,
Thyn aureat glorie, thy noblesse tenlumyne
Is be long processe brouht onto ruyne. (II.4467-4473)

The elegy processes with further architectural images of gold and of light, lights which have gone out: 'thy temple of christal bright shewing / made half of gold' (4484-5), 'Tullius, cheeff lanterne off thi toun' (4488), but there is no disposition to take Rome as an image of anything other than rebellion against the Christian god; the pagan does not serve as an allegory of the present, except insofar that the ruined city, in a change from the *ubi sunt* to a direct address as though it was still present, is urged to 'ley doun thi pride' (4523) and is in the final line of the Book (4592) seen as an example to noble princes to see that 'ye ber nat hennes but your disseruyng' (4590).

Lydgate's *Fall of Princes* translates Premierfait, so that it says what 'Iohn Bochas' has said and done, and how visions appeared to him. The Prologue culminates in praise of the Duke of Gloucester, who upholds the church so much that 'in this land no Lollard dar abide' (403).[33] The text attempts to centre itself around the patron, following the point that 'that heretik dar noon come in his siht' (410) by saying that Humphrey is given to 'Reedyng off bookis [...]' which 'Makith a prynce to haue experience, To know hymsilff [...] ' (I. 416-9). As with Hoccleve, this asserts the Lancastrian orthodoxy; so the text breaks off from the account of the end of Troy to refer to Lydgate's *Troy Book*, saying that Henry the Fifth commissioned it ('thyng of old tyme to putte in remembraunce' 1.5961) and that he, 'to stroie Lollards ... sette al his labour' 1.55968). Heresy is also the reason for the downfall of the Emperor Heraclius (9.558-567) and his son Constantine (9.599), in whose case heresy combined with sexual lust, so that his knights killed him standing naked in a bath in a brothel (9.603-616). Constantine's son, however, who kills these conspirators, was busy 'al heretikes manli to withstand' (9.639): 'manli', which should be superfluous for a man, will be noted.

The poetry aligns right thinking, right morality and masculinity, and associates perverse sexuality with heresy. Yet weeding out heresy has its own ironies, based both on the non-legitimacy of the Lancastrian dynasty, and on Humphrey Duke of Gloucester's

---

[33] See K.H. Vickers, *Humphrey, Duke of Gloucester* (London, 1907) pp. 15-16, 222-223, 224, 269-70 and 322 for some details of these executions of Lollards; note too the association of Lollardy with witchcraft.

personally ambitious part within that.[34] Larry Scanlon discusses the 'figural power' that Gloucester has in Lydgate's text which makes him ambiguous as the reader of a text which shows the excesses of princes, the privileged monitor of the effects of power on princes.[35] As collecting instances of the falls of princes, he is preparing for his own fall, however unconsciously. Gloucester who stands outside the poem reading it as a collection, appears, however, also in it:

> This myhti prynce, riht manli & riht wis
> Gaff me charge in his prudent auys,
>
> That I sholde in eueri tragedie
> Afftir the processe made mencioun,
> At the eende sette a remedie,
> With a lenvoie conueied by resoun,
> And afftir that, with humble affeccioun,
> To noble pryncis lowli it directe,
> Bi othres fallyng thei myght themsilff correcte'.
> (II. Prologue 153-4)

Gloucester's role seems to be allegorical of Reason, and the thesis of *The Fall of Princes* subtly changes. In the Prologue to Book I, after the passage about heretics, Gloucester is said to have read Boccaccio's book (in Premierfait's version) as 'onto pryncis gretli necessarie / To *yuive exaumple* how this world doth varie' (I.426-7), 'to *shewe* thuntrust off al worldli thyng' (I.429), 'to *shewe* the chaung of worldi variaunce' (I.434). The italics I have provided indicate the moralism, and the pageant-nature of the text.

The Prologue to Book II says that 'vicious lyung' not 'gouerned by resoun' (II. 46,56) is what destroys princes, rather than 'fals Fortune' turning her wheel (II.43). The effect and perhaps intention of that Prologue is to centre Gloucester, yet Gloucester in himself demonstrates that his own relation to power is not transparent, which better demonstrates the impossibility of a thesis which sees princes brought low by Fortune. This model reader neither has the complete power of a 'myhti prynce' or of reason, and his actions show his own disposition towards an aggrandisement of power which is exactly half of the subject-matter of *The Fall of Princes*, before the loss of power and of life, the other half. Yet Gloucester, except by having this moralism introduced, does not actually change the thesis, for there has been no consistency in the first book, whether Fortune strikes

---

[34] On Humphrey's conduct during the years of Henry VI's minority, see E.F. Jacob, *The Fifteenth Century* (Oxford; Clarendon Press, 1961), pp. 211-234.

[35] Larry Scanlon, *Narrative, Authority and Power: The Medieval Exemplum and the Chaucerian Tradition* (Cambridge: Cambridge University Press, 194), p. 326.

down the guiltless, or the guilty, and that pattern continues in the following books.

Gloucester reappears in the Prologue to Book III. 70-91, where Lydgate indicates in the line 'mi lordis fredam and bounteous largesse' (74) that he has rewarded him financially, but nonetheless Book III also contains a begging letter (3837-81) which appears in a long sequence following on the narrative of the death of Alcibiades - an exclamation on his death, an envoy, a discussion of the desires of the people who forget that 'Fortune is double' (3752). This leads Lydgate towards the prerogative of princes, and another section on what different people joy to do, which then takes him towards poets, and to Gloucester as a 'welle of fredam' (III.3865). But as Pearsall points out, there is no more money after Book III.[36] Instead, Books IV and V begin with reference to Bochas, and Book VI opens with him, and with Fortune appearing to him, the effect of which is to make it clear that she has not only been the agent who has displaced princes, but she is also the subject of the text.[37]

VI - FORTUNE

Fortune appears as a monstrosity, 'Hir heer vntressid, hard, sharp & horrible / Froward or shappe, lothsum & odible' (VI.32,33), and with an hundred hands, and ambiguous in her dress 'of manyfold colours' (VI.43), ambiguous in her appearance and movements, and ambiguously gendered:

> Now lik Ector, now dreedful Thersites,
> Now was she Cresus, now Agamemoun,
> Sardanapallus off condicioun;
> Now was she mannysh, now was she femynyne,
> Now coude she reyne, now koude she falsi shyne. (VI.59-63)

The shapes continue to change: angel, mermaid, lamb, wolf, Siren. She addresses Bochas and identifies herself with the woman of the House of Fame (109).[38] Fame is the goddess of *The House of Fame* (III.1360-1418), and 'Dame Fortune' (III.1547) is said to be her sister.[39] She brings Boccaccio and Chaucer into alignment, and *The*

---

[36] Pearsall, p. 237.

[37] On Fortune, see Howard R. Patch, *The Goddess Fortune in Mediaeval Literature* (Cambridge, Mass.: Harvard University Press, 1927).

[38] Lydgate has already referred to *The House of Fame* III.1130 in *The Fall of Princes* V.588; and sees Chaucer as having written 'Dante in Inglissh' in *The House of Fame* (I.302). *The Temple of Glass* (c.1400-1410) seems to be Lydgate's version of *The House of Fame*.

[39] 'As numerous medieval allegories attest, it is only a slight step from the deification of Fortune to the deification of her gifts - Fame, Honours, Riches - who take on the generic attributes of Fortune as well as the particular qualities of the gifts themselves' - B.G. Koonce, *Chaucer and the Tradition of*

House of Fame, as a text whose substance is much to do with the power of rumour and of talk, and hence productive of paranoia, is brought into the fifteenth century. Fortune repeatedly says of herself that she is double (131,163,175,190,191,202,207), a point which he then responds to (221,395). Bochas replies with feeling to her rebuke that he defames her, and, emboldened, asks her to help him with the book that he might attain fame. She responds with a comment on the slanders he has said about her in his book, including the description of her which has just been given; she also refers to his account of her struggle with Poverty (493)[40]. However, she agrees to help, and makes him start the sixth book with the character of Saturnine, dictating stories to him till she disappears, having been visible for nearly a thousand lines, over a quarter of the book. Her last action is to point out Cicero as an example of rhetoric, and the narrative of Book VI then follows through a narrative of Rome to culminate with Cicero and the praise of rhetoric (3277-3500).

The energy of the account makes evident that not Gloucester but something much more vivid is the unstable and destabilizing centre of this book. Fortune's appearance as a series of allegories, all impossible to sustain on account of her doubleness, gives fame and takes it away, but at the end of her meeting with Bochas she says

> Yit of my chaunges no man taketh heed
> Nor how vnseurli I caste my dreedful look,
> Sauf thou art besi to sette hem in thi book. (VI.964-6)

- which implies that the corollary to giving Bochas fame is that she has none unless he writes of her: hence the significance of Cicero as a figure of poetry. She is not important, save as represented; so that she becomes the signified of poetry. The principle of change, of instability, which includes the instability of meaning which allegory speaks of and which appears in her varied appearances, conveys the sense that nothing can motivate events save a basic instability at the heart of the text which has already displaced Gloucester from the scene. There is no Prologue to the short Book VII, but Book VIII shows that though she is absent she is also present. The Prologue opens with John Bochas lying on his couch in a state of internal self-division, reminiscent, in Lydgate's version, of Hoccleve's internal

---

Fame: Symbolism in The House of Fame (Princeton: Princeton University Press, 1966), p. 44. Alistair Minnis, *Oxford Guides to Chaucer: The Shorter Poems* (Oxford: Clarendon Press, 1995) p. 187 says that making Fame and Fortune sisters was Chaucer's originality.

[40] The reference is to a fable told by Andalus the Black, a doctor of astronomy, who tells of the contest between Glad Poverty and Fortune, in which Fortune is worsted, in III. 20-707.

divisions. This state of conflict compares with the refrain to the envoi which commented on Oedipus and Jocasta: 'Kyngdams deuyded may no while endure' (I.3822), and be a reminder that it is the nature of kingdoms always to be divided. One part of Bochas, the subject, is thinking of the effort that is involved in writing the eighth book, but then the 'ladi Slouthe' (VIII.49) reminds him of the House of Fame before telling him that his labour shall 'wexe derk' (43). The Lady Sloth seems another form in which Fortune appears, in which case, if she may also be identified with melancholy (through *acedia* which is both sloth and melancholy), she also connects with allegory, which may be what is signified by Fortune. Allegory then becomes a feminine form. At the point where allegory - which would be a recognition of the impossibility of writing to the end - and melancholy intersect, another figure has to intervene: Petrarch, brought in as the allegory of the laureate poet, the poet crowned with fame, who reminds him of his book 'of lyffe solitarye / ... which in sekirnesse / Techeth the weie of vertuous besynesse' (108-110). Solitude becomes the only condition from which any writing can take place. The Prologue ends with Lydgate identifying himself and showing that he follows on from this example of Bochas and Petrarch. And Petrarch's influence is referred to again in the opening of Book IX. Not till the end is the Duke of Gloucester invoked again.

In the envoi to Book IX, he speaks of his limitations, and distinguishes himself from such writers as Gower, Stroode and 'Richard Hermyte', author of *The Prick of Conscience*, and most from Chaucer:

[...] my mayster hadde nevir pere, -
I mene Chauceer – in storyes that he tolde;
And he also wrote tragedyes olde.

The Fal of Prynces gan pitously compleyne,
As Petrark did, and also Iohn Bochas;
Laureat Fraunceys, poetys bothe tweyne
Toold how prynces for ther greet trespace
Were ovirthrowe, rehersyng al the caas.
As Chaucer dide in the Monkys Tale.
But I that stonde lowe doon in the vale,

So greet a book in Ynglissh to translate,
Did it be constreynt and no presumpcioun.
Born in a village which callyd is Lydgate [...](9. 3419-31)

Having spoken about himself he concludes 'with whyte and blak / And where I faylle let Lydgate ber the lack'

Off this translacyoun considred the matere,
The processe is in party lamentable;
Wooful clausys of custom they requere,
No rhetoryques nor florysshynges delyctable:

> Lettrys of compleynt requere colour sable,
> And tragedyes in especial
> Be rad and songe at feestys funeral. IX. 3443-3449

Tragedy is linked again to 'compleynt' as also at the earlier quoted line IX. 3419, and so to the *Trauerspiel* motif. The text needs no rhetoric or adding of flourishes, as if denying or repressing something of what was said in Book VI; what has been written are 'letters of complaint', and tragedies are declared to be fit for funeral recitations.

Though the text ends, effectively, with the envoy to Gloucester, it has also withdrawn from him with a deepened interest in Fortune, making for an ambiguity which repeats - or which is - the subject-matter of the book: the displacement of the prince by Fortune. The desire to centre Gloucester fails as the text extends its interest from the examples given to showing that there is a process of writing taking place, which is a discovery of Fortune herself. Since Fortune inverts everything, since she is double and a figure of mutability (VI.205, 359, 399, 486, ('contrarious mutabilite' 633), 865,911) and of 'ambiguite' (VI.866), she may approach the condition of carnival that Bakhtin discusses. Perhaps that is the poem's strange honesty. One specific point may be made connecting carnival to Lydgate's text. Bakhtin argues that nothing originates the carnival:

> instead a signal is given for each and every one to play the fool and madman as he pleases. This is extremely important for the carnival atmosphere - that even in its beginning, it has no serious or pious tone. Nor is it set in motion by an order [i.e. there is no hierarchy beginning it]; it opens simply with a signal marking the beginning of merriment and foolery.[41]

Whatever the signal might be, the point is that carnival and the *de casibus* tradition – 'the logic of crownings and uncrownings' as Bakhtin calls it, with reference to Shakespearian tragedy,[42] have this in common, that they begin with the premise of instability, not with order. What is originary is not reason, as the Duke of Gloucester would want to imply, but a difference which might be expressed as madness or folly, or as by the doubleness which may be epitomised in the doubling of allegory and melancholy, whose name in this text may be Fortune, and who, while she destabilizes gender altogether, is also feminine. Perhaps Dürer's *Melencolia* portrays Fortune. Fortune is a woman, as Machiavelli stresses, just as, for Nietzsche, truth may

---

[41] Mikhail Bakhtin, *Rabelais and his World*, trans. by Hélène Iswolsky (Bloomington: Indiana University Press, 1968), p. 246.
[42] Bakhtin, p. 275.

be a woman.[43] The poem has to show the setting aside of the Duke of Gloucester, whose personal reluctance to fund Lydgate therefore demonstrated retrospectively his displacement from a position of originating or authorizing. The complete text could be seen as about him. To say this is to note an irony within the text whose effect is to make the text more true than it knows.

Death is another name for the allegory of Fortune, as in Lydgate's *The Daunce of Machabree* they have identical functions: the half-quotation of the end of *The Monk's Tale* (2766), as said about Fortune, will also be noted in the fifth line:

> Death spareth nought low ne high degre,
> Popes, kynges, ne worthye Emperours;
> Whan they shine most in felicite
> He can abate the freshnes of her flours,
> Her brighte sunne clipsen with his shours
> Make them plunge fro her sees lowe; -
> Mauger the might of al these conquerours,
> Fortune hath them from her whele ythrow. ("The Prologue" 9-16)[44]

Death and Fortune may also be alike in gender, Death being a woman, as in the pre-1348 fresco in the Campo Santo in Pisa.[45] In this, the living join in a round dance or a line dance with the dead, though the dead are in hierarchical order, The difference in Holbein's 'Dance of Death' woodcuts of 1523-1526, published in 1538, is that Death now, in a set of scenes, comes as a skeleton, not, as before, as a cadaver, to visit each soul. Further, there is a significant attention paid now to the individual setting in which he appears. The dance of the dead before that has something within it of carnival, as popular art, in that it portrays a levelling, as *de casibus* tragedy also shows.[46]

Yet in Lydgate this carnival spirit, which ironizes his work and makes it an allegory of the fall of the prince, which explores the ambiguity that makes it impossible to give a moral centre to narratives of destruction, and which is a part of melancholy, does not become other than a record of collapse. It says that 'this world is a

---

[43] Machiavelli, *The Prince*, ed. and trans. by Quentin Skinner and Russell Price (Cambridge: Cambridge University Press, 1988), p. 87 (chapter 25); Nietzsche, *The Gay Science*, trans. by Walter Kaufmann (New York: Vintage, 1974), p. 38 (Preface to the second edition).

[44] See also Patch, pp. 117-120 for further examples.

[45] See Michael Camille, *Master of Death: The Lifeless Art of Pierre Remiet, Illuminator* (New Haven: Yale University Press, 1996), pp. 133-138. See also Philippe Aries, for the Campo Santo.

[46] For the popularity of the motif see Sarah Webster Goodwin, *Kitsch and Culture: The Dance of Death in Nineteenth Century Literature and Graphic Arts* (New York: Garland, 1988), pp. 25-57.

thoruhfare full of woe' (I.795) - quoting *The Knight's Tale*. It corresponds to a softening of issues throughout Lydgate and a preservation of a conservative order which marks out the text as repressed. The melancholia that runs through the text is thus nostalgic, equally as much as it sees everything as fragmented by death. In that repression Lydgate is different from Chaucer.

This appears in his censure of 'cherlis' (4.2684-2716) which appears in his account of the low-born tyrant Agathocles. The word 'cherle' recurs again and again (2659, 2686, 2693 ('Of cherel & gentil make this dyuisioun'), and 2701: 'Froward techchis [traits] been euer in cherlis founde'. Cognate terms circulate in the passage: knave and fool. The churl is both the peasant, the villein, (OED 3: 'A tenant in pure villeinage; a serf, a bondman [The position to which most of the Old English ceorlas (free men) were reduced after the Norman conquest]) and he may be Saturn, himself pictured as a peasant, perhaps like the ploughman of 'March' in the 'Très Riches Heures', the agent of change, a manifestation of time, as real as the chariot going across the heavens in the picture's lunette. Dante elides Saturn and Fortune, when responding to Brunetto Latini's warnings of his impending change, being exiled from Florence:

> Non è nuova a li orecchi miei tal arra:
> però giri Fortuna la sua rota
> come le piace, e'l villan la sua marra. (*Inf.* 15.94-96)
> [Such earnest (of news) is not new to my ears;
> therefore let Fortune turn her wheel
> as she chooses and the peasant his mattock.][47]

Churls reappear when Fortune speaks to 'Bochas' – first about Athenion whom she allowed to gather 'robbours' and 'cherlis' (6.725-6), then with the conspiracy of Spartacus, who 'gadred cherlis' (6.771), a churl himself (6.838), and because he was a churl, thrown from Fortune's wheel, it being cruel 'whan a cherl hath domynacioun' (6.780). Though Fortune has shown a principle of instability, she shows in that a desire for stability. Lydgate returns to the topos in the Envoi following the fate of Agathocles, when he warns against taking everything that shines brightly as gold: 'Lat

---

[47] See the discussion of this passage in Amilcare A. Iannucci, 'Saturn in Dante', in Massimo Ciavolella and Amilcare A. Iannucci, *Saturn from Antiquity to the Renaissance* (University of Toronto Italian Studies: Dovehouse Editiond inc., 1992), pp. 51-67. Iannucci, who makes the identification of Greek Chronos with the Roman Saturn Kronos, takes the 'villano' as Kronos - Saturn - and so paraphrases the lines as "let Fortune turn her wheel as she pleases, and Time continue its relentless course" (p. 59). See also Erwin Panofsky, "Father Time" in *Studies in Iconology: Humanistic Themes in the Art of the Renaissance* (New York: Harper and Rowe 1972).

men bewar of counterfeit coignage / techchis schewyng of cherlissh low lynage' (4.2946-7). Boccaccio regards his princes with contempt and aversion; Lydgate accepts state rule, which does not include the rule of the 'commons' (3.2203). The Envoi for the tragedies of Miltiades and Themistocles, banished by their subjects, equates the community ('comounte') with Fortune: it is difficult to say that Fortune controls the commons; rather, their nature is to be like Fortune, and that makes the principle of 'change' natural, as the image in the last lines, leading to the repetition in the refrain of the last line itself implies:

> The stormy trust of eueri comounte,
> Ther geri corages & troublid constaunce,
> In this tragedie men may beholde & see,
> Now vp, now doun, as Fortune cast hir chaunce.
> For thei off custom haue ioie & most plesaunce,
> In ther desirs onstedfast and ontrewe,
> To seen ech day a chaung of pryncis newe ....

> Noble Pryncis, in your prosperite,
> On sodeyn chaungis set your remembraunce,
> Fresshnesse off floures, off braunchis the beute
> Haue ai on chaung a tremblyng attendaunce,
> In trust off comouns is no perseurance:
> As wynter & somer be dyuers off ther hewe,
> So be thei dyuers in chaung of pryncis newe. (3. 2164-2170, 2199-2206)

Lydgate softens any discredit on the church; he softens violence and sexual passion; he omits or cuts out references to homosexuality, as with Vitellius in Book 7, 929-1103, especially 7.978, 'From al vertu Vitelli dide varye'. So too with Ptolemy Philopator (5.841-875, where Lydgate writes 'it is contagious the processe to endite, / Because the exaumple doth harm & no good' (5.864-5). Wright points out a similar repression in the case of Alexander (3.4760).[48] Homosexuality seems to have been a marker of the Duc de Berry, and perhaps relates to his collecting: so Camille argues (see above, note 9). Lydgate, who shows no sense of how strange it is that he should be collecting, accumulating ceaselessly, becomes most contemptuous of homosexuality in the case of Nero, who would, however, outgo the Duc de Berry, and certainly Gloucester, in his commitment to a carnival existence. Lydgate's literal-mindedness about the power of literature to shock and a willingness to follow authority produces the following self-censorship as a further form of repression:

> Be my writyng men shal neuer reede,
> The mateer is so foul & outragous

---

[48] Herbert G. Wright, *Boccaccio in England from Chaucer to Tennyson* (London: Athlone 1957), p. 10.

> To be rehersed, & the horrible deede
> Which Nero usid whilom on Sporus
> And on another callid Ompharus:
> Both male children, as bookis telle can,
> Them to transfforme to liknesse of woman. (7.721-725) [49]

Homosexuality in the way Lydgate describes it, might destabilize gender in a way equivalent to Fortune, and so be a form of carnival. It is interesting to watch Lydgate miss this within Nero. He comments on the first of two palaces that Nero built which was called 'the Transitorie' (655) – 'For this cause, as is put in memorie / The said palesi aftirward was brent / Therefore was it callid Transitorie' (656-8), but the wit which should attend this is missing. (The palace could only be so named after it was burned, so that 'Transitory' would be an appropriate name that could not relate to anything having physical existence.) It is absent even though Nero himself gives a hint how his life should be taken when he suddenly gave himself to 'ribaudie' (683) and to jugglers, as if in a carnival inversion of what he had been:

> Of Grece and Egipt with dyuers ionglours
> And among vileyns hymsilfe disprting,
> Left the presence of olde senatours
> And among ribaudis he wolde harp & synge,
> Made comedies dishonestli sownyng,
> At the bordel dide hymsilf auaunce
> With comoun women openli to daunce (684-91)

The carnival spirit, which, perhaps oddly, recalls Langland's minstrels, puts on comedies in brothels, identifying the theatre with the whorehouse. [50] It is the reverse of the tragic, which, it seems, Lydgate might not have associated with the theatre at all. And perhaps Lydgate was right to associate the theatre with the brothel:

> When Pushkin said that the art of the theatre was 'born in the public square', the square he had in mind was that of 'the common people', the square of bazaars, puppet theatres, taverns, that is the square of European cities in the thirteenth, fourteenth and subsequent centuries. He also had in mind the fact that the state and 'official society' [...] were located by and large beyond the square [...]. [51]

The tavern and the brothel relate to each other, no doubt. Nero steps out of official culture into another richer, popular culture. The text

---

[49] For these points, see Wright pp. 3-28. See also Willard Farnham, *The Medieval Heritage of Elizabethan Tragedy* (Oxford: Basil Blackwell 1963) pp. 160-170.

[50] See the discussion by Henry Ansgar Kelly, *Chaucerian Tragedy* (Cambridge: D.S. Brewer 1997) p. 174.

[51] Mikhail Bakhtin, *The Dialogic Imagination* trans. Michael Holquist and Caryl Emerson (Austin: University of Texas Press 1981) p. 132.

reads the carnival, though it denies its interest, when, it continues with Nero, who collects transgressions, and who like a 'ribaude horrible & detestable'[52] carved up the womb of his mother. Nero is identified in the text with 'woodnesse' (738) and then with 'malencolie' (743). He is seen also identifying with the madman (754-60), before taking his own life. Kelly and Scanlon both note the prevalence of suicide in the fall of princes.[53] 'To reede the processe no prince sholde haue ioye' (777) the Envoy asserts, but despite or because of the leaden telling, where the poet protests that he is ashamed to put him in the book (739), the text has failed to dull his interest, bringing out instead an alliance between the writing of comedies and gender-inversion, and an abject fascination with the corpse of the mother - the corpse being Benjamin's supreme allegorical emblem - in relation to madness and melancholia. Whether the text can allow the insight or no, what it has described is like a case of schizophrenia. It is in sequence with Hoccleve's account of his madness, if it is radically unlike it in character; it is like the madness of the King of France, Charles VI, where that madness would emblemize the point that the rule of the kingdom divides internally the monarch whose single being is supposed to express its unity.

Nero as the prince exemplifies the heresy that the text must repress, as Gloucester is praised for repressing it, but he shows the alliance between madness and otherness that the formal allegory of the text cannot work with, because if it did it would have to surrender its moralism. At this point, another allegory is at work within the text. The collector cannot find that everything he collects has the same unity within it.

---

[52] The OED gives as one meaning of 'ribald' a lowly retainer in a court, and also, though marked as obsolescent, '*king of the ribalds*, an officer of the royal household of France, who had jurisdiction over crimes committed within it, vagrants resorting to it, and all brothels and gaming-houses about the court. Hence used allusively'. Its first citation is 1400.

[53] Scanlon, pp. 347-8, Kelly, pp. 186-7.

CHAPTER 5

The Testament of Cresseid: Reading Henryson with Baldung

I - AGE

> Be it Paris who dies or Helen,
> Whoever dies dies in such pain
> The wind is knocked out of him,
> His gall breaks on his heart,
> And he sweats God knows what sweat
> And noone can relieve his pain,
> For he hasn't child, brother or sister
> Willing to stand in for him then.
>
> Death makes him shudder and blanch,
> Makes his nostrils curl, his veins stand out,
> His neck puff and flesh go limp,
> Joints and sinews swell and stretch:
> O female body which is so precious
> So smooth, delicate and soft,
> Will you too come to these agonies?
> Yes, or rise in the flesh up to heaven.[1]

In Robert Henryson's *The Testament of Cresseid*, written in Scotland near the end of the fifteenth century[2] - the narrator, a 'man of age' (29) tells what happened to Cresseid after she left Troilus for

---

[1] Translation from Villon by Galway Kinnell, *The Poems of Francois Villon* (New York: Signet Classics, 1965), p. 67. A better edition of the French appears in *Francois Villon: Complete Poems*, ed. by Barbara N. Sargent-Baur (Toronto: University of Toronto Press, 1994).

[2] Quotations from Henryson are from his edition of *The Testament of Cresseid*, ed. by Denton Fox (London: Nelson, 1968) with line references and page references given in the text, and from *Poems*, ed. by Denton Fox (Oxford: Clarendon Press, 1981). I have also referred to the *Selected Poems*, ed. by W.R.J. Barron (Manchester: Carcanet 1991). On Henryson's milieu, see John Macqueen, *Robert Henryson: A Study of the Narrative Poems* (Oxford: Clarendon Press, 1967), pp. 1-23; for the relationship between the Medieval and the Renaissance see A.C. Spearing, *Medieval to Renaissance in English Poetry* (Cambridge: Cambridge University Press, 1985), pp. 164-199. See also for the milieu, Douglas Gray, *Robert Henryson* (Leiden: E.J. Brill, 1979), pp. 2-30, 162-208. Another set of contexts comes in Piero Boitani, ed., *The European Tragedy of Troilus* (Oxford: Clarendon 1989), especially the essays by C. David Benson, 'True Troilus and False Cresseid', pp. 153-170, and Anna Torti, 'From "History" to "Tragedy": The Story of Troilus and Criseyde in Lydgate's *Troy Book* and Henryson's *Testament of Cresseid'*, pp. 171-198, which discusses Medieval views of tragedy, using Chaucer's *Monk's Tale* lines 1973-7; compare *Testament* line 63. For a summary of scholarship see Louise O. Fradenberg, 'Henryson Scholarship: The Recent Decades' in Robert F. Yeager, ed., *Fifteenth-Century Studies: Recent Essays* (Hamden, Conn.: Archon Books, 1984), pp. 65-92.

Diomed. Like Villon in 1461, whose verses quoted above end an 'ubi sunt' section which began eleven stanzas before, and which produces afterwards the 'Ballade' beginning 'Dictes moy ou, n'en quel paÿs, / Est Flora la belle Romaine' with its refrain 'Mais ou sont les neiges d'antan?' the text is fascinated by death.[3] It documents a crisis, medical and sexual, impacting on its unconscious presuppositions and drives, and shows an embodied subject marked by age and sickness.

The title *The Testament of Cresseid* refers to Cresseid's will, which is also part of a testimony, and so it is also a confession, made under the constraint of her sickness: for after her affair with Diomed, the gods strike her with leprosy. In her will she fragments herself, as she speaks separately of her body, her spirit, and her goods. But the 'man of age' will speak for the young woman, telling her end and making public her secret. The tone, unlike that of Villon, is tendentially misogynistic. But this polarization, and splitting of interest between the two figures in the text does not hold, for both the old man and Cresseid are the text's fictional creations, and the text cannot separate itself from the woman, for the narrator is, we shall see, Cresseid-like, his experiences ghosting hers. He calls the text, in an assumption of dignity, a 'tragedy' and stages himself in the self-deprecatory tone of a man of no illusions, a mode adopted from Chaucer, his model, whom he says he has been reading. Since, as Walter Benjamin says, 'what draws the reader to the novel is the hope of warming his shivering life with a death he reads about',[4] his existence may be said to be based on her death. Half-confessional in intention, he declares himself inadequate in relation to Venus, whose star is 'the bewtie of the nicht'; who has a 'goldin face', (11, 13) and is 'luifis quene / To quhome sum tyme I hecht obedience' (23,24). In contrast to this unreachable stellar figure, worshipped from the margin of his text, Cresseid is excluded in the text's body, like the Venus who appears in Cresseid's dream, and has no claim to reverence.

The 'quair' the man has been reading is Chaucer's *Troilus and Criseyde* of the 1380s. The point has been made that *this* poem assumes Cresseid's death from the opening announcement of its theme: 'the double sorwes ... / Of Troilus in lovynge of Criseyde / And how that she forsook hym ere she deyde' (I.54-56).[5] Chaucer

---

[3] Villon: 'Tell me, where, in what country, / Is Flora the beautiful Roman ... But where are the snows of last year?'

[4] Walter Benjamin, 'The Storyteller', *Illuminations*, trans. by Harry Zohn (London: Jonathan Cape, 1970), p. 101.

[5] See Gayle Margherita, 'Criseyde's Remains: Romance and the Question of Justice', *Exemplaria* 12 (2000), 257-297. Another feminist reading appears in Catherine S. Cox, 'Froward Language and Wanton Play: The "Commoun" Text

says no more of Criseyde's death; the end focuses on Troilus. Henryson's 'vther quair'[6] which he reads to find out what happened to Cresseid – whether this book is real or imaginary – leads to the announcing of *his* theme, like another tragedy in the *de casibus* tradition, as:

> the lamentatioun
> And woful end of this lustie Cresseid
> And quhat distres scho thoillit, and quhat deid'. (68-70)

So, the last line of the text runs: 'Sen scho is deid I speik of hir no moir' (616) - after lamentation, woe and distress. Is the poem a testimony of love? But she has been dead since before the beginning of the narrated events; from the moment when he takes up Chaucer's text to read it; dead in Chaucer, dead in the 'uther quair', dead long before she dies - her voice cut off as she speaks her testament - and is memorialized in the epitaph which admonishes 'fair ladyis': that Cresseid 'Vunder this stane, lait lipper, lyis deid' (609). This line is pleonastic as is the brief last line, which contains the unconscious proposition: I can now stop writing because she is dead, because the purpose of writing is to bring her to death. But she was dead before he began writing, it is more strange that he should apostrophize her in lines 78-91, as though she were still alive – 'I haue pietie thow sud fall sic mischance' (84). He revives the dead world in the form of a mask, as Benjamin would say, in the action of the allegorist, who busies himself with books.

The narrator and his obsessions reappear uncannily in fragmented form in his story. His private 'orature', and the glass through which he sees the star, recur as the mirror in which Cresseid sees herself, and in Cresseid's orature. 'Phebus' disappears in both the sunset of the introduction and in Cresseid's experience (14,400), with all that follows. Venus is referred to by him, by Cresseid; his hope for his

---

of Henryson's *Testament of Cresseid*', *Studies in Scottish Literature* 29 (1996), 58-72. On the relationship with Chaucer, see also Lee W. Patterson, 'Christian and Pagan in *The Testament of Cresseid*', *Philological Quarterly* 52 (1973), 696-714 and the essays by Louise O. Fradenburg, 'The Scottish Chaucer', Tim William Machan, 'Textual Authority and the Works of Hoccleve, Lydgate and Henryson', C. David Benson, 'Critic and Poet: What Lydgate and Henryson Did to Chaucer's *Troilus and Criseyde*' in Daniel J. Pinti, *Writing After Chaucer: Essential Readings in Chaucer and the Fifteenth Century* (New York: Garland, 1998), pp. 167-176; 177-200; 227-242; for a view critical of Cresseid, see Edwin D. Craun, 'Blaspheming her "Awin God": Cresseid's "Lamentatioun" in Henryson's *Testament*', *Studies in Philology* 82 (1985), 25-41.

6 On this 'book', see a review of the literature in Robert L. Kindrick, 'Henryson's "Uther Quair" Again: A Possible Candidate and the Nature of the Tradition', *Chaucer Review* 33 (1998), 190-220.

heart to be made green is echoed by Cresseid in her angry prayer (24, 138). Similarly, the violence of the hailstones recurs (6,168). An old man, he is doubled by Calchas and by Saturn: for as the narrator, he inflicts Cresseid with the leprosy which Saturn gives her. Other links are the winter fire, missing in the cold of the body of the narrative, and the physic which he takes (to increase sexual desire), but which Cresseid cannot.[7] These, and more fragments from his short narrative of himself reappear as if in a rebus, as if the poem of Cresseid is the narrator's experiences changed into dream-form. Both parts together are his confession; he is Cresseid, even if, as a man of age, he is not one of the 'youtheid' (youths) (30), his sexual desire ('curage') being 'doif and deid' (32); as Villon implies his was. But Villon's text is more ironic, more inflected by the 'dance' character of the dance of the dead, more aware of the possibility of arguing back, as in the 'Ballade' – 'Dites moy' - tell me.

Perhaps Henryson's text practises a partially unconscious resentment against 'youtheid', which develops from the problematic ending of *Troilus and Criseyde*:

> O yonge fresshe folkes, he or she
> In whom that love up groweth with your age
> Repeyreth hom from worldly vanyte [...]' (V.1835-7)[8]

Resentment against age prompts resentment against youth. Cresseid's fate confirms the sense that this 'cairfull dyte' should be written in the 'doolie sessoun' of Lent - penitential, antagonistic to the body, excluding it and the woman.

II - ABJECTION

Cresseid is an individual subject, the mirror of the writer whose private 'orature' and 'chalmer'with the fire, and solitary reading are his way of making himself the private, individual subject. Her privacy, violated by his revelations, her ability to reflect upon herself and to comment on her situation make her the subject whose unjust treatment is felt. The narrator shows signs of sympathy but

---

[7] For the glass image, see Philippa Tristram's treatment of the poem in *Figures of Life and Death in Medieval English Literature* (London: Paul Elek, 1976), p. 148. The book's treatment of the *'ubi sunt'* motif is also relevant (pp. 113-128). Tristram (p. 66) compares with the opening of the poem the confession of Lust in *Piers Plowman* (C.VII, 192-4):

> Ich lay by the lovelokeste, and loved hem never after.
> Whenne ich was old and hor, and hadde lore that kynde,
> Ich had lykynge to lauhe of lecherous tales.

[8] For a summary of critical views of the end of the poem (from at least V.1786 on), see Barry Windeatt, *Oxford Guides to Chaucer: Troilus and Criseyde* (Oxford: Clarendon Press, 1992), pp. 310-3.

formally declares Cresseid's repudiation, continuing the process Diomed initiated in sending her a 'libell of repudy' (74). The verb from 'exclusion' appears first when Diomed has sent the libell of repudy:

> And hir excludid from his companie. (75)

Her exclusion is registered spatially, when she leaves, disguised, walking 'a mile or twa' outside the town to her father's house. When she speaks 'angerly' upon Venus and Cupid, she says that in relation to Diomed and Troylus, she is

> [...] clene excludit, as abiect odious. (133)

'Abject' was a new word: its first English appearance is recorded as 1534. But Cresseid cannot be its first user, for she responds to how she has been named and considered, or constructed. If she is abject, that is the result of a prior naming, in which the narrator seems collusive. Exclusion appears again when Saturn lays his frosty wand on Cresseid's head, in judgment of her and says 'lawfullie' – the word recalling Diomed's recourse to law:

> Thy greit fairnes and all thy bewtie gay,
> Thy wantoun blude, and eik thy golden hair,
> Heir I exclude fra the for euermair. (313-5)

The public punishment of leprosy imposed on her by Saturn and Cynthia – making her body so odious that she cannot appear in public except as an object of display – intensifies and disallows her desire to be single, private. It drives her from her 'secreit orature' (120) 'in secreit wyse' (381) through a 'secreit get' to a 'spittaill hous' half a mile away in a village (388-91). Her 'Complaint' is uttered in an 'ane dark corner of the hous allone' (405); but she must enter the public sphere of begging; by which time melancholy has so taken her over as to have driven her out of her mind.

Her desire for privacy (94), disguise, (95), secrecy (116-120), confidentiality (365-6), secrecy again in leaving her father's house (381,388), the dark corner and ultimately the tomb, contrast with the time when, dropped by Diomed, she comes 'into the court, commoun' (77), i.e. 'promiscuous'. She is a split subject, both a public sexual being, a commodity, and desiring a private and autonomous subjectivity. 'Court' is part of this contrasted geography: open and public, in contrast to the private spaces she retreats to. Splitting, which shows the unsustainable position of a woman who can be of neither in the private nor public sphere, appears in her melancholy. Leprous, with identity so lost that Troylus, cannot recognise her, she must '*clap* her *clap*per to and fro' (479). This repetition, backwards-forwards, repeats the treadmill movement of going around 'air and lait' (82). She becomes a 'rank beggar' (483) – the adjective is loaded - as before she had been a prostitute. There seems to be a sense of repetition: mimed in the text's backwards-and forwards words, and showing that what she is declared to be in the first part of the poem is what she is condemned to be in its second.

Like Hoccleve, and Arcite, Cresseid, awakened from sleep, goes to her polished glass

> and hir shaddow culd luik;
> And quhen scho saw hir face sa deformait
> Gif scho in hart was wa aneuch, God wait! (348-50)

In lines 347-343, judgment was pronounced: Cresseid has become a leper, her *crystall* eyes now mingled with blood, her *clear* voice unpleasant, hoar and hoarse, and her face covered with 'spottis blak', aligning her with the moon-goddess Cynthia, whose gown is full of 'spottis blak' (260). Cresseid's 'lumpis haw' – lead-coloured lumps - also recall Cynthia, 'haw as the leid' (257). Lead, associated with Saturn also – 'his lyre [face] was lyke the leid' (155) – gives her face saturnine, melancholic, features. Jupiter, 'far different' from his father Saturn (172), has a clear voice and crystal eyes (176): Cresseid, her hair lost, has moved towards the status of the old man, away from Jupiter, changing both gender and age. Hoccleve cannot register a change in his face: it may be the same, it may be different, but the text keeps silent whether there is a change or not, with the implied sense that it would not necessarily make any difference if there was. Cresseid's face, however, *has* changed. The spoiled face is only one of the markers of a change upon her in a text whose events may look more medieval than what happens to Hoccleve, whose text appears more modern since he records an attempt to prove that he is sane, in the absence of anything that could validate that. But perhaps *The Testament of Cresseid* also registers something different and more modern still, because of its sense of a changing discourse of the body of the subject.

After Cresseid has become 'commoun' the narrator apostrophizes her: 'how was thou fortunait / To change in filth all thy feminity / And be with fleschely lust sa maculait ... taking thy foull plesance' (79-83). Does 'feminity' imply that Cresseid, becoming a prostitute, is no longer a woman? (Denton Fox, (p. 29): 'Cresseid trades her beautiful femininity for the genderless filth of a leprous body'.) She will regain her 'womanheid' only as dead (608). The change is from the human to the monstrous, the indescribable. The stanza following, referring to her 'womanheid' seems evasive or ironic, or an expression of ambiguity felt towards her as a woman, for though the idea that she has become 'commoun' is only what 'sum men sayis' (77), the stanza cannot do anything to change the sense that what has

151

been said by 'men' (males) is true, and that she has not simply been injured by slander:

> Yit nevertheles, whatever men deme or say
> In scornefull langage of thy brukkilnes,
> I sall excuse, als far furth as I may
> Thy womanheid, thy wisdome and fairnes,
> The whilk Fortoun hes put to sic distres
> As hir pleisit, and nathinh throw the gilt
> Of the – throw wickit langage to be split! (85-91)

'Filth', 'maculait' and 'foull' make Cresseid as if always-already leprous. Her moral contagion is allegorized by her leprosy. These implications are, however, left ambiguous, as much as the moral status of catching venereal disease is usually ambiguous in discourse (leaving open the question how responsible the person is for becoming infected, but in even raising it as a question, settling it also to the prejudice of the person infected). So the text indicates that she has excluded herself in making herself 'foull', as much as she has been excluded by the man who, it seems from the lines 'Quhen Diomeid had all his appetyte / And mair, fulfillit of this fair ladie' (71-72) has repudiated as abject what his appetite has consumed.

She diagnoses her leprosy; no doctors appear in this text.[9] But the text shows the doctor's discourse in its awareness of physicality and of the power of disease. Imposition of leprosy, as an act of violence and revenge (294), is the principal form of her exclusion; as an imposition of pain, it follows what Foucault discusses in *Discipline and Punish* of earlier, pre-modern regimes of state punishment. It demonstrates the might of the sovereign gods who stand in for the power of the state, acting upon the body of the woman.[10] Cupid, who demands recompense, shows his self-hatred (hatred for sexual love), in calling Cresseid 'wretchit' (278) and 'vnclene and lecherous' (285): out of such judgmentalism, which implies the inability of power to justify itself, and which sustains its own definition of love by dismissing Cresseid's, condemnation falls. Yet readers of the text have continued to justify Henryson's text by justifying Cresseid's leprosy – even if they say she is 'redeemed' at the end – and join in the accusations of blasphemy, or lack of trueness, or promiscuity

---

[9]   Mercury is seen as a satire on physicians: 'doctour in phisick, cled in ane skarlot goun / And furrit weill, as sic ane aucht to be; / Honest and gude, and not ane word culd lie' (250-52). See on this John B. Friedman, 'Henryson's *Testament of Cresseid* and the *Judicio Solis in Conviviis Saturni* of Simon of Couvin', *Modern Philology* 83 (1985), 12-21.

[10] A.C. Spearing draws attention to the word 'pane' used by the gods as meaning both 'penalty' and 'pain' in lines 277, 291, 299, 306; see *Criticism and Medieval Poetry* (London: Edward Arnold, 1964), pp. 118-144, (p. 140).

within the woman. To side against Cresseid, as a blasphemer, so as a heretic, or for her sexuality, colludes with such exclusionary practices, and criticism needs to ask whether it could proceed otherwise, in a way that would not further empower the empowered. The text quotes no doctor, for such evidence of a secular response to the disease would imply a critique of its purpose. We can surmise what that purpose is when it is recalled that the exclusion of leprosy in the twelfth to the fifteenth centuries could be seen, historically, as part of a 'wider crusade against heretics, Jews, homosexuals, and anyone else whose conduct or beliefs gave rise to suspicion. [...] [so that] the heretic was frequently described in medical terms as a spiritual leper, infected by a poisonous contagion from which his soul was unlikely to recover'.[11] The exclusion of lepers from towns, and the demand that they be isolated, had been a feature of the Third Lateran Council of 1179; 'leprosy' had appeared in Europe a century before; and R.I. Moore argues that the church in the twelfth century began to direct and to construct a persecutory and violent attitude towards the leper as the other — a move intensified in the Fourth Lateran Council's demand, in 1215, for annual confession from all believers.[12]

III - LEPROSY

Leprosy is barely described in the poem. As Cresseid becomes leprous, Saturn and Cynthia are always-already leprous. Saturn allegorizes leprosy and old age:

> And first of all Saturne gaue his sentence,
> Quhilk gaue to Cupide litell reuerence,
> Bot as ane busteous churle on his maneir
> Come crabitlie with auster luik and cheir.
>
> His face fronsit, his lure was lyke the leid,
> His teith chatterit and cheuerit with the chin,

---

11 Carol Rawcliffe, *Medicine and Society in Later Medieval England* (Stroud: Sutton Publishing, 1995), p. 14. That the Medieval church said the burial rites over the leper, which idea circulated through Rotha Mary Clay's influential *The Medieval Hospitals of England* (1909, last reprinted in 1966), is questioned in Nicholas Orme and Margaret Webster, *The English Hospital* (New Haven: Yale University Press, 1995), pp. 29-31. For their discussion of leper hospitals, see pp. 23-48.

12 R.I. Moore, *The Formation of a Persecuting Society: Power and Deviance in Western Europe, 950-1250* (Oxford: Blackwell, 1987), pp. 45-59 for discussion of lepers. On the appropriation of Foucault for medieval studies, and the interest in alterity this has produced, an attention 'not only to the marginal but to the grotesque', see Paul Freedman and Gabrielle M. Spiegel, 'Medievalisms Old and New: The Rediscovery of Alterity in North American Medieval Studies', *American Historical Review* (1993), 677-704 (p.699 for quotation).

Hie ene drowpit, how sonkin in his heid,
Out of his nois the meldrop fast can rin,
With lippis blaand cheikis leine and thin;
The ice schoklis that fra his hair doun hang
Was wonder greit, and as ane speir als lang:

Atouir his belt his lyart lokkis lay
Felterit vnfair, ouirfret with froistis hoir,
His garmound and his gyte full gay of gray,
His widderit weid fra him the wind out woir,
Ane busteous bow within his hand he boir,
Vnder his girdill ane flasche of felloun flanis
Fedderit with ice and heidit with hailstanis.   (151-168)

Old age is disgusting, abject, the discharge from the nose an image of the body's waste, and the body seen as waste. The critique of these gods as loathsome makes them abject because of their bodies: that is also true of Cresseid, and it may even be true of the narrator's attitude to his body, part of the abjection of the text, in which the old narrator cannot be excluded from Cresseid's condition. Leprosy, old age and the body as failing, disgusting, recall Julia Kristeva on the abject:

As in true theatre, without make-up or masks, refuse and corpses show me what I permanently thrust aside in order to live. These body fluids, this defilement, this shit are what life withstands, hardly and with difficulty, on the part of death. There I am at the border of my condition as a living being. Such wastes drop that I might live, until, from loss to loss, nothing remains in me and my entire body falls beyond the limit. Cadere – cadaver. If dung signifies the other side of the border, the place where I am not and which permits me to be, the corpse, the most sickening of wastes, is a border that has encroached upon everything.[13]

---

[13]   Julia Kristeva, *Powers of Horror: An Essay on Abjection*, trans. by Leon Roudiez (New York: Columbia University Press, 1982), p. 3. Further references in the text. This is cited also in Felicity Riddy's feminist reading, '"Abject Odious": Feminine and Masculine in Henryson's *Testament of Cresseid*', in Helen Cooper and Sally Mapstone, eds., *The Long Fifteenth-Century* (Oxford: Clarendon, 1997), pp. 229-248. This is a valuable essay, though Riddy says that 'what is obscurely at stake in the story of the much-loved woman who is cast out is the very making of masculinity' (p. 235), by which she means Troilus's; an emphasis I find less relevant, and also making abjection a completed operation, which in Kristeva it cannot possibly be. I also find her account of the casting out of the woman de-historicizing; and to underestimate the critique of old age. I am grateful to the essay, however, for three points: that leprosy is seen as old age (quoting Lesley Johnson, 'Whatever Happened to Cresseid? Henryson's *Testament of Cresseid*' in Keith Busby and Erik Hooper, *Courtly Literature: Culture and Contexts* (Amsterdam: John Benjamins, 1990), pp. 313-321, quoted p. 233); and for her use of Joan Cadden, *Sex Difference in the Middle Ages: Medicine, Science and Culture* (Cambridge: Cambridge University Press, 1993) p. 208, with pp. 170-173 on

Yet such repugnance from the body is not natural, nor essential, but constructed and historical. The discourse within the text *needs* to associate feminine sexuality, Cresseid, 'so giglotlike takand thy foull plesance' (83), with disease. Hence the leprosy, which is textually created, is a mirror of that plesance. But leprosy evokes an interior state too: melancholy, which has superimposed on it the nauseated state of abjection; the text keeping these two constitutive elements - leprosy and melancholia together. Saturn says:

I change thy mirth into melancholy. (316)

Denton Fox comments: 'Henryson uses the term here as the opposite of *mirth*, but also with reference to its more technical meaning, the excess of black bile, which is the cause of leprosy [...] as well as of sadness'.[14] Leprosy on Cresscid's body expresses age which is inside the sphere of death. Melancholy, which physiologically, according to humoural medicine, causes the leprosy (is both the cause and the consequence), is 'the mother of all pensiuenes' (317), the dominant maternal feminine whose existence increases abjection in an attempt to escape such an overpowering and all-absorbing mother.

Loss of mirth underlines the text being Cresseid's 'lamentatioun' (68), which, begun in her anger, continues in her Complaint (407-469). As her leprosy remains unrepresented, so in the Complaint, written in seven nine-line stanzas, and so standing out from the rest of the text, she never mentions it, though speaking about dwelling among lepers in: 'This lipper ludge tak for thy burley bour' (438) and in 'Ludgeit amang the lipper leid, "Allace!"' (451). Her change is taken as part of a more general reversal of fortune. She is not "common" with the leper-folk; she makes no identification with them. Leprosy externalizes female melancholia, physical and psychic in its effects. Melancholia, individuating and so seeming to constitute subjectivity, also severs the subject's unity, as an intrusion of otherness into the body, disturbing its clarity and crystal-like quality, so that the subject comprises disparate fragments, double: life and death, the old man and the young woman; Troylus when he views her as the leper sees a double figure, and the text takes four stanzas (498-525) to indicate how he must read the

---

the use of coldness to make Saturn appear androgynous (p. 247); and last, I am grateful for the fifteenth-century illustration of Eve from the museum in Strassbourg. Here, though Riddy does not say so, the toad that penetrates Eve's genitalia seems phallic, and further ironizes the woman.

14 Fox, pp. 112-3. See also p. 45, where he gives the references to mirth: lines 355, 368, 384-5, 409. Mirth, associated in Langland with sloth and so acedia, is definitional for youth in Henryson's 'The Ressoning Betuix Aige and Yowth'.

image of Cresseid dialectically, as two opposite things together – like Shakespeare's Troilus: 'This is, and is not Crisseid'.[15]

Earlier, after her blasphemy of the gods: 'doun in ane extasie / Rauischit in spreit, intill a dreame scho fell' (141-2). Melancholia associates with madness and delirium, for when Troylus appears, she sits 'not witting what scho was' (497).[16] She has blanked out. It illustrates Elaine Scarry's point: 'the presence of pain is the absence of world'.[17] Delirium contrasts with her previous secretive, disguised or private behaviour, which was motivated by feelings of shame. With no split between public and private subjectivity, she is a thing, an irony repeated by the mode in which Troylus pays her, unconsciously treating her as a prostitute by flinging the money into her lap. The knowledge that it was Troylus produces two further lamentations. The first (541-574), despairing, ending 'Nane but myself as now I will accuse', which repudiates the narrator's half-felt 'excuse' made for her (87), takes on the language of 'brukkilnes' for herself (86, 569). It constrains her to accept her condition as though her state embodied a single allegorical image of transgression punished. In the unfinished second lament, her testament, she considers from the standpoint of being alive, how her body after death will be 'rent', as the *corps morcelé*.[18] She had thought of

---

[15] Shakespeare, *Troilus and Cressida*, ed. Alan Palmer (London: Methuen, 1982), V.ii. 146.

[16] The point is made by Malcolm Pittock, 'The Complexity of Henryson's *The Testament of Cresseid*', *Essays in Criticism* 40 (1990), 198-221 (p. 206). Michael W. Dols, 'The Leper in Medieval Islamic Society', *Speculum* 58 (1983), 891-916 (p. 897) notes that in Islam, the leper was treated as if mentally ill.

[17] Elaine Scarry, *The Body in Pain: The Making and Unmaking of the World* (Oxford: Oxford University Press, 1985), p. 37.

[18] Referring to Lacan on the mirror-stage: when the subject is constituted by its ability to see itself in a glass – as Cresseid is forced to – phantasmatically as entire, complete, not as a fragmented *corps morcelé*: the mirror-stage 'manufactures for the subject, caught in the lure of spatial identification, the succession of phantasies that extends from a fragmented body-image to a form of its totality that I shall call orthopaedic – and lastly to the assumption of the armour of an alienating identity [...]' – Jacques Lacan, *Écrits: A Selection*, trans. by Alan Sheridan (London: Tavistock, 1977), p. 4. Though bodies were fragmented after death, as Miri Rubin shows, in 'The Body, Whole and Vulnerable in Fifteenth Century England', in Barbara A. Hanawalt and David Wallace, eds., *Bodies and Disciplines: Intersections of Literature and History in Fifteenth-Century England* (Minneapolis: University of Minnesota Press, 1996), p. 23, I do not think this negates the pathological awareness in Cresseid's words. For overviews of death in the period, see Margaret Aston, 'Death', in *Fifteenth-century Attitudes: Perceptions of Society in Late Medieval England* (Cambridge: Cambridge University Press, 1994), pp. 202-28 and R.C. Finucane, 'Sacred Corpse, Profane Carrion: Social Ideals and Death Rituals in the Later Middle Ages', in Joachim Whaley, ed., *Mirrors of*

herself as 'fair', which assumes that she has had the benefit of the mirror; she has seen herself as diseased in the mirror, and she finishes by the vision of her body as fragmented, as identified with the bestial, which is the abject condition.[19]

IV - COMPLAINT

If melancholia is an accession of otherness into the body, it is not a privation, but the addition of something else. Ficino's writings on melancholia in *De Vita Triplici* (1482-89) are contemporary with Henryson's text, and give those with a saturnine temperament a capacity for divine madness, making melancholia necessary for creative awareness. But that dialectic is nowhere in *The Testament of Cresseid*, and Cresseid gains nothing from her 'madness'. Cresseid's Complaint invites comparison with Hoccleve's *Complaint*, a differently gendered text. Julia Schiesari, in *The Gendering of Melancholia* distinguishes between depression and melancholia, seeing the first as working where the self has no empowerment to articulate its position, and the second as legitimated in Western discourse, implying the ability of the subject to speak its condition. Speaking of the 'symbolically accredited category of melancholia and the devalued status of depression', she argues, following Luce Irigaray, that women are seen as depressed, and are denied access to the '"signifying economy" that is the discursive apparatus of (male) melancholia'. She also cites Kaja Silverman's view that women are constituted depressed since they have had to 'renounce a mother with whom they must *also* identify'.[20] (And Cresseid has a father, but no mother.) Schiesari argues that literary texts show virtually no examples of women's melancholia, also arguing that Dürer's

---

Mortality: Studies in the Social History of Death (London: Europa, 1981), pp. 40-60.

[19] Millard Meiss, *Painting in Florence and Siena After the Black Death* (Princeton: Princeton University Press, 1951), pp. 74-76, and the reproduction (no. 52) of Giovanni del Biondo of a Madonna and child, with in the predella, a corpse being consumed by snakes and toads. Meiss shows the fourteenth-century connection between frogs and bestiality. For further discussion of death as the subject of art, see Paul Binski, *Medieval Death: Ritual and Representation* (London: British Museum Press, 1996), pp. 123-163.

[20] Juliana Schiesari, *The Gendering of Melancholia: Feminism, Psychoanalysis and the Symbolics of Loss in Renaissance Literature* (Ithaca: Cornell University Press, 1992), p. 17. See pp. 63-77 for further development of Irigaray's position and of Silverman's.

Melencolia, *I* represents masculine creativity overcome by depression.[21] Is *The Testament of Cresseid* an exception to all this?

Before making her testament, Cresseid says that she knows 'the greit unstabilnes / Brukkill as glas' which makes her expect to find in others 'als greit unfaithfulnes' (568-70). The instability of the world, which generates the *ubi sunt* theme, discussed in the last chapter, and the motif of *contemptus mundi,* has engendered Cresseid's unfaithfulness to Troylus. It is also the substance of the Complaint, which, as in Chaucer, and Chaucerian tragedy, in Hoccleve and in texts of lamentation, is a poetry based on this perception, unable to move away from it.[22] To complain is to recognise the nature of the world as it is; it is not the egotism of the 'culture of complaint'. It is the predicament in which the present-day subject is called to exist: it can do no more than write, while knowing the impossibility of changing anything. To complain, then, becomes a heroism because it is marked by impossibility. In Cresseid's Complaint, after addressing herself as other for the first four stanzas, calling herself 'Cresseid' in the second line (408), she speaks as 'I' for three stanzas, about her voice, her singing, or her 'port':

> Now is deformit the figour of my face;
> To luik on it na leid now lyking hes. (448-9)

In the last two stanzas she addresses other women, telling them to make a mirror of her – the point recalls Langland - as she also says that she is to be an 'exempill' (465); presenting herself as an image, or an allegory:

> O ladyis fair of Troy and Grece, attend
> My miserie, quhilk nane may comprehend,
> My friuoll fortoun, my infelicitie,
> My greit mischeif, quhilk na man can amend.
> Be war in tyme, approchis neir the end,
> And in your mynd ane mirrour mak of me:
> As I am now, peraduenture that ye
> For all your micht may cum to that same end,
> Or ellis war, gif ony war may be. (452-60)

She is the mirror, the speculum that warns. R. Howard Bloch finds antifeminism 'peculiarly attracted' to medieval allegory, and amplifies this from a comment that 'the discourse of misogyny,

---

[21]   On this representation, see *Saturn and Melancholy* and Erwin Panofsky, *The Life and Art of Albrecht Dürer* (Princeton: Princeton University Press, 1955), pp. 156-171.

[22]   See Richard Danson Brown, *'The New Poet': Novelty and Tradition in Spenser's Complaints* (Liverpool: Liverpool University Press, 1999), pp. 23-30 for a summary of the 'complaint' tradition up to the 1590s.

which represents an attempt to speak of the other through the voice
of the other, is so closely allied with allegory, the literary form or
register whose very name implies "speaking other"'.[23] Allegory
enables a scapegoating of certain unacceptable emotions or states
(including femininity) within the subject or within the community
onto a single figure who becomes an allegory of those qualities.
These, however, must be visualised, as by the representation of them
as bodily sickness. A quality held to be unacceptable (such as
promiscuity) becomes disgusting, by being characterised as leprous.
As it highlights by its existence as allegory the idea that such
disgusting states exist, so it creates, within the subject itself, the
existence of qualities which can then be marginalized.

While the writing denies its melancholia, in its protestations of
humanity and humane judging, the contagion of melancholy spreads
and cannot be contained by Cresseid. When Troylus sees Cresseid,
unable to see the plurality in her, which makes it impossible to
reduce her to what personification allegory implies, he throws gifts:

> Than raid away an not ane word he spak,
> *Pensiwe* in hart, quhill he come to the toun,
> And for greit *cair* oft syis almaist fell doun. (523-5, my emphasis)

He too has become melancholic: youth has been affected with the
character of 'a man of age'; the word 'cair' returns to the narrator's
description of his 'dite' at the beginning. The 'mother of all
pensiveness' has reached him making him unable to read the image.
The northern wind at the beginning is said to have 'purifyit the air'
(17), in the context of a text whose subject is infection, but there is
more impurity around towards the end than at the beginning.

V - SYPHILIS

Dwelling on the gods - degraded from their presentation in *The
Knight's Tale* - and on leprosy, the poem seems disposed to lay aside
the body altogether. There is nothing analogous here to Bahktin's
'ever unfinished, ever creating body', as happens with the medieval
mystics such as Margery Kempe (who embraced and kissed female
lepers), where the body is 'not a closed, completed unit; it is
unfinished, outgrows itself, transgresses its own limits' and 'the
stress is laid on those parts of the body through which the world
enters the body, or emerges from it, or through which the body itself
goes out to meet the world'.[24] (Saturn's dripping nose will be

---

[23] R. Howard Bloch, *Medieval Misogyny and the Invention of Western Romantic
Love* (Chicago: University of Chicago Press, 1991), pp. 7, 201.
[24] Mikhail Bakhtin, *Rabelais and his World*, trans. by Helen Iswolsky
(Bloomington: Indiana University Press, 1985), p. 26.

remembered as the abject contrast to this.) Rather, the text stresses the materiality of leprosy by reference to fifteenth century cultural practices. Cresseid's 'spittail hous' is in a liminal position, in a village outside the town (Henryson's Dumferline). Roberta Gilchrist has drawn attention to *leprosariae* in England being placed at parish boundaries. It is not just that the leper is excluded, but – Gilchrist uses Mary Douglas – the fear of pollution was, perhaps, used to protect boundaries.[25] The presence of the lazar-house, as of the leper in the public road where such as Troylus could pass by, meant that the leper had a necessary place in society, her place outside it guaranteeing the city's purity, by being at the border, the abject place. The place of Cresseid outside the town at the end replicates the place of the prostitute, as in Chaucer's Southwark,[26] so much so that Cresseid's leprosy, which acts also as an allegory of the state of prostitution, draws attention to the place of prostitution in society. But these cultural practices are situated on the very edge of European modernity, which is the moment where Foucault starts to read, in *Histoire de la folie*, when he opens by saying that 'at the end of the Middle Ages, leprosy disappeared from the Western world'.[27]

For Foucault, the disappearance of leprosy means its power of signification has been lost. This signifying power is replaced by madness as the basis for social exclusion. The public display of the subject's corrupt body in leprosy becomes something else, the subject whose madness declares that the individual, a private subject, is marked by interiority. The sixteenth century anatomizes the corpse, opening up its secrets, like Hamlet wanting to show his mother a 'glass where you may see the inner part of you'.[28] That probing is

---

[25] Roberta Gilchrist, 'Medieval Bodies in the Material World: Gender, Stigma and the Body', in Sarah Kay and Miri Rubin, eds., *Framing Medieval Bodies* (Manchester: Manchester University Press, 1994), pp. 47-49.

[26] See Henry Ansgar Kelly, 'Bishop, Prioress, and Bawd in the Stews of Southwark', *Speculum* 75 (2000), 342-388. Further analysis of the status of prostitution in the late Middle Ages appears in Ruth Mazo Karras, *Common Women: Prostitution and Sexuality in Medieval England* (Oxford: Oxford University Press, 1996).

[27] Michel Foucault, *Madness and Civilization: A History of Insanity in the Age of Reason* trans. Richard Howard (London: Tavistock, 1967), p. 3.

[28] *Hamlet* III.iv. lines 18-19. Herbert Grabes, *The Mutable Glass: Mirror Imagery in Titles and Texts of the Middle Ages and Early Renaissance*, trans. by Gordon Collier (Cambridge: Cambridge University Press, 1982), pp. 230-34 indicates the overlap of the titles using the word "A Mirror for ..." and "An Anatomy of ...". The word "anatomy" is first cited, as meaning the science of bodily structure, in 1381; it seems first cited in 1540 as applied to the dissected body. Compare the appearance of Vesalius's *De Corporis Fabrica* in 1543. The anatomies in the Danse Macrabre, as with Holbein (first published 1538) are pre-Vesalian. On the medieval mirror, see Sister Rita Mary Bradley,

already evident in *The Testament of Cresseid*, where the heroine speaks of her reduction to becoming a 'corps and carioun' (577). Physical leprosy includes an inwardly subjective state of melancholia, and so the possibility of madness. Leprosy did not die out, for Fox refers to leprosy cases preserved in the Scottish public records for the sixteenth century, but Foucault's point holds, that leprosy lost significance.[29]

Fox, like others, regards Cresseid's leprosy as the image of venereal disease. A new discourse of disease emerged in the 1490s. In 1496, Dürer produced a woodcut, 'The Syphilitic', illustrating a broadsheet, written in Latin verse, by the physician of Nuremberg, Dr Ulsenius. It shows a knight bowed down by the pox, a vernacular term that flourished for the new disease. (The OED gives 1503 for the first citation of 'the French pox'). Above the knight's head appear the astrological constellation of Saturn and Jupiter in Scorpio (25 November 1494): a cause of syphilis.[30] Sander Gilman, who refers to this image – and who keeps to the terminology of "syphilis" when describing the "new" contagion of the 1490s – also shows the illustration to a broadside prayer of around 1500, where a melancholic sits in the depressive position that Dürer would make classic. He suffers from the pox, which afflicts him like the sores on

---

'Backgrounds of the Title *Speculum* in Medieval Literature', *Speculum* 29 (1954), 100-115.

[29] See Fox pp. 24-25. For the accuracy of this, see Peter Richards, *The Medieval Leper and his Northern Heirs* (Cambridge: D.S. Brewer, 1977), especially chapter 9, 'The Rise and Fall of the Disease' (pp. 83-97). The first leper hospital in England opened before 1089; there were 200 hospitals in the thirteenth and fourteenth centuries, but a substantial decline happened thereafter. For *The Testament of Cresseid* see pp. 6-8. See also Saul Nathaniel Brody, *The Disease of the Soul: Leprosy in Medieval Literature* (Ithaca: Cornell University Press, 1974). Penelope Doob, *Nebuchadnezzar's Children: Conventions of Madness in Medieval English Literature* (New Haven: Yale University Press, 1974), p. 2 connects perceptions of leprosy with sin. On Cresseid's leprosy and leprosy in Scotland, see Marshall W. Stearns, 'Robert Henryson and the Leper Cresseid', *Modern Language Notes* 59 (1944), 265-9, and Johnstone Parr, 'Cresseid's Leprosy Again', *Modern Language Notes* 60 (1945), 487-491. For leprosy in art, see William B. Ober, who points out the paucity of representations of leprosy in the Renaissance, in 'Can the Leper Change His Spots? The Iconography of Leprosy', pts 1 and 2, *American Journal of Dermatopathology* 5 (1983), no. 1 pp. 43-58, no. 2 pp. 173-186.

[30] See Fedja Anzelewsky, *Dürer: His Art and Life* (London: Gordon Fraser, 1982), p. 92. For the appearance of the 'Spanish pox' (so Dunbar) in Scotland, see the notes to his poem 'To the Quene' (line 30) in James Kinsley, ed., *The Poems of William Dunbar* (Oxford: Clarendon Press, 1979), pp. 306-8 (no. 30 in Bawcutt's edition). Kinsley notes that 'this cantagius seiknes' was the subject of legislation in 1497: that those infected should assemble on Leith sands for transportation to Inchkeith in the Firth of Forth.

the skin of Job. The male's symbolic capital is increased by his suffering; Gilman argues that not until the Enlightenment does the woman become illustrated as the exemplary figure of the pox, when she appears as the carrier.[31] This reinforces what is original in Henryson, for a woman is melancholic, and suffers from the pox.

It is usually considered that *The Testament of Cresseid* appeared before 1495, the date which Fox gives for the first definite mention in Scotland of syphilis, then called the French disease, the *morbus gallicus*.[32] Fox quotes the view, though doubting it, that syphilis in Europe was older than the colonization of America, which is the moment and the place generally felt to be its point of origin for European countries. But epistemic breaks cannot be worked out through dates. Some of the recent research on the great pox makes it clear that modern syphilis, a disease which is read through germ-theories of infectious diseases, cannot be compared with the disease of the end of the fifteenth century, also called syphilis. Two historians of medicine, Roger French and Jon Arrizabalaga, state flatly, 'we cannot hope to identify the French pox with a modern disease'.[33] These researchers decline to say whether the disease which spiralled into such prominence at the end of the fifteenth century was pre-Columbian or not.[34] A date of writing prior to 1490 is retainable

---

[31] Sander Gilman, *Disease and Representation: Images of Illness from Madness to AIDS* (Ithaca: Cornell University Press, 1988), pp. 248-57. With reference to Dürer's image of 1496, Gilman argues that the scorpion was the sign of perverse sexuality (p. 311), and finds in the picture the sufferer constructed as 'visually recognisable by his signs and symptoms, and sexually deviant' (p. 250).

[32] See Claude Quétel, *History of Syphilis*, trans. by Judith Bradock and Brian Pike (Oxford: Polity Press, 1990), who indicates how syphilis was first thought of as a leprosy (p. 43) and was identified with Saturn's influence (p. 34). Its ascription to the Americas seems to have been made some thirty years after 1492.

[33] 'Coping with French Diseases: University Practitioners's Strategies and Tactics in the Transmission from the Fifteenth to the Sixteenth Centuries', in Roger French, Jon Arrizabalaga, Andrew Cunningham and Luis Garcia-Ballester, eds., *Medicine From the Black Death to the French Disease* (Aldershot: Ashgate, 1998), p. 254. It becomes evident (see p. 266, from the question whether the French disease was the elephantiasis of Galen) that part of the controversy over the disease, which the authors refuse to call syphilis, was whether it was new or not.

[34] Jon Arrizabalaga, John Henderson and Roger French, *The Great Pox: The French Disease in Renaissance Europe* (New Haven: Yale University Press, 1997), p. 16. A recent piece appearing in the London *Guardian* (31 May 2001) said: 'A girl's bones dating back to the middle ages appear to disprove the theory that Christopher Columbus brought syphilis to Europe, researchers for English Heritage said yesterday. The bones, from a churchyard at Rivenhall, Essex, show traces of the disease and have been dated to between 1295 and 1445. Columbus discovered America in 1492'.

for *The Testament of Cresseid*, which sees evidences in it of an anxiety associated with the arrival of a new contagion, whose symptoms were there before. The crisis is not a new disease but a new construction of disease. This, in individualizing attention onto the subject of disease, the patient, would be partly constitutive of a modernity beyond the medieval. The text becomes then, an unconscious evidence of, and the construction of a crisis, and the attempt to deal with it by objectifying it in relation to the woman, the feminine. The evidence of this textual tendency appears a century later, when leper-hospitals had become places to treat the French disease. Pistol, in *King Henry V* (1599) tells Nym that he cannot marry Mistress Quickly, and says to him: 'to the spital go / And from the powdering-tub of infamy / Fetch forth the lazar kite of Cressid's kind'.[35] The woman he means is Doll Tearsheet. Henryson's text seems to have led to Cresseid being diminished to a single image, an infected bawd in a leper-hospital. She has been condemned twice. If this text were purely of the Middle Ages, she would simply have been a leper. If the text was purely early modern, she would be a syphilitic in whatever sense the word had then. Registering a crisis brought on by the new, the text calls her a leper, while on the evidence of the readings of the sixteenth-century, it becomes evident that it means also at least the newer form of disease.

In the Complaint, *The Testament of Cresseid* returns to Chaucer for an older world-view, to contrast it with this new one, centred in the leper-hospital, place of the birth of the clinic, place for dealing with the pox. The point is repressed from the text, and displaced onto the *ubi sunt* motifs of the Complaint which register a nostalgia for a Medieval formation and mode of thought which has disappeared:

> Quhair is thy garding with thir greissis gay
> And fresche flowris, quhilk the quene Floray
> Had paintit plesandly in euerie pane,
> Quhair thou was wont full merilye in May
> To walk and tak the dew be it was day,
> And heir the merle and mawis mony ane
> With ladyis fair in carrolling to gane
> And se the royall rinkis in thair ray,
> In garmentis gay garnischit on euerie grane? (425-433)

From the *hortus conclusus* to the excluded subject in a dark corner of a hospital - Cresseid's nostalgia is for a lost youth: recalling the

---

[35]   Shakespeare, *King Henry V* II.i, lines 74-6; ed. J.H. Walter (London: Methuen, 1954), p. 34. For the prevalence of syphilis in Shakespeare, often referred to still as leprosy, see Greg W. Bentley, *Shakespeare and the New Disease: The Dramatic Function of Syphilis in ' Troilus and Cressida', 'Measure for Measure' and 'Timon of Athens'* (New York: Peter Lang, 1989).

description of Jupiter (170), it is for a figure she can no longer identify with. Perhaps it implies the narrator's nostalgia, for the garden of courtly romance excluded Old Age.[36] It implies the end of a particular form of allegory signalled in 'the quene Floray', and such non-individuating terms as are implied in this description – 'gay' (repeated), 'fresche', 'faire,' 'royall'. The loss of a readable equivalence between the signifier and the signified may be what is indicated in passing from leprosy as a master-discourse of disease to the 'French disease'. The latter disease is not so easily identifiable nor separable from in terms of excluding the other, and works more like allegory in pulling down apparent, surface, established meanings.

As though in prosopopoeia, Henryson makes Cresseid in the last two verses of her Complaint, speak to other women as though she were the dead addressing the living, creating in them the same melancholia that is in herself. As the speculum that edifies by example, an allegory, Cresseid is part of the dance of the dead, that fifteenth-century form where the dead and the living are in continuity with each other, and the dead mirror the living.[37] In the beginning of the Complaint, she named herself and evoked an imagined past, so creating an autobiography, centred on the device of the proper name and its uniqueness. As with modern autobiography, it is all spoken as if from the standpoint of death, from a life that is finished. For Fox says of her warnings to the living, that 'it is usually a corpse who is made to speak this way', and he adds, in a way which has implications for the use of the mirror as image, that 'she is both the warner and the warned: both the *memento mori* and the young person who is taught mortality by being made to consider the *memento mori*' (pp. 44, 45). He compares Henryson's 'The Deid Pollis', where the heads of three dead corpses address the living, from the standpoint of the anonymity of the dead, and also the old man as the mirror of mortality in 'The Ressoning Betuix Age and Yowth'. In Henryson's "The Ressoning Betuix Deth and Man," Death (Mors) begins a debate by addressing Man:

---

[36]   C.S. Lewis, *The Allegory of Love* (Oxford: Oxford University Press, 1938), p. 126, using *Le Roman de la Rose* lines 339-406.

[37]   For the dance of death, see J.M. Clark, *The Dance of Death in the Middle Ages and Renaissance* (Glasgow: University of Glasgow Press, 1950); Philippe Ariès, *The Hour of our Death* (New York: Knopf, 1981), pp. 116-118 (and pp. 110-132 for the 'macabre', and for his argument that fifteenth century 'images of death and destruction do not signify fear of death or of the beyond ... they are the sign of a passionate love for this world and a painful awareness of the failure to which each human life is condemned' (p. 130). My reading of *The Testament* suggests a more depressed attitude.

> O mortall man, behald, tak tent to me,
> Quhilk sall thi myrrour be baith day and nycht [...]

and, mirror-like, Man (Homo) begins his side in the following stanza by asking:

> Now quhat art thow that biddis me thus tak tent
> And mak ane myrrour day and nycht of the [...]

Here, the mirror is a *memento mori*. Cresseid has become like that: a death's head.

The excluded body returns as the corpse; Cresseid's 'corps and carioun' (577). Though that does not quite account for everything in her, since in a final splitting from her body her spirit will walk with Diana 'in waist woddis and wellis' (588), nonetheless, 'sen scho is deid I speik of her no moir' (616). No more can be said; the body is beyond the power of symbolization, though it is still to be penetrated by phallic toads; the text forces it into representation.

VI – BALDUNG

There seems little erotic in the death of Cresseid. A comparison could be made with Hans Baldung (c.1484-1541), an artist trained in Dürer's studio, and mentioned in chapter 2 in relation to the figures of death and the knight, parallel to Dürer's *The Knight, Death and the Devil*. Baldung's work comprises several studies of the woman and of death: as with *The Three Ages of Life and Death* (Vienna, 1509-10) and *Maiden, with Death Pursuing* (Florence,) and *Death and Maiden* (Basel, 1517), and *Death and the Woman* (Basel, 1518-20) and *Eve, the Serpent and Death as Adam* (Ottawa) and the *Stages of Human Life and Death* (Madrid, 1544). In the first of these, the young woman looks in her mirror, ignoring the hourglass that the dead figure holds up to her. In the second, the hourglass is capped by a clock which gives the hour of twelve, 'dead midnight' and death holds the woman's lower arm in his left hand, while bringing his right, holding the hourglass, under the same arm, so that the two seem to be in a dance together. In the third and fourth, death grasps the woman; by the hair in the third, while pointing to the ground; more erotically in the fourth, his mouth biting into her cheek, while her garments are coming off her lower half, as though equating the grave-clothes being put on with garments being taken off. In the fifth, Eve looks lasciviously at Adam, who is a figure of death, bound to the tree by the snake, who wrapped twice around it, bites into his arm. And in the last, a young woman on the left is pulled by an old woman in the centre. Her left arm has death's right arm passed under it, and death holds in that right hand an hourglass with a clock with no hands above it, as though it was a sacrament. An owl below

165

looks at the spectator as though pensive, with the melancholy of wisdom and the wisdom of melancholy, and there is a dead child to the right in the lower foreground. Henryson's art moves in the same area of thought as does the slightly later Baldung, but it is interesting to see that with him, there is no allegorization of death in relation to this woman.[38]

In each of Baldung's pictures, an erotic desire for the woman (Eve, Venus) is a desire for death, and there is an erotic attraction in seeing the woman as dying, perhaps as the victim of the sexual disease of Dürer's woodcut, or through childbirth. Or the woman and the dead figure, who may be a revenant, a figure violently cut off, may be the same, mirrors of each other. In the first picture, *The Three Ages of Life*, and Death, the boy hides away from the vision of death and the old woman tries to push him away (but the 'him' is problematic, for death here is not gendered), so that death, which pulls at the veil which goes round the pudendum of the woman and which the boy holds to conceal himself or look through, is in this way connected to the young woman, while he ignores the old woman (as the old man in *The Pardoner's Tale* cannot die). Removing the veil is the work of melancholy; if death supports the veil, as Koerner says, that is the work of allegory.[39] In the second picture, *Maiden with Death Pursuing*, the eyes of death are wide open and staring; those of the woman shut. Her virtual nakedness versus his (or hers, for again the gender is indecisive), makes the two mirrors of each other. Death is in possession of the woman in the third picture, swinging her round to his right, towards an open grave, while in the fourth picture, he seems to have come upon her unawares. The picture of Eve and Adam fuses the temptation to eat with death; it literalizes the warning of God 'in the day that thou eatest thereof, thou shalt surely die' (Genesis 2.17). The woman who holds an apple is death to the man. Death as male - for Adam / Death also has an apple - is the destruction of the woman. Two images of the male become one: life and death.

In Blanchot's *récit, Arrêt de mort*, which was discussed in relation to *Piers Plowman*, the mutuality of life and death are stressed, and

---

[38]   For these paintings, see Gert von der Osten, *Hans Baldung Grien: Gemälde und Documente* (Berlin: Verein für Kunstwissen, 1983), plates 10,24,44,48 and 54 and 7b. See also James H. Marrow and Alan Shestack, eds., *Hans Baldung Grien: Prints and Drawings* (New Haven: Yale University Art Gallery, 1981) essay by Charles W. Talbot, pp. 36-37; Karl S. Guthke, *The Gender of Death: A Cultural History in Art and Literature* (Cambridge: Cambridge University Press, 1999), pp. 95-104.

[39]   Joseph Leo Koerner, *The Moment of Self-Portraiture in German Renaissance Art* (Chicago: Chicago University Press, 1993), p. 309. This is a decisive discussion of Baldung.

166

Derrida's neologism: 'life death' was cited. In a later *récit*, *L'instant de ma mort* (1994), written fifty years after an apparently autobiographical episode where Blanchot was put before a Nazi firing squad and then accidentally released, making the rest of his life 'l'instant de ma mort désormais toujours en instance' (the moment of my death always in abeyance), he speaks of a double power of death: 'Comme si la mort hors de lui ne pouvait désormais que se heurter à la mort en lui. "Je suis vivant. Non, tu es mort"'. [As if the death outside him henceforth could do nothing but collide with the death in him. 'I am living. No, you are dead'.][40] This later narrative 'explains' perhaps the idea of an arrest of death, which Baldung shows graphically, and which despite the absence of death outside Cresseid is Henryson's theme. A life before being arrested by death (compare Emily Dickinson's poem: 'Because I could not stop for death / He kindly stopped for me') produces a new sense 'henceforth' of two deaths: outside, and inside, where the accidents of death outside meet a sense of death within, and death as structuring life. In Baldung, such a mutuality is made more complex by the investment in the woman as erotic, and so as objectified; her death in life realised by the approach from behind of Adam who is the double of death but also her double. But the complexity of what the woman is, even in Baldung, makes it difficult to read an absolute difference between the moment that he portrays and that Blanchot memorializes.

VII - THE CORPSE

Joseph Koerner quotes from Blanchot, 'At first sight, the image does not resemble a cadaver, but it could be that the strangeness of the cadaver is the strangeness of the image'.[41] The image is nothing natural; to portray death at all is an act of catachresis; and the appearance of death in representation, then, indicates the non-natural - allegorical - nature of the image. Death is an image and a meta-image. And Koerner prompts another thought: that the appearance of the cadaver as an allegory of death at the very time when portraiture is becoming so crucial - Dürer's self-portrait is 1500, a foundational moment for a foundational conception indeed - that 'the instant of my death' may be 'the moment of self-portraiture'. To learn what the subject is means learning death. There may be little distinction

---

[40] Maurice Blanchot, *The Instant of My Death* and Jacques Derrida, *Demeure: Fiction and Testimony*, trans. by Elizabeth Rottenberg (Stanford: Stanford University Press, 2000), pp. 10, 8. My translations of Blanchot.

[41] Maurice Blanchot, 'Two Versions of the Imaginary', *The Gaze of Orpheus and Other Literary Essays*, trans. by Lydia Davis (New York: Station Hill, 1981), p. 81.

between the portrait of the living and the dead: the latter being the corpse.

This thought about the corpse articulates with Benjamin. As Cresseid's Complaint finishes, she embodies death, which is her truth, as in Baldung. Since Henryson's Cresseid has always been considered from the standpoint of a dead body, her testament returns her to the state from which the text began, so that the model for the text may be that sixteenth-century form which works on the dead body: anatomy. If everything in the text – the leprosy, the melancholy, the grotesque condition into which Cresseid is brought - finds its final image in the corpse, then the corpse is indeed 'the pre-eminent emblematic property' (Benjamin, p. 218). The ultimate husk, ruin, or shard, it cannot be used as a symbol, for it cannot be idealized, but speaks of the emptying out of meaning, from which no meaning, including the values of the narrator, is likely to escape. Empty in itself, it has no residue of meaning, or signified, attached to it, and the toads that penetrate it intensify the sense that the destructive character is at work, breaking down further any system of thought. In Kristeva, 'the corpse, seen without God and outside science, is the utmost of abjection. It is death infecting life' (*Powers of Horror* 4). She carries her analysis of the dead body as silencing commentary to its furthest in her analysis of Holbein's picture of 1522, 'The Body of the Dead Christ in the Tomb' which she reads as produced out of a melancholia which can only see and read literally. She sees such a portrayal as an attempt to portray a state of 'severance', the opposite of desire, reflecting a will towards 'utmost sobriety and austerity [...] a mastery of harmony and measure'.[42] The single image of the corpse implies, in the narrative of the poem, finality and definiteness, the resolution of what is felt about the woman, but it also indicates that everything is evacuated of meaning that the narrator set out to represent. This bringing to nothing is the part of a death-drive within the text.

Empty in itself, Benjamin implies that the corpse as allegorical can be re-allegorized. This may be hinted at through another figure of the macabre that appeared in the fifteenth-century: the *transi* tomb. Here the vile body is presented as emaciated and shrivelled; however, as a double image, the *transi* tomb shows both the recumbent dead figure (the 'representacion de la mort'), as the object eaten by worms, or as the skeleton, or as a figure wrapped in a shroud, with above this statuary, another of the blessed soul in

---

[42] Julia Kristeva, *Black Sun: Depression and Melancholia*, trans. by Leon Roudiez (New York: Columbia University Press, 1989), p. 136.

paradise (the 'representacion au vif').[43] These two representations are metonyms, existing in contiguity and separable; they are not metaphors for each other, they do not make a single image. Juxtaposed, the figures of the *transi* tomb point out a plurality in ways of seeing. Like Mors, and Homo, they mirror each other, but not as signifier and signified. The *transi* tomb means the addition of the destructive element, beyond the idealization of the body in heaven; as such it points to the destruction of any idealization. As in that other element of Baroque imagery, the skull, what appears here is the ending of a meaning that can be read from the surface. But the image that is above, of the soul in Paradise, is still an image. It does not get away from the fixing power of images. Though the medieval world could pair pictures of Christ dead and Christ in resurrection, that does not mean that the medieval had a more 'optimistic' view of death than secular modernity.[44] An image of resurrection is still overcoded by the unconscious thought that the strangeness of the image is because it is dead, and that like the cadaver its fate is to lose significance.

Though the text ends with the closure of 'I speik of her no moir', confirming the supremacy of the tomb, the corpse means that even that subject-position, of the 'I' who can speak, is threatened. For as Benjamin argues, at the end of *The Origin of German Tragic Drama*, 'in all mourning there is a tendency to silence' (Benjamin, p. 224). The one who mourns is not just Cresseid, but the narrator whose move towards an ending shows a single-minded drive to lament not only the woman's loss, but the loss of his semi-assured position. In Cresseid's narrative appears his own allegory, in her image his own.

---

[43] For the *transi* tomb, see Erwin Panofsky, *Tomb Sculpture: Its Changing Aspects from Ancient Egypt to Bernini* (London: Thames and Hudson, 1964), pp. 63-66. Panofsky quotes example of a mayor from Straubing (Lower Bavaria) who died in 1482, showing 'an almost skeletonized cadaver [...] violently attacked by vermin [...] and addressing [in inscription] the beholder as follows: "Sum speculum vitae, Johannes Gmainer, et rite / Tales vos eritis, fueram quandoque quod estis" [In me behold the looking-glass of life / Such you will be, for I was what you are]'. See also Ariès, pp. 113-4. See also Kathleen Cohen, *Metamorphoses of a Death Symbol: The Transi Tomb in the late Middle Ages and the Renaissance* (Berkeley: University of California Press, 1977).

[44] This is to disagree with Gregg M. Horowitz, *Sustaining Loss: Art and Mournful Life* (Stanford: Stanford University Press, 2001), p. 2, that 'for every dead Christ in the history of art there is a Christ resurrected [...] the image of the dead Christ is only one joint of the great Christian narrative of death and rebirth'.

CHAPTER 6

Signs of the Apocalypse: Shakespeare's *Henry VI*

> And this great king that doth divide his land,
> And change the course of his descending crown,
> And yields the reign into his children's hand,
> From blissful state of joy and great renown,
> A mirror shall become to princes all,
> To learn to shun the cause of such a fall.[1]

> Base Fortune, now I see that in thy wheel
> There is a point to which when men aspire
> They tumble headlong down. That point I touched,
> And, seeing there was no place to mount up further,
> Why should I grieve at my declining fall?[2]

> Where is thy husband now? Where be thy brothers?
> Where are thy two sons? Wherein dost thou joy?
> Who sues and kneels, and says, 'God save the Queen?'
> Where be the bending peers that flatter'd thee?
> Where be the thronging troops that follow'd thee? [...]
> Thus hath the course of justice whirl'd about
> And left thee but a very prey to time[3]

> 'Tis thought the king is dead. We will not stay.
> The bay trees in our country are all withered,
> And meteors fright the fixed stars of heaven;
> The pale-faced moon looks bloody on the earth,
> And lean-looked prophets whisper fearful change;
> Rich men look sad, and ruffians dance and leap,

---

[1] Thomas Sackville and Thomas Norton, *Gorboduc or Ferrex and Porrex*, ed. by Irby B. Cauthen, jr. (Lincoln: University of Nebraska Press, 1970), I.ii, 388-393. The play is datable to 1561.

[2] *Edward II* V.6.59-63, in David Bevington and Eric Rasmussen, eds., *Christopher Marlowe: Doctor Faustus and Other Plays* (Oxford: Oxford University Press, 1995). I have also taken quotations from *Tamburlaine* (written c. 1587-8, published 1590) from this edition. See also *Edward II* in *The Complete Works of Christopher Marlowe*, ed. by Richard Rowland (Oxford: Clarendon Press, 1994). Rowland assumes a date of 1592 for this play; Charles R. Forker, in his edition for the Revels plays (Manchester: Manchester University Press, 1994) assumes 1591, and pushes back the three *Henry VI* plays accordingly, arguing that *Edward II* was influenced by them.

[3] Shakespeare, *Richard III* ed. Antony Hammond (Arden Shakespeare, London: Methuen, 1981), IV.iv.92-96, 105-106. *Richard III* exists in eight quartos, the first 1597 and the last 1634, as well as the Folio, and the dual presence of the Quarto and the Folio presents problems in itself. The Arden edition dates *Richard III* to 1591 alongside the *HVI* plays and thinks that it and they influenced *Edward II*. The New Cambridge edition, ed. by Janis Lull (1999) is inclined to agree, dating the play between 1588 and 1593. The Cambridge edition of the First Quarto, ed. by Peter Davison (1996) makes the Quarto a memorial reconstruction of the play for and by actors on tour. (I have also used the old Cambridge edition, edited by J. Dover Wilson (1961). None of these seems satisfactory, and it is not to elevate the old style to find dumbing down taking place in the New.)

The one in fear to lose what they enjoy,
The other to enjoy by rage and war.
These signs foretell the death or fall of kings.[4]

I - APOCALYPSE

I move towards the end with the three parts of *Henry VI*, and, in the Conclusion, a coda on *Richard III*.[5] These texts demonstrate how

---

[4]   Shakespeare, *Richard II*, ed. Charles R. Forker (London: Thomson, 2002) II.iv.9-15. Forker dates the play to 1595.

[5]   I refer to these plays as solely Shakespeare's, perhaps for inadequate reasons, and follow the text of the Arden editions edited by Andrew S. Cairncross (1957-1964). The New Cambridge edition edited by Michael Hattaway (1990-1993) refines this and agrees in giving the plays a single authorship, but the New Arden (part 1 edited by Edward Burns, 2000, part 2 by Ronald Knowles 1999) and part 3 by John D. Cox and Eric Rasmussen, 2001) does not, nor, predictably, does the Oxford Shakespeare (part 3 edited by Randall Martin, 2001). (I have drawn freely on all these editions.) The difficulties focus on the apparent newness of part I, relative to points 2 and 3. It was mentioned by Henslowe on March 3 1592, while part 3 was well known enough for Greene to cite it before his death at the beginning of September 1592, while the plague had closed theatres from June 23 to December. From this, and the existence of parts 2 and 3 in quarto form (1594 and 1595) it has been assumed that parts 2 and 3 were written first (note the quarto title of part 2: *The First Part of the Contention betwixt the Two Famous Houses of Yorke and Lancaster*). Dover Wilson argued that if part 2 was subsequent in writing to part 1 it would have contained a reference to Talbot. The topicality of Talbot appears in Thomas Nashe's *Pierce Penniless* of 8 August 1592. One view that seems to emerge is that part 1 was subsequent to parts 2 and 3 and used multiple authors, and was added to complete the cycle of the two other plays. Part-authorship would be necessary to explain the intense growth in the writing which takes place between parts 1 to 3, but could not explain the sense of thematic development which takes place throughout the three. Cairncross's and the old Arden editions seem of their period in their standpoints: the older taking a more 'new critical' stance, the newer Arden and Oxford a position which fragments the author and sees establishing a single text as an impossibility. Hattaway argues for a difference between the time of writing and of production and following E. J. A. Honigmann, assigns part 1 to 1589-91, following the second edition of Holinshed in 1587; and thinks of the whole sequence completed before March 1592, with the quartos as a condensation of the plays for performance perhaps outside London. This assumes that the first part was staged by Lord Strange's men at the Rose in 1592, and the other toured with a related company, Lord Pembroke's (referred to in the Quarto title for the third play, called *The True Tragedie of Richard Duke of Yorke*). Pembroke's men also performed *Edward II*, it appears. The sympathies in my account are with Hattaway, but every issue seems mired in uncertainty.

One source of irritation with the newer editions is their constant referencing of and endorsing contemporary productions especially the Royal Shakespeare. Emphasis on 'how it was done' in the modern theatre trivializes and is uncritical. While highlighting those aspects which give a fallacious sense of the plays' accessibility and contemporaneity, they take up a position which disallows the function of criticism. These editions assume that the plays can

medieval interests continue into the first works of Shakespeare and making them analogous to *Trauerspiel*. The epigraphs given indicate how much medieval themes of the mirror, of *ubi sunt* and *de casibus* tragedy and lamentation remained active within the history-plays of the beginning of the 1590s, that dramatic form apparently initiated by Shakespeare.[6] Here, the medieval lives on but in a self-reflexive state, and it has its rhetoric commented on.[7] And the plays are supplemented by something else seen in the epitaphs, the apocalyptic, though that strain was also to be found in the medieval, and was discussed with Langland.

In 1498, there appeared in book-form Dürer's woodcuts, illustrating the Apocalypse appeared in book-form. The volume, with the title *Apocalypsis cum figuris* was 'the first book conceived, illustrated and published by an artist'. The first book, then, portrays the last book. Its illustration of the Four Horsemen of the Apocalypse (Revelation chapter 6) has been credited as the one which has done most to modify the meaning of *apokalypsis* from 'revelation' to 'impending doom'.[8] 'Catastrophe' is noted by the OED as appearing first in Spenser, in 1579; however, it is a new word; it is used only four times by Shakespeare. But if it does not appear in the *Henry VI* plays, the sense of an impending fall does.

What is apocalyptic discourse? Derrida, in an essay entitled 'On a Newly Arisen Apocalyptic Tone in Philosophy', begins by noting that the Greek *apocalypsis*, [unveiling] renders, in the Greek translation of the Hebrew text, the Septuagint, the Hebrew 'gala', which has a similar sense. It does not imply the language of 'fearsome catastrophe' but rather of 'contemplation'.[9] Derrida discusses a

---

now be brought to stage presence, and I assume that it may be better for readers to contest that.

[6] See Forker, *Edward II* p. 18. See also the dating of *King John*, which E.A.J. Honigmann (London: Methuen, 1954) gives 1590/91 (pp. xix, lviii) before the anonymous *The Troublesome Raigne of Iohn King of England* which was first published in 1591. (Before that play was John Bale's *King John*, a morality c.1540.) The more usual dating is 1596; see Stanley Wells and Gary Taylor, eds, *William Shakespeare: A Textual Companion* (Oxford: Clarendon, 1987), pp. 317-8.

[7] The classic reading of Shakespeare's histories in the light of *The Mirror for Magistrates* (by William Baldwin, first published in 1559, and added to in 1563, 1578 and 1587) is by E.M.W. Tillyard, *Shakespeare's History Play* (1944; Harmondsworth: Penguin, 1962). See also Irving Ribner, *The English History Play in the Age of Shakespeare* (London: Methuen, 1965).

[8] Walter L. Strauss, ed., *Albrecht Dürer: Woodcuts and Woodblocks* (New York: Abaris Books, 1980), p. 153, and p. 186.

[9] In *Raising the Tone of Philosophy: Late Essays by Immanuel Kant, Transformative Critique by Jacques Derrida*, ed. by Peter Fenves

polemic by Kant with the English title 'On a Newly Arisen Superior Tone in Philosophy'. Kant critiques those philosophers who see truth in intuitional terms, rather than as a matter of public demonstration, and who 'pervert the voice of reason by mixing the two voices of the other in us: the voice of reason and the voice of the oracle' (130). Philosophy, for Kant, has 'no power to give orders' (130) - that is, to interfere, to become political; it must repress the voice of the oracle. Something of the debate between philosophy and literature appears here: Derrida might be seen by philosophers as one of those who take a superior tone since he insists that deconstruction always implies a political intervention, is even something oracular. Kant identifies those who adopt such a tone as wishing to unveil the sacred goddess of wisdom in a drive to reveal absolute truth. This act of disclosure is read as a desire to bring about the end and Derrida turns to 'discourses of the end' so prevalent now (the 'end of history', the 'end of art', the 'end of man' discourses), instancing Heidegger, who 'says of thought, here distinct from philosophy, that it is essentially "eschatological"' (146). So,

> whoever takes on the apocalyptic tone comes to signify to you, if not tell you something. What? The truth, of course, and to signify to you that it reveals the truth to you; tone is revelatory of some unveiling in process. Unveiling, or truth, apophantics of the imminence of the end, of whatever comes down, finally, to the end of the world. (151)

Derrida shows that in the Biblical Apocalypse, there are many letters sent and messengers (angels) flying, and a number of modes of writing - mixed modes - so that something strange emerges in apocalyptic writing: the indeterminacy of sender and receiver that goes beyond 'a distinct and calculable plurality' so that 'as soon as one no longer knows who speaks or who writes, the text becomes apocalyptic' (156). The issue of 'truth' is taken away as soon as stated; the apocalyptic, far from unveiling truth, presents the reader with more text. A recent study, *The Apocalypse in English Renaissance Thought and Literature* begins by noting that 'an important characteristic of apocalypses is the "bookish" nature of the revealed message. In several cases the revelation was originally contained in written tablets or books; in others, the seer's obligation to write the message down is noted'.[10] Derrida could be glossing that:

(Baltimore: Johns Hopkins University Press, 1993), p. 120. Further references in the text.

[10] Bernard McGinn, in C.A. Patrides and Joseph Wittreich, eds., *The Apocalypse in English Renaissance Thought and Literature* (Manchester: Manchester University Press, 1984), p. 5. See in this volume Joseph Wittreich, '"Image of that Horror": Apocalypse in *King Lear*', pp. 175-206.

> And if the *envois* always refer to other *envois* without decidable destination, the destination remaining to come, then isn't this completely angelic structure, that of the Johannine apocalypse, isn't it also the structure of every scene of writing in general? (156)

The apocalyptic becomes not an exception within discourse, but a feature within writing itself. It announces truth and unveiling, but defers, or delays that within itself; implying a single truth it pluralizes the message. Derrida refers to the prevalence of apocalyptic writing within periods of censorship to say that 'it is a challenge to the established receivability of messages and to the policing of destination, in short, to the postal police or the monopoly of posts' (160). Here, it may be noted, in parenthesis, that in Shakespeare's time, the one book of the New Testament not read in Anglican churches during the course of the year was Revelation.[11] The increase of information within printing in the sixteenth century illustrates the link between apocalyptic thinking and what Derrida calls 'dissemination'. Dürer's illustrations link the apocalypse theme to the development of print; his woodcuts circulated widely before becoming part of a Bible (1511), and the Apocalypse series gave him international status.[12] A print-revolution, which destroys control of information, produces urgency and violent disorder, and alternative forms of thought. At the time, the sixteenth century was seen as giving a fulfilment of what was said to Daniel when the angel said 'shut up the words, and seal the book, even to the time of the end: many shall run to and fro and knowledge shall be increased' (Daniel 12.4).The contents of the printing revolution may announce the apocalypse to the sixteenth century, but perhaps the dissemination of information *was* the sixteenth century apocalypse. And 'dissemination' implies that the study of any moment could never deliver a decidable message, or one that could be decoded in terms of some truth, but that its value would be an increase in terms of possibilities of thought which would go outside all the coded forms of discourse allowed by the given subject.

The apocalyptic is both revelation and destruction. Malcolm Bull defines the apocalyptic as an unveiling, as a revelation of what has been excluded from thought, as 'the reincorporation of excluded

---

[11] Helen Morris, 'Shakespeare and Dürer's Apocalypse', *Shakespeare Studies* 4 (1968), 253.

[12] For print, see Andrew Cunningham and Ole Peter Grell, *The Four Horsemen of the Apocalypse: Religion, War, Famine and Death in Reformation Europe* (Cambridge: Cambridge University Press, 2000), pp. 16-18. The thesis of this book seems weak: that the apocalyptic period which the authors take as the 1490s to 1648 (p. 11) was marked out by an objective rise in the numbers of wars, famine and disease and by a crisis in religion: those things symbolised in the four horsemen.

contradiction',[13] which means that the possibility of thinking in binary opposites has gone. He refers to Julia Kristeva's *Powers of Horror* on the violent exclusion of otherness within the subject which is contained through the power of the taboo which Kristeva calls:

> [a] facet of religious, moral and ideological codes on which rest the sleep of individuals and the breathing spells of societies. Such codes are abjection's purification and repression. But the return of their repressed makes up our 'apocalypse'.

In the same paragraph Kristeva discusses 'the veil of the communitarian mystery'. The apocalypse unveils what has been radically excluded. Apocalyptic discourse, then, reintroduces the heterogeneous. Enlightenment history may seem to lead towards the Hegelian 'totality', proceeding on the basis that history displays rationality. Kant's anxiety about 'tone' however, indicates that rational statements conceal something, that a totality could only be a repressive structure. Revealing that repression, the apocalyptic is the opposite of the 'end of history' and gives not the sense of order framing everything but "the frame of disorder'.[14] Since the apocalyptic works against the totality, it aligns itself with the allegorical, which does the same: as Benjamin puts it, in allegory 'the false appearance of totality is extinguished' (*Origin* 176). Allegorical thinking is different from thinking the totality, its interest in the fragment as other is fascination with the heterogeneous; what is excluded in totalizing systems of thought, while its obsession with the past is opposite to a thought of progress. Malcolm Bull associates the anti-totality strain in twentieth-century critical thinking with its 'anti-ocularism'; both the dominant regime of vision and the thought of totality exclude the hidden. Apocalypse which is an unveiling, and allegory which is a veiling and therefore a deferral of meaning, may be similar, in that neither work to set up a single truth.

---

[13] Malcolm Bull, *Seeing Things Hidden: Apocalypse, Vision and Totality* (London: Verso, 1999), p. 100.

[14] The title of Philip Brockbank's discussion of the plays, *On Shakespeare* (Oxford: Blackwell, 1989). Another excellent account of the plays appears in A.C. Hamilton, *The Early Shakespeare* (San Marino: The Huntingdon Library 1967). See also John D. Cox, *Shakespeare and the Dramaturgy of Power* (Princeton: Princeton University Press, 1989), pp. 82-103, and E. Pearlman, 'The Invention of Richard of Gloucester', *Shakespeare Quarterly* 43 (1992), 410-29, and Ian Frederick Moulton, '"A Monster Great Deformed": The Unruly Masculinity of Richard III', *Shakespeare Quarterly* 47 (1996), 251-68. As recent discussion of the plays has proliferated, like productions, see Thomas A. Pendleton, ed., *Henry VI: Critical Essays* (London: Routledge, 2001) and the bibliography there.

Henry VI part 1 begins with the funeral of Henry the Fifth and the line 'Hung be the heavens with black, yield, day to night'. Bedford's initial words have made the stage a church and the world a stage with the heavens hung with black curtains. If the ending of a tragedy evokes the apocalypse, what *King Lear* calls 'the promised end', this play, first of three - or perhaps four - in terms of chronology, begins there; because it implies that another play has already finished. Lamenting over a dead body, Bedford desires apocalypse and night, and his prophecy looks straight towards the weeping queens of *Richard III*:

> Posterity, await for wretched years,
> When at their mothers' moist eyes babes shall suck,
> Our isle be made a nourish of salt tears,
> And none but women left to wail the dead. (48-51)

The commitment to the apocalyptic is towards the new, which will be 'wretched years', marked out by 'massacre', which is heard of in this scene (I.i.135), and was then a new word (the OED cites 1586 for its first use), implying a new scale of slaughter and indiscriminate destruction which is also apocalyptic.[15] The apocalyptic also opens the way to civil war and disorder, as part of the lifting of taboos, and however destructive, it is also productive of heterogeneity, if it is assumed that order is repressive. So 'fear frames disorder' as young Clifford says before seeing the dead body of his father, which makes his melancholia the 'destructive character', which also turns towards the apocalyptic:

> O! let the vile world end
> And the premised flames of the last day
> Knit earth and heaven together;
> Now let the general trumpet blow his blast,
> Particularities and petty sounds
> To cease [...].
> [...]   Even at this sight
> My heart is turn'd to stone: and while 'tis mine
> It shall be stony [...].   (V.ii. 40-45, 48-50)

The desire for the apocalyptic is for the end of distinction, which is the ultimate in disorder, and the end of feeling. But nothing ceases:

---

[15] The word reappears at II.ii.18 (see below) and V.iv. 160 when Alencon is proposing to Charles a truce which can be broken, 'to save your subjects from such massacre / And ruthless slaughters as are daily seen [...]' - as if the word summed up the events of the play. It appears twice in *Richard III* (II.iv.53, IV.iii.2) and twice in *Titus Andronicus* (1594 in performance; but its writing could go back as far as to 1588) and only once later, in *I Henry IV*. Marlowe's *The Massacre at Paris* seems to have been performed by the Lord Strange's men at the Rose in January 1592/3, after *I Henry VI*.

another play is yet to come, like another trumpet-blast, and there will be no clarification and resolution.

Clifford's words compare with the lament of Spencer in *Edward II* after the king's arrest, when he has been betrayed by the gloomy 'mower', the figure of Death[16]:

> O is he gone! Is noble Edward gone,
> Parted from hence, never to see us more?
> Rend, sphere of heaven, and fire forsake thy orb,
> Earth melt to air! Gone is my sovereign,
> Gone, gone, alas, never to make return. (IV.vii.99-103)

This complaint, which envisages fragmentation, was cited by Wolfgang Clemen as part of the 'note of lamentation [that] resounds throughout the whole of pre-Shakespearian [and Shakespearian] tragedy'. As *Gorboduc* has as its music for the third act, flutes, and for its fourth, hautboys, both intensifying mourning, and then for its fifth act, drums and flutes - giving the combination of arms and weeping in civil war - these plays may be aligned to *Trauerspiel*, as mourning-plays, while the mourning is also apocalyptic in character.[17]

The first part ends with Joan La Pucelle led off to death and by the semi-comedy of Suffolk's engineering Henry's marriage to Margaret while wooing her for himself. The play fulfils Malcolm Bull's definition of an apocalyptic plot. In the non-apocalyptic, 'endings resolve the unbearable uncertainty that has earlier been created by the narrative. But apocalyptic texts describe a world that grows ever more confusing and may culminate in a new world that is quite unlike the old'.[18] That is true of each of the three plays of the trilogy, though not quite with *Richard III*, even if it is not possible in that play to identify with Richmond, or to feel that the play's resolution is unqualified, or that it has settled accounts with injustice. In each of the three plays, the ending resolves nothing but induces a more extraordinary play next time. The end of *3 Henry VI*, ending with an apparent peace and an unsuitable marriage, replays the end of *1*

---

[16] Forker, *Edward II*, p. 262 quotes the OED on this as the first time 'gloomy' is applied to a person. On the emblematic significance of this scene, see David Bevington and James Shapiro, '"What are Kings when Regiment is Gone?": The Decay of Ceremony in *Edward II*', in Kenneth Friedenreich, Roma Gill and Constance B. Kuriyama, *A Poet and a Filthy Play-maker: New Essays on Christopher Marlowe* (New York: AMS Press, 1988), pp. 263-278.

[17] Wolfgang Clemen, *English Tragedy Before Shakespeare: The Development of Dramatic Speech*, trans. by T.S. Dorsch (London: Methuen, 1961), p. 214; see pp. 211-286 for Clemen's discussion, including this speech and that of Clifford's.

[18] Malcolm Bull, *Seeing Things Hidden: Apocalypse, Vision and Totality* (London: Verso, 1999), p. 84.

Henry VI in a more convoluted manner. The plays begin asserting difference: England / France; blue coats / tawny coats, white rose / red, and showing that difference can exist. By the third play, civil war means that differentiation has broken down to a point where it is impossible to identify people since their names are those of places, and it is not clear whether people with place-names in part 3 are the same, or on the same side, as the people who existed in part 1. As the war enters a second generation stage (York is killed and his sons replace him), so people change sides, further destroying distinctions. And the breakdown in narrative chronology is part of the same issue, for the apocalypse includes within it the words of the angel that 'there should be time no longer' (Revelation 10.6).

The centre of part 2 is the death of Lydgate's patron, Gloucester, who anticipates his murder by the other lords with a comment on these post-mortem times. Beginning with balanced allegorical abstractions, he then names his accusers (Beaufort, Suffolk and Bukingham):

> Virtue is chok'd with foul Ambition,
> And Charity chas'd hence by Rancour's hand;
> Foul Subornation is predominant,
> And Equity exil'd your Highness' land,
> I know their complot is to have my life;
> And if my death might make this island happy,
> And prove the period of their tyranny,
> I would expend it with all willingness.
> But mine is made the prologue to their play;
> For thousands more, that yet suspect no peril,
> Will not conclude their plotted tragedy.
> Beaufort's red sparkling eyes blab his heart's malice [...]. (2.III.i.143-154)

Their 'complot' will produce his death in their 'play', which is their 'plotted tragedy', and which does not mean the death of just one person - even though Warwick calls Gloucester's death a 'tragedy' (2.III.ii.193). Tragedy now envisages the thousands who will die; it has no 'period': indeed, in part 1, Warwick has prophesied - prophecy being part of the apocalyptic - that the 'brawl' between the Red and the White Rose will send 'a thousand souls to death and deadly night' (1.II.iv.127). This is not lament: he rather seems to want such an end, for he has just plucked the white rose himself. The speech of Warwick is echoed, only a little after Gloucester's words, by York: 'I will stir up in England some black storm / Shall blow ten thousand souls to heaven, or hell' (2. III.i.349-50). The storm is Jack Cade's rebellion, which runs through Act IV, and it is only the beginning of things: Henry continues the point when prophesying of Richard of Gloucester, who follows on from his father, that 'many a thousand' will 'rue the hour that ever thou wast born' (3. V.vi.37, 43).

II - POST-MORTEM STATES

The revelation also unveils what lies beyond death, the post-mortem state. For Exeter at the funeral of Henry the Fifth:

> Henry is dead and never shall revive.
> Upon a wooden coffin we attend;
> And death's dishonourable victory
> We with our stately presence glorify,
> Like captives bound to a triumphant car. (1.I. i. 18-22)

The triumph of death modifies the nostalgic praise of Henry that 'he ne'er lifted up his hand but conquered' (I.i.16). At no point in the scene is a direction given for the funeral car to go offstage; it seems to be an interrupted ceremony, like two other scenes of ceremony in *1Henry VI*, the openings of Acts III and IV; but perhaps here it means that this funeral can never come to an end: its implications persist. So, in I.iv, the firing of cannon at Orleans kills Sir Thomas Gargrave outright, and wounds fatally the Earl of Salisbury. Talbot, recalling that Salisbury trained Henry the Fifth to the wars, calls the event 'this woeful tragedy' (76). The tragedy includes the ending of that chivalric order which gunpowder displaces. A dead march follows for Salisbury (II.ii) as if placing that death inside Henry's funeral, just as Talbot has just carried out a 'bloody massacre' of the French (II.ii.18). At the end of Act II dies 'the dusky torch of Mortimer', who was brought in sick in a chair; in Act III.ii, Bedford in his turn appears sick in a chair, and dies, but not before Joan La Pucelle has asked if he will 'run a tilt at Death within a chair?' (III.ii.51). Talbot's elegy at the end of the scene has to ensure that the funeral of Bedford will not be forgotten. At the end of Act IV.vi, Talbot and his son go off to fight, but Talbot is brought on, wounded, 'led' by a servant in the following scene, like the blinded Gloucester in *King Lear*, while the body of his son is brought onto the stage a moment later. Talbot apostrophizes 'antic Death, which laugh'st us here to scorn' (IV.i.18) and dies cradling his son (IV.vii.32), so evoking the comment of Burgundy, 'See where he [the son] lies inhearsed in the arms / Of the most bloody nurser of his harms' (IV.vii. 45-46). The English soldier Lucy gives a full epitaph of Talbot's titles, but Joan la Pucelle reduces all this with 'Him that thou magnifiest with all these titles / Stinking and fly-blown lies here at our feet' (IV.vii.75-76). The body is no more than the corpse, and to show that is the spirit of *Trauerspiel*. But then, no more is the state anything but a state of living death, imaged here in a speech by Exeter in terms that evoke the 'representacion de la mort' in the transi tomb:

> This late dissension grown betwixt the peers
> Burns under the feigned ashes of forg'd love,
> And will at last break out into a flame;
> As fester'd members rot but by degree
> Till bones and flesh and sinews fall away,
> So will this base and envious discord breed. (III. i. 189-194)

In *2 Henry VI*, Gloucester is literally, probably, choked by foul ambition, and Henry responds by saying that now he will find 'in life but double death, now Gloucester's dead' (III.ii.54). That life is death already increases the apocalyptic awareness which is inseparable from a sense of being posthumous. Later, Henry says on viewing the body, which is shown with apocalyptic force, when the bed-curtains are pulled back – 'seeing him, I see my life in death' (III.ii.151). That is, he sees his life in a state of death: it is as if he looks at his own dead body. Gloucester's body is an allegory of him: he too will be murdered. The statement means 'I see my life as dead'; for the dead body is the allegorical object, which produces the melancholic vision that characterises Henry. That melancholy, in a comparable moment in a later play, *Richard II* marks Richard when he is thinking about the murder of kings. In the speech which I quote, it will be seen that Richard's face is destined to become that of the other, i.e. death. That is, the king's body becomes an allegory of something other than the king:

> For within the hollow crown
> That rounds the mortal temples of a king
> Keeps Death his court, and there the antic sits,
> Scoffing his state and grinning at his pomp,
> Allowing him a breath, a little scene,
> To monarchise, be feared and kill with looks,
> Infusing him with self and vain conceit,
> As if this flesh which walls about our life
> Were brass impregnable; and humoured thus,
> Comes at the last, and with a little pin,
> Bores though his castle wall, and farewell, king!
> (*Richard II* III.ii.160-170)

The king is brought down by the 'antic' – that which speaks of madness, and which is also the other. But in 1-3 *Henry VI*, the king is also the antic. The point seals the link between the king, as the absolute image, and death.

III - ALLEGORY

The First Part, in Act V scene 3, sees a symmetry, where York captures Joan la Pucelle, followed by Suffolk capturing Margaret of Anjou. Perhaps the same actor played both women; for Joan's curses on York, which produce his fearful but fascinated reaction, 'Fell banning hag, enchantress, hold thy tongue' (1.V.iii.42) segue into the next two plays, haunting him with the power of the feminine and perhaps maddening him in a way which relates to the death-drive that he ultimately suffers from (see below). The woman who will kill him, Margaret, doubly 'other' in being French and in being female, appears straight after, but it is not the end of Joan, for she reappears for a last scene in V.iv.1-91, so that if the same actor did play both parts, the sense of the double identity of Margaret could only have received reinforcement thereby. York's words as Joan goes to be burned – 'Break thou in pieces and consume to ashes / Thou foul accursed minister of hell' (V.iv.92-3) only invites the thought that this *sparagmos* will breed something worse in the future and something worse rise from out the holocaust.

Margaret generates in Henry sexual feelings which make him self-conflictual, so much so that he draws on Exeter's word 'dissension' to describe the civil war within him:

> I feel such sharp dissension in my breast
> Such fierce alarums both of hope and fear,
> As I am sick with working of my thoughts. (1.V.v.84-86)

This splitting reappears in part 3, in the battle of Towton, whose ferocity, historically, may have given Malory a context for the last battle between Arthur and Mordred.[19] Henry withdraws to sit on a molehill and is followed by the son who has killed his father. Henry bids him mourn, saying he will aid him, 'And let our hearts and eyes, like civil war, / Be blind with tears and break o'ercharged with grief' (3.II.v.77-8). Division of the body into hearts and eyes and the division between the two are explained as the effects of 'civil war' - a term which came into currency in the mid sixteenth century. Hearts and eyes produce a chiasmus which divides, then joins in the next line: the eyes are blind with tears and the hearts break. Civil war produces a bodily division which replicates the father/son division in the scene. Hearts and eyes work against the rest of the body; the eyes blind the body, the heart breaks it. That is another aspect of the comparison with the civil war; but isolating eyes and hearts which are doing the same thing (grieving) and separating them both from each other - which the chiasmus reinforces - and from the body, is characteristic of allegory. As when Hoccleve personifies Thought, allegorical qualities divide. Allegory expresses a state of civil war, correspondent to madness. Whereas Gloucester's abstract allegorical terms were opposites, now eyes and heart are seen to be doing the

---

19   See P. J. C. Field, 'Malory and the Battle of Towton', in D. Thomas Hanks, jr, *The Social and Literary Contexts of Malory's Morte Darthur* (Cambridge: D.S. Brewer, 2000), pp. 68-74. The battle, fought on Palm Sunday 1461, killed between 28,000 and 38,000 people.

same thing, but oppositionally (as the son has killed the father and the father the son). Civil war can now make no distinction. Allegory now names qualities that can have no separate meaning, as the allegorical roses, distinctive and distinguishing in Part 1, have virtually disappeared by part 3.

IV - MELANCHOLY

Henry comments in part 1 on the outbreak of the York / Lancaster dispute, 'what madness rules in brainsick men' (IV.i.111) before showing his own lack of reason in taking the red rose for himself, thus showing himself to be part of a party, not a figure of unification. In part 2, Richard of York styles himself a 'madman' (III.i.347), and says there will be no cessation to the 'fury of this mad-bred flaw' (354), till he is crowned. After Gloucester's death, Beaufort, Bishop of Winchester and Cardinal is 'discovered' in his bed, mad, and that is another apocalyptic state, in that it presses beyond all behavioural taboos. His madness makes him blab his guilt, while the scene plays on the *ars moriendi* and the dance of the dead motifs in revealing to the Cardinal the face of death, which he identifies with Henry's face in the line: 'If thou be'est death, I'll give thee England's treasure [...]' (III.iii.2). But then, Henry *is* a figure of death: that is what kingship, as a form of absoluteness and otherness, means in these plays.

The face - the death's head - becomes Winchester's own, so that Warwick says of him: 'See how the pangs of death do make him grin' (24). Engaging with otherness in his madness, the Cardinal also fantasises that the ghost of Gloucester, that which is beyond death, has appeared to him. It is a post-mortem moment and a melancholic and apocalyptic state all at once.

Winchester's death in 'black despair' (23) is succeeded by a fight at sea. The triumphant lieutenant, who holds Suffolk as prisoner, begins a speech which by reference to Gloucester's speech and the word 'blabbing' alludes unconsciously to Winchester's death:

> The gaudy, blabbing and remorseful day
> Is crept into the bosom of the sea,
> And now loud-howling wolves arouse the jades
> That drag the tragic melancholy night;
> Who with their drowsy, slow and flagging wings
> Clip dead men's graves, and from their misty jaws
> Breathe foul contagious darkness in the air. (IV.i. 1-7)

There seems to be a continued move towards black (compare 'melancholy') night, which is tragic, and the source of a sluggish melancholia (note 'drag') which induces melancholia in others as well as the sense of being haunted.

182

But melancholia has started earlier. The centre of *2 Henry VI*, is the death of Gloucester, the melancholy man, who was seen in mourning before the time in Act II.iv.[20] Eleanor, his wife asks him at the beginning of the play 'Why droops my lord', referring to him 'hanging the head', and to his brows which are 'knit' 'as frowning at the favours of the world' and to his eyes 'fixed to the sullen earth / Gazing at that which seems to dim thy sight' (I.ii.1-7). As the Viceroy who falls to the ground in *The Spanish Tragedy* says, the earth is the 'image of melancholy' (I.iii.300). That explains Gloucester's action, and it also anticipates Richard II sitting on the ground. 'The downward gaze is characteristic of the Saturnine man' writes Benjamin (*Origin*, p. 152). Further, hanging the head picks up from a stage direction in *IHVI*.V.iii, when Joan la Pucelle invokes the spirits to help France 'get the field', but the fiends 'walk and speak not' and then 'they hang their heads' before shaking them and departing. Benjamin says that 'the image of the court is not so different from the image of hell, which is, after all, known as the place of eternal mournfulness' (144).

The play illustrates the king's inability to act: but such a phenomenon is not unique to him. Richard, Duke of York, who has already shown some diffidence in allowing Henry to reign throughout his lifetime so long as the succession then passes to York (I.i), dies not because he cannot get away but because he gives up:

> Ah hark! the fatal followers do pursue,
> And I am faint and cannot fly their fury;
> And were I strong I would not shun their fury.
> The sands are number'd that makes up my life;
> Here must I stay and here my life must end. (3.i.iv.22-26)

and when Margaret, young Clifford and Northumberland and the young Prince enter, he invites them: 'I dare your quenchless fury [the third use of fury in that scene] to more rage. / I am your butt and I abide your shot' (I.iv.29-29).

When Benjamin refers to the downward gaze, his argument associates indecision with *acedia*, melancholia as sloth, and he says that 'the fall of the tyrant is caused by indolence of the heart' (156). The phrase associates with what he writes in the 'Theses on the Philosophy of History' discussing historicism as possible only when historians have blotted out everything they know of the later course of history. 'It is a process of empathy whose origin is the indolence of the heart, *acedia*, which despairs of grasping and holding the genuine historical image as it flares up briefly. Among medieval

---

[20] Compare the mourning in 3.II.i.161, and in *Edward II* I.iv.305 and III.i, 'Enter Gaveston mourning'.

theologians it was regarded as the root cause of sadness'. Historicists empathize 'with the victor. And all victors are the heirs of those who conquered before them. Hence empathy with the victor invariably benefits the rulers'.[21] *Acedia* as discussed in the *Trauerspiel* book is 'comparable in kind to the bite of a mad dog, for whoever is bitten by the same is immediately assailed by horrible dreams, he is terrified in his sleep, becomes enraged and senseless, rejects all drink, is afraid of water, barks like a dog, and becomes so fearful that he falls down in terror. Such men die very soon if they receive no help'.[22] In this alliance of melancholia and madness appears a process of phantasmatic fear followed by a decline into inaction which cannot be recovered from. This seems to be, in differing modes, the fate of Joan, and of Richard of York and his son Richard III, while descent into madness is the fate of Winchester. What is interesting in each of these deaths is a reflectiveness on the part of the sufferer that is missing in the deaths of Talbot, or Suffolk, or even Warwick in the battle of Barnet.

The main figure of indecision in the plays is Henry. The king is impotent when faced with the son that has killed his father and the father that has killed his son. Something of this emerges in his soliloquy seated on the molehill (which aligns him with York, enthroned on a molehill by the Lancastrians before he is killed), thrown out of the battle by his wife and son, doomed to see neither again. Turning, like York, to the idea of numbering, he thinks it were a happy life 'to be no better than a homely swain', while his sitting down parodies the idea of kingship and shows the king as little better than a madman, who calls the sheep 'fools' as if their character (dumb, having no logos) parallels him:

> To sit upon a hill, as I do now,
> To carve out dials quaintly, point by point,
> Thereby to see the minutes how they run -
> How many makes the hour full complete,
> How many hours brings about the day,
> How many days will finish up the year,
> How many years a mortal man may live.
> When this is known, thus to divide the times -
> So many hours must I tend my flock;
> So many hours must I take my rest;
> So many hours must I contemplate;
> So many hours must I sport myself [...].
> So minutes, hours, weeks, months and years,

---

[21] Walter Benjamin, *Illuminations*, trans. by Harry Zohn (London: Jonathan Cape, 1970), p. 258.

[22] *Origin*, p.152 quotes Aegidius Albertinus, whom Benjamin calls 'the Munich didacticist' (144), from his *Lucifers Königreich und Seelengejäidt* [1612], p.156.

Pass'd over to the end they were created,
Would bring white hairs unto a quiet grave. (II.v. 23-40)

The interest is in division: dividing existence up being characteristic of the allegorical disposition which works by soliloquy. If he could know his period of life, that would mean that he was already past death; in the light of that he could divide up the time he has to wait for death. Henry's melancholia as one who sees his life in death, from the standpoint of death, is the spirit of *acedia*: 'so many hours *must I* tend my flock' shows the unwillingness to act; a fascination with clock time and with time as repetition and with each activity as empty, carried out as a meaningless ritual. The hope is nihilistic, to become a 'timely-parted ghost' (*2HVI.* III.ii. 160), whereas Gloucester's death was 'timeless' (III.ii. 186), untimely, or interrupting a sense of time, having no time since time assumes orderly progression and murder is outside time, has no time. Henry's division of the times makes no room for that which cannot be put into 'so many hours'. So too, York seems to have settled with himself that his time has finished *before* he is killed. In both Lancastrian and Yorkist, a failure associates them with a melancholia which is nostalgic, as Henry hollowly views the shepherd's life to be preferable to a king's. It is an idealizing view, suggestive of being held by a different form of fear from that of the war.

In Benjamin's 'Theses on the Philosophy of History', 'the concept of the historical progress of mankind cannot be sundered from the concept of its progression though a homogeneous empty time' (263). So 'A critique of the concept of such a progression must be the basis of any criticism of the concept of progress itself' (*Illuminations* 263). The concept of progress is Hegelian: Enlightenment, non-apocalyptic.[23] The phrase 'homogeneous, empty time' runs through Benjamin's writings on history; Benjamin says that until the instantiation of such a concept of time, the notion of progress could not be thought.[24] 'Empty homogeneous time' seems to be Henry's

---

[23] 'World history is the progress in the consciousness of freedom - a progress that we must come to know in its necessity', G. W. F. Hegel 'Introduction', in *The Philosophy of History*, trans. by J. Sibree (New York: Dover Publications 1956), p.19.

[24] Yet it may be argued that 'progress' itself is tainted by thought of the apocalypse. If Löwith is right, then Enlightenment thought is the repression of apocalyptic thought. Karl Löwith in *Meaning in History*, 'philosophy of history originates with the Hebrew and Christian faith in a fulfilment, and [...] it ends with the secularization of its eschatological pattern' (Chicago 1949, p.2). His view was contested by Hans Blumenberg in *The Legitimacy of the Modern Age* which is a defence of progress as not dependent on a prior rhetoric of Christian eschatology. Yet even Blumenberg says that this rhetoric, because of what he calls 'poverty of words' appears in the structuring of ideas

concept too, and to be non-apocalyptic; he only alters his perception of time when he prophesies at the moment of his murder. To accept 'homogeneous, empty time', which means not thinking in terms of discontinuities, is *acedia*, denying the possibility of the alternative - the idea of redemption of the past; it forgets history. Yet even the idea of 'progress' may be apocalyptic, based on a Christian understanding of history, as Karl Löwith argued; 'progress' is a metaphysical idea which implies the ability to read what results from the sequence of time. It is as if it is impossible not to think of history in terms which are outside history.[25] For Hegel to think in terms of progress means to think forwards towards the totality, which implies a resolution of opposites. This holism, which suppresses the heterogeneous within history, Benjamin questions as an idealizing process. The passage which follows was cited earlier, in the Introduction, but will bear repetition:

> In the field of allegorical intuition the image is a fragment, a rune. Its beauty as a symbol evaporates when the light of divine learning falls upon it. The false appearance of totality is extinguished. For the *eidos* disappears, the simile ceases to exist, and the cosmos it contained shrivels up. The dry rebuses which remain contain an insight [...] (176)

Progress is shot through with what aligns it with something else, which is opposite: 'the concept of progress should be grounded in the idea of catastrophe. That things "just keep on going" *is* the catastrophe'.[26] The catastrophe is the norm.

A history which emphasises ascent, or development, or ages of improvement becomes complicit with the catastrophe. Elsewhere Benjamin wrote that 'Marx says that revolutions are the locomotives of world history. Things are entirely different. Perhaps revolutions are the human race, who is travelling in this train, reaching for the emergency brake' (quoted, Smith 201). The catastrophe is things

---

of progress. 'The sphere of sacral language outlives that of the consecrated objects and is anxiously conserved and used as a cover precisely where philosophically, politically and scientifically new thinking is being done'. Malcolm Bull, ed., *Apocalypse Theory and the Ends of the World* (Oxford: Blackwell, 1995), p. 14, quotes this and calls it 'linguistic anachronism'. If the thought of the apocalypse is anachronistic in the modern age, which is what Blumenberg would say, the modern age is also anachronistic in that its language cannot free itself from an earlier formation, and the modern attack on anachrony partakes of anachrony.

[25] See the discussion of Löwith's position in relation to that of Hans Blumenberg by Giuseppe Tassone, *A Study on the Idea of Progress in Nietzsche, Heidegger and Critical Theory* (Lewiston: Edwin Mellen Press, 2002), pp. 9-32.

[26] Re the Theory of Knowledge, Theory of Progress', in *Benjamin: Philosophy, History, Aesthetics*, ed. by Gary Smith (Chicago: University of Chicago Press, 1983), p. 64, N9a,1. This is one of the notes for the 'Arcades' project.

continuing as they are, the train speeding on. Applying the brake is breaking with the idea of progress which even Marxism has adopted: it is the end of history. It breaks with an order of things premised on continuance in time; bringing about the untimely. This requires a violent disruption, the imposition of discontinuity. Applying the brake arrests 'the march of events' and it is the philosophy which breaks with a sense of events being linked; it argues instead for the power of the epistemological caesura interrupting historical narrative.[27]

One form of melancholia in the play is the sloth that loses the ability to think of change, accepting the hegemony of homogeneous empty time, and a history of slaughters. That sense of time contrasts with the memory of the carnival-like 'merry world' (2.IV.ii.8) which Jack Cade intends to bring back when he says that 'our enemies shall fall before us, inspir'd with the spirit of putting down kings and princes' (IV.ii.33,34). It seems then that the inspiration which makes these kings and princes fall is both carnivalesque *and* the spirit of witchcraft which has already been seen in Joan and in Eleanor of Cobham. It is both heterogeneous (we 'are in order when we are most out of order' [IV.ii.182-3]) and also melancholic.[28] The opposition to the sloth that takes over and destroys people before they die comes in those moments of anger or passion or poetry which surface: such as with Henry at the time of his death, of Clarence, in *Richard III* in the scene of his death. They point to another form of melancholy, which exists in a state of ruin, but which has not lost a sense of the possibility of another history.

V - SOLILOQUY

Listening to this play means catching many different tones and becoming aware of different intensities which are characteristically spoken in soliloquy form. The first, short, soliloquy in the First Part comes at the end of the first scene: it is the conspiratorial planning

---

27 The 'Theses on the Philosophy of History' is full of references to an emergency, or to what is also called 'a moment of danger' (257). The danger affects 'both the content of the tradition' - the archive – 'and its receivers. The same threat hangs over both: that of becoming a tool of the ruling classes'. If the tradition is taught as just that: as calm, received tradition, and not as the record of catastrophe, it affects the receivers too: and 'the tradition of the oppressed teaches us that the "state of emergency" [...] is not the exception but the rule' (259). The state of emergency as normal is of course a catastrophic situation.

28 Note the occurrences of 'decay' and 'decayed', which Cade's name allegorises: 1.I.i.34; II.v.1; 2.III.i.194; 3.IV.iv.16. There are numerous uses of the 'fall' of princes; the best is Richard's carnivalesque game with the clerics who will keep him from 'the fall of vanity' (*RIII* III.vii.96).

of Winchester. A second comes from Richard of York after the death of Mortimer (II.v) and it suits his melancholia that he should have the most in the three plays. Two soliloquies, both expressions of despair, are spoken by Exeter, a dying figure from the age of Henry V (III.i and IV.i), and the scene with Joan la Pucelle and the silent spirits (V.iii.1-28) may also be seen as a soliloquy. The only other person who speaks soliloquies is the plotter Suffolk, once at the end of V.iii and in the last few lines of the play.

In Part 2, the first scene ends with a soliloquy by York, while an alternative plotter, Hume, speaks alone at the end of I.ii. As the mood shifts away from France to England as the site of contest, III.i contains the soliloquy by York which has been quoted from already, while Cade has a prose soliloquy before his death in IV.x. Clifford's soliloquy over the body of his father in V.ii, quoted from for its desire to bring down the apocalypse, makes the near-conclusion to the play. In Part 3, York's soliloquy before his death in I.iv has been discussed. There are no more till Henry's 54-line speech on time in II.v. Clifford dies with a soliloquy in II.vi which complements his earlier one; Henry has another long soliloquy as the martyr before his arrest in III.i and Warwick speaks alone at the end of III.iii, while having a soliloquy before his death in V.ii. Richard has the last soliloquy at the end of V.vi after he has killed Henry.

These links between melancholia, soliloquy and death are pervasive, and the plotter and or intriguer stands with the tyrant and martyr in the *Trauerspiel* (*Origin* 95) while Benjamin adds that 'the gloomy note of intrigue' (97) awakens 'a mood of mourning [*Trauer*] in the creature stripped of all naive impulses' (98). Something of that appears in Richard, the son of Richard of York, and even more obsessive than his father about wanting the crown. Appearing first in the last act of Part 2, and killing Somerset, his legacy in Part 3 is to receive the title of Duke of Gloucester, which belonged to the Duke slaughtered in part 2, and whose opposite he is. The difference haunts him, as though with the power of the other. It makes him utter his only ever 'foolish' comment (3.II.vi.107-8), in trying to evade being given the title of Gloucester. How much more haunted than his father he is appears soon after in his mad and self-conflictual rhetoric which envelops him in his long soliloquy of some 71 lines (3.III.ii.124-195), where he says he 'dreams on sovereignty' and the dream becomes frustrated and irrational passion:

> Like one that stands upon a promontory,
> And spies a far-off shore where he would tread,
> Wishing his foot were equal with his eye;
> And chides the sea, that sunders him from thence,
> Saying, he'll lade it dry to have his way:
> So do I wish the crown, being far off,

> And so I chide the means that keeps me from it;
> And so I say I'll cut the causes off,
> Flattering me with impossibilities. (III.ii. 135-142)

The anger (chiding) returns in fiercer form, after he has appeared to be so clear-sighted in rejecting sexual relations as a possibility for him. To choose love would be a 'monstrous fault' - except that the monstrosity in the woman cannot be separated from his own monstrosity, which he has also commented on.[29] Despite the disavowal he may be still entangled by the sexual, that which he has disowned:

> And I - like one lost in a thorny wood,
> That rents the thorns and is rent with the thorns
> Seeking a way, and straying from the way;
> Not knowing how to find the open air,
> But toiling desperately to find it out -
> Torment myself to catch the English crown
> And from that torment I will free myself,
> Or hew my way out with a bloody axe. (III.ii.174-181)

The desire to catch the crown, which Richard first advanced in *Tamburlaine*-like terms in I.ii.28-31, is so much more restless, more manic than anything in Tamburlaine's rhetoric (*I Tamburlaine* II.vii. 18-29), perhaps because the relation of the desire to the other frustrated possibility, the sexual - cannot be owned. The word 'crown' appears seven times in this speech in total; Richard's most plain declaration is that this world is hell 'Until this misshap'd trunk, which bears this head / Be round impaled with a glorious crown' (170-171). Yet, if the body was impaled, it would be dead: the desire for the absolute single-subject position is one of death. That is true of what possession of the crown as a complete image would mean anyway: it is also true of being a king, as Henry VI knows he allegorizes death.

In the quotation about the 'thorny wood', internal division and injustice to himself ('I [...] torment myself') is marked through the use of an allegorical image which recalls Yvain's madness and desire for the wood, caused in his case by a failure in relation to the erotic. But what the wood means is obscure, not sayable, any more than Dante's *selva oscura* may be wholly interpreted. Once within the wood, Richard forgets that he is inside an image and as the 'bloody axe' implies, he literalizes what he thinks: he does not get out of allegory, as he cannot get out of the wood. The passage's word-repetitions produce the unreal choice of actions in the last two lines,

---

[29] Hattaway and the New Arden both take 'monstrous fault' to include the meaning 'unnatural vagina' - as the allegorical characterisation of the woman that would love him.

marking the split subject, who identifies the wood with other people
- or, because the axe may also be used on himself - with himself.
Richard is differentiated from his brothers but made a continuation
of his father, by a melancholia released in soliloquy-form rather than
public activity, and which might be inseparable from that new form
of expression.[30]

The word 'soliloquy' comes from Augustine's *Liber Soliloquiorum*,
one of the dialogues written at Cassiciacum in 387, a little before the
Confessions (397). In the *Confessions*, he speaks to God of 'my
discussions with those present and with myself alone before you'.[31]
Both texts, soliloquies and confessions, are ways of exploring
divisions and attempt to close the gap between the subject who writes
and the subject who is written about. The opening of the *Soliloquies*
reveals the 'I' who 'was turning over in my mind many and divers
matters' when 'all at once a voice spoke to me - whether it was
myself or another inside or outside of me I do not know, for that is
the very thing I am trying to find out. Reason therefore spoke to me
[...]'[32] and soon this allegorical Reason (*Ratio*) causes Augustine to
speak to God. The soliloquy form in Augustine is a dialogue form;
indeed Reason may represent a force in the subject which is also felt
to be external to it. Just as there is no need to think of a soliloquy
requiring nobody else to be on stage, or requiring nobody else to be
listening (as with Joan speaking to the demons) it is a mistake to
think of the person speaking in soliloquy as a single subject; two or
three subject-positions speak in dialogue form and the 'soliloquy'
dramatizes several voices within one body. Just as Augustine in the
Confessions never addresses his readers, so the soliloquy does not
come from a unified subject who is speaking to another unified
subject, the audience. Instead, it dramatizes a multiplicity of voices
within the individual, while the audience, if it is addressed, which
need not be the case, dramatizes the multitudinous voices of the
other that the individual on stage uses to try to set up some form of
identity, however partial. Marlovian drama makes one part of the

---

[30] There is no essential definition of soliloquy (a word the OED gives as c.1597),
or mode of distinguishing it from monologue (a later word): see Raymond
Williams, *Writing in Society* (London: Verso, 1983), pp. 31-64. See James
Hirsh, 'Shakespeare and the History of Soliloquies', *Modern Language
Quarterly* 58 (1997), 1-26 for the view that for Shakespeare 'soliloquies
represented speeches by characters and did not represent the thoughts of
characters' (p.1), which I accept if the split nature of the 'character' is also
accepted.

[31] Augustine, *Confessions* IX.iv.7, trans. by Henry Chadwick (Oxford: Oxford
University Press, 1991), p. 159.

[32] *Soliloquies* Book 1, ch.1, trans. by Thomas F. Gilligan OSA in *Writings of St
Augustine* vol. 1 (New York: CIMA Publishing, 1948), p. 343.

subject address another as though that was the whole – 'Settle thy studies, Faustus, and begin [...]' (*Dr Faustus* I.i.1), or sets up part of the self as an image to be admired ('Weep not for Mortimer' *Edward II* V.vi.64). The mode in the *Henry VI* plays, however, speaks of 'I' but then shows how conflictual a subject that 'I' is. 'I' is no more than an allegorical name and even that is not consistent. Thus, in Richard's soliloquy, after the image of the sea which stands between him and his desire, he says:

> My eye's too quick, my heart o'erweens too much,
> Unless my hand and strength could equal them.
> Well, say there is no kingdom then for Richard;
> What other pleasure can the world afford? (III.ii.144-174)

The first two lines are a satement yet they are indicative that what (we cannot say who) is speaking perceives divisions in what is individual (the body that cannot be divided) - in the eye, the heart, the hand. The third line invites something in the individual to say, as a proposition, 'there is no kingdom for Richard'. The name attempts to describe the self which is other than the part that speaks. The fourth line implies a counter-question, coming from somewhere else.

In the two extended images of the sea and the thorny wood (and how much more investment there is in the second image than the first), there appears the attempt to look at an imaginary self ('Like one' – 'And I, like one lost'), judging and commenting on it. But in the second comparison, with the man lost in the wood, the subject that looks on identifies with that other self: there is no return, as in the previous image to 'So do I'. He will never be out of the wood. The earlier scenes of the plays had shown the subject looking on and speaking objectively about the self as caught between allegorical abstractions, as with Henry on hope and fear, or Gloucester reflecting on the antagonisms within himself. The soliloquy form, however, goes further since it sets up a split between the self speaking and another self standing on a promontory, and who which wishes itself elsewhere, fantasising 'treading' and having its way (both sexual terms). In other words, the self imagines a subject already split. In the 'thorny wood', the observed subject is split between being *in* the wood and *being* the wood. Melancholy produces allegory because that expresses a splitting so intense that it confounds the question whether the splits are internal or external.

VI - DEFORMITY

The point about splitting appears through consideration of another line, which appears earlier in the soliloquy: 'Where sits Deformity to mock my body' (III.ii. 158). With or without the capital letter, the deformity is part of the body and outside it, mocking it. In *Richard*

191

III III.i.130-131, the boy Duke of York mocks his uncle: 'Because that I am little like an ape, / He thinks that you should bear me on your shoulders!' which allegorizes the deformity as a mocking ape that is carried by a fool, and which therefore says that the subject is not in charge of himself, but is held by something else that mocks him or apes him, that certainly constructs him and makes him a fool. And of course, we have seen that the fool is linked to death, as will also be the case in *Hamlet*: in one of Holbein's *Dance of Death* woodcuts, 'The Queen', Death appears as the jester.

As constructed in these plays, the deformity is an excess of the subject which may express what the subject is. The body, as the expression of the subject's dream of unity, is mocked by what is expressed as an allegorical part, where deformity is not neutral but means active vice (the sense it has in its first OED citation, c.1400, in Mandeville). In *Much Ado About Nothing* (c.1598) the villain Borachio calls fashion a "deformed thief" and the watchman who is listening in to what Borachio says, but who does not quite follow it, extends the allegorization into a complete subject called Deformed when he says to his companion: 'I know that Deformed; 'a has been a vile thief this seven year; 'a goes up and down like a gentleman: I remember his name'.[33] The deformity that marks out Richard does indeed thieve from him, since it - as contingent to him - becomes the whole truth of him. The character is dominated by an allegorical part when deformity becomes the symbol of moral deformity. In *Richard III*, the character who speaks of himself as 'deformed, unfinished' (I.i.20) is even more than now held by this partial image, like Hoccleve fearful that his face may betray him. Unable to 'court an amorous looking-glass', Richard can only think to 'spy my shadow in the sun / And descant on my own deformity' (I.i.15, 26-27). Similarly, Lady Anne refers to him as allegorical object, when she says 'Blush, blush, thou lump of foul deformity' (I.ii.57).

In the soliloquy in *3 Henry VI*, the dominance of the allegorical induces a sense of knowing the self to be split, and this Richard commits himself to – 'Why, I can smile, and murder whiles I smile' (182), like Chaucer's "smyler with the knyf under the cloke" (*Knight's Tale* 1999). It also brings in the sense of how much he can outdo other figures, and in the movement from fabulous images to an historical one, we will note the apocalyptic language of the repeated 'more' and the sense of the power he has to accumulate:

> I'll drown more sailors than the Mermaid shall;
> I'll slay more gazers than the basilisk,

---

[33] Shakespeare, *Much Ado About Nothing*, ed. by A.R. Humphreys (Arden Shakespeare; London, Methuen, 1981) III.ii. 121-4.

> I'll play the orator as well as Nestor;
> Deceive more slily than Ulysses could,
> And, like a Sinon, take another Troy.
> I can add colours to the chameleon,
> Change shapes with Proteus for advantages,
> And set the murderous Machiavel to school. (186-193)

Machiavel as the divider of morality from power is an instance of the split subject, accepting itself as split. But the subject who declares these abilities forgets that this 'I' is not identical with the 'I' that speaks. In his last soliloquy in the play he says:

> I have no brother, I am like no brother;
> And this word 'love', which greybeards call divine
> Be resident in men like one another,
> And not in me: I am myself alone. (V.vi.80-83)

That conclusion gives the sense that he has closed the gap between the subject who speaks and the "I" that is represented in his speech, and that may be the marker of the subject who fantasises for himself what Lacan calls 'the armour of an alienating identity',[34] whose solipsism separates him altogether from others. 'I have no brother, I am like no brother' (V.vi.80) not only denies differential relationship with others (which is the denial of a place within the symbolic order), in contrast to the fraternity that underpins *The Knight's Tale*, but also asserts a monstrosity that cannot be equalled: there can be no brother to it. Undoubtedly the subject is a victim of his own language, and it is that sense of mastery, which enables him to go below all surfaces, and yet conceals the point that he is held by something of which he is unaware, which is under his own surface, and which can therefore only be spoken of allegorically, which constitutes his melancholia.

---

[34] Jacques Lacan, *Écrits*, trans. by Alan Sheridan (London: Tavistock, 1977), p. 4.

CONCLUSION

Richard III, Mourning and Memory

I - VICE

> Prince: Is it upon record, or else reported
> Successively from age to age, he [Caesar] built it? [the Tower]
> Buckingham: Upon record, my gracious lord.
> Prince: But say, my lord, it were not register'd,
> Methinks the truth should live from age to age,
> As 'twere retailed to all posterity,
> Even to the general all-ending day.
> Richard: [*Aside*] So wise, so young, they say, do ne'er live long.
> Prince: What say you, uncle?
> Richard: I say, without characters, fame lives long.
> [*Aside*] Thus, like the formal Vice, Iniquity,
> I moralise two meanings in one word. (*Richard III* III.i.72-83)

The Vice, figure of mid-sixteenth century morality drama, moralizes,
yet he prompts people towards evil. Richard, identifying himself with
this older, 'formal' figure of the Vice, Iniquity, first cites a proverb,
'so wise, so young they say do ne'er live long' in an aside. The
proverbial form seems, then, to be subversive, overturning. He then
speaks openly: 'I say, without characters, fame lives long'. This
reverses the negative sense of the proverb. So, even without
characters (writing), even without an archive, fame lives long. Or
perhaps not: 'ne'er lives long' and 'lives long' are the 'one word'
which can go either way. The Prince thinks of fame up to the
apocalyptic moment; but whether fame lives or does not live long is
ambiguous. And the ambiguity is not in Richard's power to control,
for the fame of the boys, however character-less, and whom Richard
meant to leave unrecorded, has not died. The Vice interprets
(moralizes, he calls it, where one moralization subverts the other
moral) in dual senses - as an allegorist does.[1] He ironizes - and

---

[1]   Falstaff is the Vice in *I Henry IV* – 'that reverend vice, that grey iniquity'
(ed. by A.R. Humphreys, Arden Shakespeare, London: Methuen, 1960)
II.iv.457, and Feste the fool calls himself the Vice in Twelfth Night, ed. J.M.
Lothian and T.W. Craik (The Arden Shakespeare, London: Methuen, 1975)
IV.ii.127. The Vice appears in the morality play, such as *The Castle of
Perseverance* (c.1400-1425) or *Mankind* (c.1471);   see the discussion by
Antony Hammond in *Richard III* pp. 100-102; Hammond refers to the research
of Peter Happé, who finds the Vice's greatest popularity to have been between
1550 and 1580. See also Robert Weimann, *Shakespeare and the Popular
Tradition in the Theatre: Studies in the Social Dimension of Dramatic Form
and Function* (Baltimore: Johns Hopkins University Press, 1978) whose
discussion brings out the split nature of the allegorical figure: 'on the one
hand   he   provides   a   clowning   re-enactment   of   semiritual   sport   and
showmanship, but on the other he carries within himself an element of
homiletic condemnation, Insofar as the Vice is an allegorical manifestation of
sin, this conflict cuts through his motley being, drawing sustenance from quite
orthodox   sources: the   Psychomachia,   traditions   of   allegory   like   the   Seven

perhaps irony may be 'the trope of mourning, or rather, of the inability to mourn'.[2]

Richard at this moment in the play is separate from its events, the downstage player who speaks aside, just as he started his play with thirteen lines of commentary that showed his separation from everything in the court. His opening speech makes him both Marlovian Prologue and then principal character, like Faustus. The logic of the play, however, draws him into a position of no separation from the events in it, while the lamenting Queens become the auditors of the action and so separate from it. His solipsism virtually goes; even if the creation of the subject marked by deep interiority which separates him from others, and which is deeply melancholic or saturnine, has been at the heart of these plays. An evidence of that is a new word that appears thirteen times in *Richard III* and which associates with melancholia: conscience, a word used only six times in all of the three *Henry VI* plays.

Richard first uses 'conscience' in relation to Anne and her inability to heed it (I.ii.239). In I.iii.222, Margaret, the revenant, the voice of the past, the almost-ghost, an unreal presence in the Yorkist court where she is also the conscience of those who are Lancastrians in disguise, wishes that 'the worm of conscience' may begnaw Richard's soul. Called a 'foul wrinkled witch' (I.iii.164), she repeats upon Richard the effect that Joan la Pucelle, the witch, had had upon his father. The murderers in I.iv use 'conscience' three times, in a carnivalesque discussion of its meddling power and in the context of the Judgement Day; and Buckingham and Richard both use it in the theatrical display by which Richard becomes king (II.vii. 173, 225). The murderers of the Princes are struck by conscience (IV.iii.20) and it is used by Oxford to Richmond (V.ii.17). Finally, Richard uses it twice in his speech to his soldiers: 'Conscience is but a word that cowards use / Devis'd at first to keep the strong in awe / Or strong arms be our conscience [..]' (V.iii.310-12).

Its most striking use however is in the moment when Richard wakes from his dream, where the first three sentences are proleptic, assuming his death on the battlefield, so that he speaks then, virtually, as having come back from the dead:

Deadly Sins and contemporary sermons' (pp. 153-4). See also Bernard Spivack, *Shakespeare and the Allegory of Evil: The History of a Metaphor in Relation to his Major Villains* (New York: Columbia University Press, 1958), pp. 386-407.

[2] Peter Homans, *The Ability to Mourn: Disillusionment and the Social Origins of Psychoanalysis* (Chciago: University of Chicago Press, 1989), p. 268. Insofar as irony links to mourning, it also links to allegory - see the discussion of *Piers Plowman*.

Give me another horse! Bind up my wounds!
Have mercy, Jesu - Soft, I did but dream.
O coward conscience, how doest thou afflict me!
The lights burn blue; it is now dead midnight.
Cold, fearful drops stand on my trembling flesh.
What do I fear? Myself? There's none else by;
Richard loves Richard, that is, I and [Q1] am [Q2, F] I.
Is there a murderer here? No. Yes, I am!
Then fly. What, from myself? Great reason why,
Lest I revenge. What, myself upon myself?
Alack, I love myself. Wherefore? For any good
That I myself have done unto myself?
O no alas, I rather hate myself
For hateful deeds committed by myself.
I am a villain - yet I lie, I am not!
Fool, of thyself speak well! Fool, do not flatter.
My conscience hath a thousand several tongues,
And every tongue brings in a several tale,
And every tale condemns me for a villain:
Perjury, perjury, in the highest degree;
Murder, stern murder, in the direst degree;
All several sins, all us'd in each degree,
Throng all to the bar, crying all, 'Guilty, guilty!'
I shall despair. There is no creature loves me
And if I die, no soul will pity me -
And wherefore should they, since that I myself
Find in myself no pity to myself?
Methought the souls of all that I had murder'd
Came to my tent, and everyone did threat
Tomorrow's vengeance on the head of Richard. (V.iii.178-207)

A coward conscience produces fearful drops, hence 'what do I fear?'
The answer is: 'myself' - a word that appears twelve times in the
speech, pluralizing the subject both as it stands (my self) and then as
it becomes myself versus myself, like the plural in 'Richard loves
Richard', and in 'I am I' and in 'Fool of thyself speak well' and in
'Fool do not flatter' and in 'I myself [and how many subjects are
here?] / Find in myself [another self, objectified] no pity to myself'.
Conscience is plural: it has a thousand several tongues, like Rumour
in the Prologue to *2 Henry IV*. Conscience seems indeed, like a figure
from the *House of Fame*, bringing plural messages that overwhelm
and offer no clarity; dividing, instead, the soul, which has plural
names: I, myself, Richard (repeated three times), murderer, villain
(twice), fool.

The word 'villain' recalls another moment: 'I am determined to be
a villain' (I.i.30), but for the force of contrast, and it also recalls
both of Richard's brothers' accession of conscience. At the beginning
of the play, Edward is 'sick, weak and melancholy' (I.i.136).
Clarence's dream, another production of conscience, is ghosted in
Richard's speech. Clarence at first, in his dream, cannot drown, like

the old man in *The Pardoner's Tale* who cannot die, but when he arrives in 'the kingdom of perpetual night', his father-in-law, Warwick, asks 'What scourge for perjury / Can this dark monarchy afford false Clarence?' (I.iv.50-51). The echoes of Seneca are, like Edward's mental state, *Trauerspiel*-like. Clarence's dream of being rebuked after his death by those he had betrayed is repeated in Richard's dream of the souls he has destroyed demanding revenge on him. Even more so than Richard later, Clarence dies twice: once in dream (death by drowning) and then he wakes to drown again. Richard is caught not so much by the march of events but by something strange which appears in the ghosts on the eve of the battle of Bosworth, and which shows how what was in the past returns, threatening 'despair'. Having thought about revenge on himself (187), he finishes by speaking of apocalyptically of 'tomorrow's vengeance' as though the revenge was predestined, already a certainty.

It evokes a pattern noticeable in the play, of how people have lived through or at the least anticipated their deaths: Clarence, Hastings, who ignores warnings,[3] Buckingham, who says 'That high All-seer which I dallied with / Has turn'd my feigned prayer on my head / And given in earnest what I begg'd in jest' (V.i.22-22). Such therefore return as ghosts, figures of 'living on', but also figures of injustice suffered. The ghost of Richard III, who has lived through his death, if he could be imagined, would be an interesting addition to these. For even he, a product of the heterogeneity released in apocalyptic thinking, could be considered a victim of injustice, and a figure who has been mocked by deformity. The ghost, however, is produced by the play, one of Shakespeare's most enduring, and most susceptible to reaccentuation on stage.

II - MEMORY

Conscience is associated with memory. In the passage quoted at the opening of this chapter, the young Prince Edward wishes memory to endure as long as the future. His uncle is unconcerned with memory. The situation replicates itself in a later, more famous Shakespearian play where a Prince's obsession is that no one can remember his father's death two - certainly not four - months after it has taken place. His uncle is unconcerned, and though everyone knows the uncle's name from the list of characters, yet he is never named in the

---

[3] Compare A.P. Rossiter, *Angel with Horns: Fifteen Essays on Shakespeare*, ed. by Graham Storey (London: Longman, 1989) p. 3: 'Hastings [...] says he will see "this crown of mine hewn from its shoulders / Before I see the crown so foul misplaced" (on Richard's head) - and *does* (if a man can be said to see his own decapitation)'.

play, which means he has been reduced within it to a certain anonymity, unlike his nephew, young Hamlet. Retaining memory is analogous to becoming melancholic, but in *Hamlet* it is the absence of mourning, or what Lacan calls 'insufficient mourning',[4] because people are buried in 'hugger-mugger', with the intention that their deaths should be forgotten, that induces melancholia. Gertrude thinks that Hamlet should no longer mourn:

> Do not for ever, with thy veil'd lids,
> Seek for thy noble father in the dust.
> Thou know'st 'tis common: all that lives must die,
> Passing through nature to eternity.
> Hamlet: Ay, madam, it is common.
> Queen: If it be,
> Why seems it so particular with thee? (*Hamlet* I.ii. 70-75)

Hamlet's answer shows that even though mourning is not his only affect, and does not explain his melancholia, since 'I have that within which passeth show' (85), it cannot be stopped as easily as the Queen or King wants.

The texts studied here have each focussed on mourning: whether in Will in *Piers Plowman*, or in the complaints and the lamentings that make the image of burning dominant for *The Knight's Tale* or in the *Complaint* of Thomas Hoccleve, or the memorializations of death in *The Fall of Princes* and Cresseid's death, or the lamentations that run through the *Henry VI* triad. The *Trauerspiel* links with the *Trauerarbeit*, which implies the primacy of mourning, though it should be added here that while Freud speaks of 'normal mourning' (259) it is not so clear from 'Mourning and Melancholia' that mourning is a normal state. Freud says:

> Although mourning involves grave departures from the normal attitude to life, it never occurs to us to regard it as a pathological condition and to refer it to medical treatment. We rely on its being overcome [Derrida would link this to the 'triumph' that takes place in mourning and melancholia] after a certain lapse of time, and we look upon any interference with it as useless or even harmful.

Yet a paragraph later concludes:

> This inhibition and circumscription of the ego is the expression of an exclusive devotion to mourning which leaves nothing over for other purposes or other interests. It is really only because we know so well how to explain it that this attitude does not seem to us pathological. (252)

---

4   Jacques Lacan, 'Desire and the Interpretation of Desire in *Hamlet*', *Yale French Studies* 55/56 (1977), 39.

This is tantamount to saying that perhaps mourning may not be normal; that it needs as much explanation as the melancholia from which Freud has separated it. Perhaps it is not a separable state; perhaps it is melancholia already. That would, of course, recall the relation of *Trauerspiel* to melancholy. But why mourning exists at all remains something to be asked. Can a society be envisaged which has no mourning?[5] But that would mean the abolition of memory, of which mourning is a part. And is melancholia a part of memory then?

One reason for our mourning is made apparent in the *récit* by Blanchot, *L'instance de ma mort*, which was discussed in chapter 5 in relation to Henryson and Baldung. The man who lives on after being put in front of the firing-squad owes his survival perhaps to 'l'erreur de l'injustice' (2) - the error of injustice. He survives; three young farmers who have done nothing are shot. Survival, then, becomes contingent on injustice. The point links with another: that mourning and deconstruction seem intricately related. To quote Derrida here:

> all I have recently read and reread by Paul de Man seems to be traversed by an insistent reflection upon mourning, a meditation in which bereaved memory is deeply engraved. Funerary speech and writing do not follow upon death; they work upon life in what we call autobiography.[6]

Why should mourning and deconstruction be linked? Freud linked mourning and psychoanalysis because in the death of another is discovered the subject's ambivalence towards the one who has died, an ambivalence which psychoanalysis must work through.[7] Pyschoanalysis and deconstruction may have in common the discovery of gaps within the subject, something learned also within autobiography. As with Langland and Hoccleve and perhaps Henryson, the attempt to write 'autobiography' is attended by the sense that there is no present subject, or subject marked by presence, so that to speak about the death of another is to trace an arbitrary line wherein the distinction between the living and the dead can only be maintained through the enlargement of the single ego, which is the perpetuation of a certain injustice. Richard's conscience-stricken

---

5   Peter M. Sacks, *The English Elegy: Studies in the Genre from Spenser to Yeats* (Baltimore: Johns Hopkins University Press, 1985), p. 37 points out how the right to mourn could be related to the right to inherit: he links this with *Hamlet*.

6   Jacques Derrida, *Memoires for Paul de Man*, trans. by Cecile Lindsay, Jonathan Culler, Eduardo Cadava (New York: Columbia University Press, 1986), p. 22.

7   'What released the spirit of inquiry in man was [...] the conflict of feeling at the death of loved yet alien and hated persons' - Freud, 'Thoughts for the Times on War and Death', *The Penguin Freud* 12 (Harmondsworth: Penguin, 1985), p. 82.

speech 'Give me another horse' is the recognition of his existence as unjust where personified sins, like the ghosts, 'throng all to the bar' and declare him guilty. The perception makes him end with the chance-taking of: 'I have set my life upon a cast / And I will stand the hazard of the die' (V.iv.9, 10).

To recall the Freudian distinction between mourning and melancholia quoted in the Introduction: 'in mourning it is the world that has become poor and empty; in melancholia it is the ego itself'. This distinction turns upon the maintenance of an inside / outside dichotomy. But deconstruction, by adding to the emptiness of the world a gap, or *béance* within the subject, and so questioning the logic whereby there is an inside and outside, may imply the primacy of melancholia within mourning. Mourning, within deconstruction's understanding, may proceed from melancholia, and so cannot be taken away. And neither mourning nor melancholia may be so relevant to the past, as to the present and to the future.

III - HISTORY

Benjamin discusses Richard and the speech about the 'Vice Iniquity' (and one meaning the OED gives for 'iniquity' is 'injustice') in the *Trauerspiel* study. This is after saying that Lucifer, who is the 'ruler of deep mournfulness' is the 'original allegorical figure' (228). He quotes the view of the dramatist Julius Leopold Klein (1810-1876), that only as allegorical can Richard be understood. Richard links himself to an allegorical figure, the Vice, and behind him is another, Lucifer, whose foundational character is that of mourning.

Thinking through Benjamin, perhaps Richard as an allegory may also be linked to what Benjamin says of the hunchback. Benjamin makes this figure a clue for thinking through the distortions of history. The hunchback appears in his discussions of Kafka: he finds in Kafka's hunchbacks the figure of 'distortion' or displacement, and he finds the figure present in German folksong, such as in *Des Knaben Wunderhorn*. So, for example, 'anyone whom the little man [the hunchback] looks at pays no attention; not to himself and not to the little man. In consternation he stands before a pile of debris'.[8] That pile of debris resonates with the 'Theses on the Philosophy of History', and the perception of the 'single catastrophe which keeps piling wreckage upon wreckage and hurls it in front of [the angel of history's] face' (*Illuminations* 259). The hunchback is also at the heart of the story told at the beginning of the 'Theses on the Philosophy of History', where he activates the automaton who plays a

---

[8]   Quoted, Hannah Arendt, 'Introduction' to *Illuminations*, trans. by Harry Zohn (London: Jonathan Cape, 1970), p. 6. See the discussion of Kafka, pp. 133-4.

winning game of chess no matter what the opponent. 'Actually, a little hunchback who was an expert chess player sat inside and guided the puppet's hand by means of strings'. An interpretation of this makes the puppet to be called 'historical materialism' which wins 'if it enlists the services of theology, which [...] is wizened and has to keep out of sight' (*Illuminations* 255). Apocalyptic, revelatory, thinking reveals the hunchback; but history ignores his presence. The hunchback is the distorted other who does not appear in the historical record of progress; his part is with history as the record of things 'untimely, sorrowful, unsuccessful' (Benjamin, 166) - history as the record of injustice.

In the last of the 'Theses on the Philosophy of History', Benjamin says that the Jews were prohibited from investigating the future. 'The Torah and the prayers instruct them in remembrance, however' he writes, which is the use of history. Benjamin adds: 'This did not imply, however, that for the Jews the future turned into homogeneous empty time. For every second of time was the strait gate through which the Messiah might enter' (*Illuminations* 266). This image makes the future the utterly surprising, non-fixed. The event cannot be thought or extrapolated from the study of the past; the future cannot be comparable with any thinking about it. 'Every second of time' now has something other in it, whose reality is allegorical, as Derrida in *Spectres of Marx* sees something else, heterogeneous at work in a period which has discarded Marxism. The spectre means that Marxism haunts utterance, as, in *The Communist Manifesto* Marx spoke of a spectre (of communism) haunting Europe. Cross-referencing *The Communist Manifesto* with the opening of *Hamlet* and the spectre of the murdered king Hamlet, Derrida argues that the spectre begins the play because injustice precedes everything, and makes the time 'out of joint'. Marxism thus begins *and* lives on with the force of the spectre, which both precedes the origin and confounds time, in an example of what Derrida calls the 'trace'.[9] According to Benjamin, the historian who grasps links between the present and past adds to the present: s/he 'establishes a conception of the present as the "time of the now" ("now time" [*Jetztzeit*], opposed to "empty, homogeneous time") which is shot through with chips of messianic time' (*Illuminations* 265). The splinter, or the sliver of messianic time marks or inscribes the present moment, and adds to the possibility of the future that Benjamin speaks of.

Shakespeare's tetralogy has been read with the sense of the plays bearing something 'other' within them, such as the memory of the

---

[9] Jacques Derrida, *Spectres of Marx: The State of the Debt, the Work of Mourning, and the New International*, trans. by Peggy Kamuf (New York: Routledge, 1994), p. 22.

curse of Joan la Pucelle, or the aggression of Richard of Gloucester
(with which the curse ultimately connects), quite in excess of the
events of the plays. The otherness makes it impossible to see them as
a fluent narrative, despite their movement over a period of years
whose narrative time is 1422-1485. That revelation of something
underneath which impedes narrative, makes them apocalyptic, as
Langland and other figures discussed here are too: Henryson,
Baldung and Dürer will come to mind. This breaking of narrative,
another feature of the plays, approaches what Hölderlin, writing
about tragedy, calls the 'caesura', by which he means the moment in
the work which meets and breaks an 'onrushing change of
representations'.[10] Literature as representation breaks down because
of its meeting with the unrepresentable - that which non-apocalyptic
writing keeps at bay - and it records that break, not evading it or
smoothing it over through a fictitious insistence on causal
connections. In deconstruction, and also if we follow Benjamin on
the fragment, as has been done here, literature can be nothing other
than breaks, failures or refusals to carry forward narrative and the
selective memory it implies. Literature here separates from history-
writing, which has a different narrative, and whose relation to breaks
is more problematic and which perhaps cannot invest in them. The
Henry VI plays are of their present, but just as so much of later
Shakespeare is in the tetralogy, so is much of the past, for the plays
also give images of, or to, the English fifteenth century, which is
now best known, perhaps, and certainly most persuasively, through
those plays. The plays, future to the fifteenth century, are its
archive, and carry forward something unknowable from the past they
describe.

In all these impurely kept documents, neither literature nor
history, fusions of both and neither, there exists an archive which is
both the same and different from the period they describe. An
official archive, in Derrida's sense in *Archive Fever*, which I
discussed in chapter 4 and now return to, tries to preserve
homogeneity and the singleness of history through repeated acts of
collecting materials and data. So Lydgate's work, written under the
commands of authority, presents an archive of the fall of princes. But
what stays in the mind with Lydgate are those moments of
heterogeneity (perhaps another name for Fortune) which do not
belong to that single narrative. The repetition compulsion in Freud
which collects and therefore aims to establish a history, is
inseparable from the death drive, which preys on just that interest in

---

[10] Friedrich Hölderlin, *Essays and Letters on Theory*, trans. and ed. by Thomas
Pfau (Albany: State University of New York Press, 1988), p. 102.

the proper - proper records, records which preserve or appropriate a single narrative and which expel the other. Hence Lydgate's text becomes, insofar as he keeps to his single theme, forgettable, and the collecting of time shows that time has collected him. In the death drive, as Derrida elsewhere discusses *Beyond the Pleasure Principle*, the organism 'follows its own path to death'. 'Therefore one must send away the non-proper, reappropriate oneself, make oneself come back until death. Send oneself the message of one's own death'.[11] The collection of an archive contains also its own working against itself, as if something within the activity that gathers also destroys. The death drive has the silent vocation 'to burn the archive and to incite amnesia, thus refuting the economic principle of the archive, aiming to ruin the archive as accumulation and capitalization of memory on some substrate and in an exterior place'.[12] Literature, of course, exists as an archive, and preserves a particular form of memory.

Before *Archive Fever* (1995) Derrida's interest in the 'archive' had extended over the essay on the apocalyptic tone, and also in a piece of 1984, 'No Apocalypse, not Now, (full speed ahead, seven miles, seven missiles)'.[13] One topic of this piece is the capacity of the nuclear catastrophe to destroy the archive of literature, which is 'a project of stockpiling, of building up an objective archive over and above any traditional oral base'. Weapons, too, coded with information and guided by computers, partake more and more now of the text, as if the archive of weaponry was like that of literature. Nuclear warfare faces the present with the possibility of 'irreversible destruction', leaving no traces of that archive (26), bringing about a state where there will be no capacity for remembrance. But literature as stockpiling is of the same ideology as that which produces the nuclear threat. The nuclear threat is unthinkable as to its consequences, but literature stands as an example of what is threatened by the archive fever of the nuclear. This produces the reflection that what has survival value, what will last, may be outside the archive, existing as the trace, scattered in significance, not gathered into a single homogeneous form. And so it is with the texts studied here, which parallel the *Trauerspiel*'s sense of texts speaking to conditions of ruin. What value for the future exists in those several re-writings which cannot become one in *Piers Plowman*, a text which cannot be seen as single, and which is impossible to

---

[11] Jacques Derrida, *The Post Card: From Socrates to Freud and Beyond*, trans. by Alan Bass (Chicago: University of Chicago Press, 1988), p. 355.

[12] Jacques Derrida, *Archive Fever: A Freudian Impression,* trans. by Eric Prenowitz (Chicago: University of Chicago Press, 1995), p. 12.

[13] Jacques Derrida, 'No Apocalypse, Not Now (Full Speed Ahead, Seven Missiles, Seven Missives)', *Diacritics* 14 (1984), 20-31.

categorize. Similar questionings take place in the writing of Thomas Hoccleve's *Complaint*, which implicitly critiques an archive built up on 'normal' and sane writings. The critique exists too in Shakespeare's plays which double the life of the fifteenth century and make it speak in future ways.

The texts do not exist within the institution of literature as a complete archival property set up with proprietorial rules, and are the more fascinating for it. Langland is not writing 'literature' and Chaucer's Knight finds his storytelling relativised by other elements within the Chaucerian text, within his own and others' tales; Hoccleve and Lydgate are both writing forms of history and Henryson's narrative shows its invasion by a social and cultural history which qualifies his texts. Shakespeare's plays write the history of the fifteenth and the late sixteenth centuries together. These texts start from the standpoint of death's erasure of the archive, and their fascination is with what survives. The power of the holocaust or of Fortune activates their power of mourning and memory, yet what they remember is always allegorical detail and fragment, and they pass on a knowledge that they never present as finished or as completing an archive.

BIBLIOGRAPHY

Aers, David, *Chaucer, Langland and the Creative Imagination* (London: Routledge and Kegan Paul, 1980)

----- *Medieval Literature: Criticism, Ideology and History* (New York: St Martin's Press, 1986)

----- *Community, Gender and Individual Identity: English Writing 1360-1430* (London: Routledge, 1988)

----- *Culture and History, 1350-1600: Essays on English Communities, Identities and Writing* (London: Harvester, 1992)

----- ed., *Culture and History 1350-1600: Essays on English Communities and Writing* (London: Harvester, 1992)

Aers, David and Lynn Staley, *The Powers of the Holy: Religion, Politics and Gender in Late Medieval English Culture* (Pennsylvania: Pennsylvania State University Press, 1996)

Agamben, Giorgio, *Stanzas: Word and Phantasm in Western Culture*, trans. by Ronald L. Martinez (Minneapolis: University of Minnesota Press, 1993)

Aikin, Judith Popovich, *German Baroque Drama* (Boston: Twayne, 1982)

Alford, John A., 'The Role of the Quotations in *Piers Plowman*', *Speculum* 52 (1977), 80-99

----- ed., *A Companion to Piers Plowman* (Berkeley: University of California Press, 1988)

Anderson, David, *Before The Knight's Tale: Imitation of Classical Epic in the Teseida* (Philadelphia: University of Pennsylvania Press, 1988)

Anzelewsky, Fedja, *Dürer: His Art and Life* (London: Gordon Fraser, 1982)

Ariès, Philippe, *The Hour of Our Death*, trans. by Helen Weaver (New York: Knopf, 1980)

Arrizabalaga, Jon; John Henderson and Roger French, *The Great Pox: The French Disease in Renaissance Europe* (New Haven: Yale University Press, 1997)

Artin, Tom, *The Allegory of Adventure: Reading Chrétien's Erec and Yvain* (Lewisburg: Bucknell University Press, 1974)

Aston, Margaret, 'Huizinga's Harvest: England and the Waning of the Middle Ages', *Medievalia et Humanistica* n.s., 9 (1979), 1-24

----- *Fifteenth-century Attitudes: Perceptions of Society in Late Medieval England* (Cambridge: Cambridge University Press, 1994)

Auerbach, Erich, *Mimesis: The Representation of Reality in Western Literature*, trans. by Willard Trask (Princeton: Princeton University Press, 1953)

Augustine of Hippo, *Writings of St Augustine*, vol 1, trans. by Thomas F. Gilligan (New York: CIMA Publishing, 1948)

----- *Confessions*, trans. by Henry Chadwick (Oxford: Oxford University Press, 1991)

Bachelard, G., *The Poetics of Space*, trans. by Maria Jolas (Boston: Beacon Press, 1994)

Bak, Janos, ed., *The German Peasant War of 1525* (London: Frank Cass, 1978)

Bakhtin, Mikhail, *Rabelais and his World*, trans. by Hélène Iswolsky (Bloomington: Indiana University Press, 1968)

----- The Dialogic Imagination, trans. by Michael Holquist and Caryl Emerson (Austin: University of Texas Press, 1981)

----- Rabelais and his World, trans. by Helen Iswolsky (Bloomington: Indiana University Press, 1985)

Baltrusaitis, Jurgis, *Anamorphic Art*, trans. by W.J. Strachan (Cambridge: Chadwyck-Healey,1977)

Barber, Richard, *The Knight and Chivalry* (London: Longman, 1970)

Barthes, Roland, *S/Z*, trans. by Richard Howard (New York: Hill and Wang, 1974)

Bartra, Roger, *Wild Men in the Looking Glass: The Mythic Origins of European Otherness*, trans. by Carl T. Berrisford (Ann Arbor: University of Michigan Press, 1994)

Batt, Catherine, ed., *Essays on Thomas Hoccleve* (London: Centre for Medieval and Renaissance Studies, Queen Mary and Westfield College, University of London, 1996)

Baudelaire, Charles, *Les Fleurs du Mal*, with translations by Richard Howard (London: Picador, 1982)

Bawcutt, Priscilla, *Dunbar the Makar* (Oxford: Clarendon Press, 1992)

----- *The Poems of William Dunbar*, 2 vols (Glasgow: Association for Scottish Literary Studies, 1998)

Bell, Michael Davitt, *The Development of American Romance: The Sacrifice of Relation* (Chicago: University of Chicago Press, 1980)

Benjamin, Walter, *Illuminations*, trans. by Harry Zohn (London: Jonathan Cape, 1970)

----- *Charles Baudelaire: A Lyric Poet in the Era of High Capitalism*, trans. by Harry Zohn (London: New Left Books, 1973)

----- *The Origin of German Tragic Drama*, trans. by John Osborne (London: Verso, 1977)

----- *One Way Street and Other Writings*, trans. by Edmund Jephcott and Kingsley Shorter (London: Verso, 1979)

----- 'Central Park', *New German Critique*, 34 (1985), 32-58

----- *Walter Benjamin: The Arcades Project*, trans. by Howard Eiland and Kevin McLaughlin (Cambridge Mass.: Harvard University Press, 1999)

Benson, Larry D., *Malory's Morte Darthur* (Cambridge, Mass: Harvard University Press, 1976)

Bentley, Greg W., *Shakespeare and the New Disease: The Dramatic Function of Syphilis in 'Troilus and Cressida', 'Measure for Measure' and 'Timon of Athens'* (New York: Peter Lang, 1989)

Benveniste, Emile, *Problems in General Linguistics* (Miami: University of Miami Press, 1971)

Bergin, Thomas G., *Boccaccio* (New York: Viking, 1981)

Berman, Russell, *Modern Culture and Critical Theory: Art, Policy and the Legacy of the Frankfurt School* (Madison: University of Wisconsin Press, 1989)

Bernheimer, Richard, *Wild Men of the Middle Ages: A Study in Art, Sentiment and Demonology* (Cambridge, Mass.: Harvard University Press, 1952)

Berstein, Micahel André, *Bitter Carnival: Ressentiment and the Abject Hero* (Princeton: Princeton University Press, 1992)

Bevington, David and Eric Rasmussen, eds., *Christopher Marlowe: Doctor Faustus and Other Plays* (Oxford: Oxford University Press, 1995)

Binski, Paul, *Medieval Death: Ritual and Representation* (London: British Museum Press, 1996)

Blanchot, Maurice, *The Gaze of Orpheus and Other Literary Essays*, trans. by Lydia Davis (New York: Station Hill, 1981)

----- *The Space of Literature*, trans. by Ann Smock, (Lincoln: University of Nebraska Press, 1982)

----- *The Instant of My Death* and Jacques Derrida, *Demeure: Fiction and Testimony*, trans. by Elizabeth Rottenberg (Stanford: Stanford University Press, 2000)

Blickle, Peter, *The Revolution of 1525*, trans. by Thomas A Brady, jr. and H.C. Erik Midelfort (Baltimore: Johns Hopkins University Press, 1981)

Bloom, Harold, ed., *Deconstruction and Criticism* (London: Routledge, 1979)

----- ed., *Geoffrey Chaucer: The Knight's Tale* (New York: Chelsea House, 1988)

Bloomfield, Morton W., *The Seven Deadly Sins: An Introduction to the History of a Religious Concept: With Special Reference to Medieval English Literature* (East Lansing: Michigan State University Press, 1952)

----- *Piers Plowman and a Fourteenth-Century Apocalypse* (New Brunswick: Rutgers University Press, 1961)

----- *Essays and Explorations: Structure in Ideas, Language and Literature* (Cambridge, Mass.: Harvard University Press, 1970)

Blumenberg, Hans, *The Legitimacy of the Modern Age*, trans. by Robert M. Wallace (Cambridge, Mass.: MIT Press, 1983)

Boccaccio, Giovanni, *The Fates of Illustrious Men*, trans. by Louis Brewer Hall (New York: Frederick Ungar, 1965)

----- *Decameron*, trans. by G.H. McWilliam (Harmondsworth: Penguin, 1995)

Boffey, Julia and Janet Cowen, eds., *Chaucer and Fifteenth-Century Poetry* (London: King's College London Centre for Late Antique and Medieval Studies, 1991)

Boffey, Julia and Pamela King, eds., *London and Europe in the Later Middle Ages* (London: Centre for Medieval and Renaissance Studies, Queen Mary and Westfield College, University of London, 1995)

Boitani, Piero, *Chaucer and Boccaccio* (Oxford: Society for the Study of Medieval Languages and Literature, 1977)

----- *Chaucer and the Italian Trecento* (Cambridge: Cambridge University Press, 1983)

----- ed., *The European Tragedy of Troilus* (Oxford: Clarendon, 1989)

----- *The Tragic and the Sublime in Medieval Literature* (Cambridge: Cambridge University Press, 1989)

Boitani, Piero and Anna Torti, eds., *Genres, Themes and Images in English Literature* (Tübingen: Guater Narr Verlag, 1981)

----- eds., *Religion in the Poetry and Drama of the Late Middle Ages in England* (Woodbridge: D.S. Brewer, 1990)

Bowers, John, *The Crisis of Will in Piers Plowman* (Washington DC: The Catholic University of America Press, 1986)

Bradley, Sister Rita Mary, 'Backgrounds of the Title *Speculum* in Medieval Literature', *Speculum* 29 (1954), 100-115

Brockbank, Philip, *On Shakespeare* (Oxford: Blackwell, 1989)

Brody, Saul Nathaniel, *The Disease of the Soul: Leprosy in Medieval Literature* (Ithaca: Cornell University Press, 1974)

Brown, Peter and Andrew Butcher, *The Age of Saturn: Literature and History in The Canterbury Tales* (Oxford: Blackwell, 1991)

Brown, Richard Danson, *'The New Poet': Novelty and Tradition in Spenser's Complaints* (Liverpool: Liverpool University Press, 1999)

Budra, Paul, '"Exemplify my Frailty": Representing English Women in *De Casibus* tragedy', *Philological Quarterly* 74 (1995), 359-372

Bull, Malcolm, ed., *Apocalypse Theory and the Ends of the World* (Oxford: Blackwell, 1995)

----- *Seeing Things Hidden: Apocalypse, Vision and Totality* (London: Verso, 1999)

Burrow, John, ed., *Geoffrey Chaucer* (Harmondsworth: Penguin, 1969)

----- 'The Poet as Petitioner', *Studies in the Age of Chaucer* 3 (1981), 61-75

----- *The Ages of Man: A Study in Medieval Writing and Thought* (Oxford: Clarendon, 1986)

----- 'Autobiographical Poetry in the Middle Ages: The Case of Thomas Hoccleve', *Proceedings of the British Academy* 68 (1988), 115-127

----- *Langland's Fictions* (Oxford: Clarendon Press, 1993)

----- *Thomas Hoccleve* (Authors of the Middle Ages; Aldershot: Variorum 1994)

----- 'Thomas Hoccleve: Some Redatings', *Review of English Studies* n.s. 46 (1995), 366-72

----- ed., *Thomas Hoccleve's Complaint and Dialogue* (Oxford University Press for the Early English Texts Society, 1999)

Busby, Keith and Erik Hooper, *Courtly Literature: Culture and Contexts* (Amsterdam: John Benjamins, 1990)

Bynum, Caroline Walker, *Jesus as Mother: Studies in the Spirituality of the High Middle Ages* (Berkeley: University of California Press, 1982)

Bynum, Caroline Walker, *Holy Feast and Holy Fast: The Religious Significance of Food to Medieval Women* (Berkeley: University of California Press, 1987)

Cadden, Joan, The Meanings of *Sex Difference in the Middle Ages: Medicine, Science and Culture* (Cambridge: Cambridge University Press, 1993)

Camille, Michael 'The *Très Riches Heures*: An Illuminated Manuscript in the Age of Mechanical Reproduction', *Critical Inquiry* 17 (1990), 72-107

----- *Master of Death: The Lifeless Art of Pierre Remiet, Illuminator* (New Haven: Yale University Press, 1996)

----- '"For our Objects and Pleasure": The Sexual Objects of Jean, duc de Berry', *Art History* 24 (2001), 169-194

Campbell, Lily B., ed., *The Mirror for Magistrates* (Cambridge: Cambridge University Press, 1938)

Cazelles, Raymond and Johannes Rathofer, *Illuminations of Heaven and Earth: The Glories of the Très Riches Heures du Duc de Berry* (1984; New York: Harry N. Abrams edition, 1988)

Cerquiglini-Toulet, Jacqueline, *The Color of Melancholy: The Use of Books in the Fourteenth Century*, trans. by Lydia G. Cochrane (Baltimore: Johns Hopkins University Press, 1997)

Chaucer, Geoffrey, *The Riverside Chaucer* ed. Larry D. Benson (Boston: Houghton Mifflin, 1987)

Chrétien de Troyes, *Yvain*, ed. by Jan Nelson, Carleton W. Carroll and Douglas Kelly (New York: Appleton-Century, 1968)

----- *Arthurian Romances*, trans. by D.D.R. Owen (London: Everyman, 1987)

----- *Arthurian Romances*, trans. by William W. Kibler and Carleton Carroll (Harmondsworth: Penguin, 1991)

Cervantes, Miguel de, *Don Quixote*, trans. by Charles Jervis (Oxford: Oxford University Press, 1992)

Ciavolella, Massimo and Amilcare A. Iannucci, *Saturn from Antiquity to the Renaissance* (University of Toronto Italian Studies: Dovehouse Edition Inc., 1992)

Claridge, Gordon; Ruth Pryor and Gwen Watkins, *Sounds from the Bell-Jar: Ten Psychotic Authors* (London: Macmillan, 1990)

Clark, J.M., *The Dance of Death in the Middle Ages and Renaissance* (Glasgow: University of Glasgow Press, 1950)

Clemen, Wolfgang, *English Tragedy Before Shakespeare: The Development of Dramatic Speech*, trans. by T.S. Dorsch (London: Methuen, 1961)

Clopper, Lawrence M., '*Songs of Rechelesnesse': Langland and the Franciscans* (Ann Arbor: University of Michigan Press, 1997)

Cohen, Kathleen, *Metamorphoses of a Death Symbol: The Transi Tomb in the late Middle Ages and the Renaissance* (Berkeley: University of California Press, 1977)

Cohn, Samuel K., jr., *The Cult of Remembrance and the Black Death* (Baltimore: Johns Hopkins University Press, 1992)

Condren, Edward I., *Chaucer and the Energy of Creation* (Gainesville: University Press of Florida, 1999)

Cooper, Helen, *Oxford Guides to Chaucer: The Canterbury Tales* (Oxford: Oxford University Press, 1989)

Cooper, Helen and Sally Mapstone, eds., *The Long Fifteenth-Century* (Oxford: Clarendon, 1997)

Cornell, Drucilla; Michel Rosenfeld and David Gray Carlson, eds., *Deconstruction and the Possibility of Justice*, (New York: Routledge, 1992)

Cortázar, Julio, *Hopscotch*, trans. by Gregory Rabassa (New York: Pantheon Books, 1966).

Cox, Catherine S., 'Froward Language and Wanton Play: The "Commoun" Text of Henryson's *Testament of Cresseid*', *Studies in Scottish Literature* 29 (1996), 58-72

Cox, John D., *Shakespeare and the Dramaturgy of Power* (Princeton: Princeton University Press, 1989)

Craun, Edwin D., 'Blaspheming her "Awin God": Cresseid's "Lamentatioun" in Henryson's *Testament*', *Studies in Philology* 82 (1985), 25-41

----- *Lies, Slander and Obscenity in Medieval English Literature: Pastoral Rhetoric and the Deviant Speaker* (Cambridge: Cambridge University Press, 1997)

Cunningham, Andrew, and Ole Peter Grell, *The Four Horsemen of the Apocalypse: Religion, War, Famine and Death in Reformation Europe* (Cambridge: Cambridge University Press, 2000)

David Wallace, ed., *The Cambridge History of Medieval English Literature* (Cambridge: Cambridge University Press, 1999)

De Man, Paul, *Blindness and Insight*, ed. by Wlad Godzich, 2nd edn. (Minneapolis: University of Minnesota Press, 1983)

----- *The Resistance to Theory* (Minneapolis: University of Minnesota Press, 1986)

Deleuze, Gilles and Felix Guattari, *Kafka: Towards a Minor Literature*, trans. by Dana Polan (Minneapolis: University of Minnesota Press, 1986)

----- *Thousand Plateaux*, trans. by Brian Massumi (Minneapolis: University of Minesota Press, 1987)

Derrida, Jacques, *Of Grammatology*, trans. by Gayatri Chakravorty Spivak (Baltimore: Johns Hopkins University Press, 1977)

----- *Writing and Difference*, trans. by Alan Bass (London: Routledge and Kegan Paul, 1978)

----- *Spurs: Nietzsche's Styles*, trans. by Barbara Harlow (Chicago: University of Chicago Press, 1981)

----- 'No Apocalypse, Not Now (Full Speed Ahead, Seven Missiles, Seven Missives)', *Diacritics* 14 (1984), 20-31

----- *Margins of Philosophy*, trans. by Alan Bass (Brighton: Harvester, 1986)

----- *Memoires for Paul de Man*, trans. by Cecile Lindsay, Jonathan Culler, Eduardo Cadava (New York: Columbia University Press, 1986)

----- *The Post Card: From Socrates to Freud and Beyond*, trans. by Alan Bass (Chicago: University of Chicago Press, 1988)

----- 'On a Newly Arisen Apocalyptic Tone in Philosophy' in *Raising the Tone of Philosophy: Late Essays by Immanuel Kant, Transformative Critique by Jacques Derrida*, ed. by Peter Fenves (Baltimore: Johns Hopkins University Press, 1993)

----- *Spectres of Marx: The State of the Debt, the Work of Mourning and the New International*, trans. by Peggy Kamuf (New York: Routledge, 1994)

----- *The Gift of Death*, trans. by David Wills (Chicago: University of Chicago Press, 1995)

----- *Archive Fever: A Freudian Impression*, trans. by Eric Prenowitz (Chicago: University of Chicago Press, 1996)

Dickens, A.G., *The German Nation and Luther* (London: Edward Arnold, 1974)

Dickens, Charles, *The Old Curiosity Shop*, ed. by Angus Easson (Harmondsworth: Penguin, 1972)

Dobson, R.B., *The Peasants' Revolt of 1381* (London: Macmillan, 1983)

Dols, Michael W., 'The Leper in Medieval Islamic Society', *Speculum* 58 (1983), 891-916

----- *Majunun: The Madman in Medieval Islamic Society* (Oxford: Clarendon Press, 1992)

Donaldson, E.T., *Piers Plowman: The C-Text and its Poet* (New Haven: Yale University Press, 1949)

Doob, Penelope, *Nebuchadnezzar's Children: Conventions of Madness in Medieval English Literature* (New Haven: Yale University Press, 1974)

Dudley, Edward and Maximilian Novak, eds., *The Wild Man Within: An Image in Western Thought from the Renaissance to Romanticism* (Pittsburgh: University of Pittsburgh Press, 1972)

Dunbar, William, *The Poems of William Dunbar*, ed. by James Kinsley (Oxford: Clarendon Press, 1979)

Dunning, Richard, *Theory, Culture and Society 4* (1987), 363-374

Elias, Norbert, *The Civilizing Process: The History of Manners*, trans. by Edmund Jephcott (Oxford: Blackwell, 1978)

Elsner, John and Roger Cardinal, eds., *The Cultures of Collecting* (London: Reaktion Books, 1994)

Engels, Friedrich, *The German Revolutions*, ed. by Leonard Krieger (Chicago: University of Chicago Press, 1967)

Englehardt, G.J., 'The Ecclesiastical Pilgrims of the Canterbury Tales', *Medieval Studies*, (1975), 287-315

Famiglietti, R.C., *Royal Intrigue: Crisis at the Court of Charles VI, 1392-1420* (New York: AMS Press, 1986)

Farnham, Willard, *The Medieval Heritage of Elizabethan Tragedy* (Oxford: Basil Blackwell, 1963)

Fein, Susanna, 'The Poetic Art of *Death and Life*', *Yearbook of Langland Studies* 2 (1988), 103-123

Felman, Shoshana, *Writing and Madness: Literature, Philosophy, Psychoanalysis*, trans. by Martha Noel Evans (Ithaca: Cornell University Press, 1985)

Fisher, John H., 'A Language Policy for Lancastrian England', *PMLA* 107 (1992), 1168-80

Fletcher, Angus, *Allegory: The Theory of a Symbolic Mode* (Ithaca: Cornell University Press, 1964): paperback edition 1970

Foucault, Michel, *Folie et Déraison: Histoire de la Folie à l'Age Classique* (Paris: Libraire Plon, 1961)

----- *Madness and Civilization: A History of Insanity in the Age of Reason*, trans. by Richard Howard (London: Tavistock, 1967)

----- *Discipline and Punish: The Birth of the Prison*, trans. by Alan Sheridan (Harmondsworth: Penguin, 1979)

----- 'My Body, this Paper, this Fire', *Oxford Literary Review* 4 (1979), 9-28

Fradenburg, Louise O., 'Psychoanalytic Medievalism' *New Medieval Literatures* 2 (1998), 249-76

Frank, Robert Worth, jr., 'The Hungry Gap: Crop Failure and Famine: the Fourteenth Century Agricultural Crisis and *Piers Plowman*', *Yearbook of Langland Studies* 4 (1990), 87-104

Freedman, Paul and Gabrielle M. Spiegel, 'Medievalisms Old and New: The Rediscovery of Alterity in North American Medieval Studies', *American Historical Review* (1993), 677-704

French, Roger and others, eds., *Medicine From the Black Death to the French Disease* (Aldershot: Ashgate 1998)

Freud, Sigmund, *The Interpretation of Dreams: The Penguin Freud 4* (Harmondsworth: Penguin, 1976)

----- *On Metapsychology: The Penguin Freud 11* (Harmondsworth: Penguin, 1977)

----- *Civilization, Society and Religion: The Penguin Freud 12* (Harmondsworth: Penguin, 1985)

Friedenreich, Kenneth; Roma Gill and Constance B. Kuriyama, *A Poet and a Filthy Play-maker: New Essays on Christopher Marlowe* (New York: AMS Press, 1988)

Friedman, John. B., *The Monstrous Races in Medieval Art and Thought* (Cambridge, Mass.: Harvard University Press, 1981)

----- 'Henryson's *Testament of Cresseid* and the *Judicio Solis in Conviviis Saturni* of Simon of Couvin', *Modern Philology* 83 (1985), 12-21

Friedrich, Werner P., *Dante's Fame Abroad, 1350-1850* (Roma: Edizioni di Storia e letteratura, 1950)

Froissart, John, *Chronicles*, trans. by Geoffrey Brereton (Harmondsworth: Penguin, 1878)

Frow, John, *Marxism and Literary Theory* (Oxford: Blackwell, 1986)

Geoffrey of Monmouth, *Life of Merlin* (*Vita Merlini*), ed. by Basil Clarke (Cardiff: University of Wales Press, 1973)

Gillespie, Gerald, *Daniel Casper von Lohenstein's Historical Tragedies* (Athens: Ohio State University Press, 1965)

----- ed., *German Theater Before 1750* (New York: Continuum, 1992)

Gilman, Sander, *Disease and Representation: Images of Illness from Madness to AIDS* (Ithaca: Cornell University Press, 1988)

Girard, Rene, *Violence and the Sacred*, trans. by Patrick Gregory (Baltimore: John Hopkins University Press, 1972)

Goldie, Matthew Boyd, 'Psychosomatic Illness and Identity in London, 1416-1421: Hoccleve's *Complaint* and Dialogue with a Friend', *Exemplaria* 11 (1999), 23-52

Goodwin, Sarah Webster, *Kitsch and Culture: The Dance of Death in Nineteenth Century Literature and Graphic Arts* (New York: Garland, 1988)

Gordon, Bruce and Peter Marshall, eds., *The Place of the Dead: Death and Remembrance in Late Medieval and Early Modern Europe* (Cambridge: Cambridge University Press, 2000)

Gower, John, *The Complete Works of John Gower*, ed. by G.A. Macaulay, 4 vols (Oxford: Clarendon Press, 1901)

Grabes, Herbert, *The Mutable Glass: Mirror Imagery in Titles and Texts of the Middle Ages and Early Renaissance*, trans. by Gordon Collier (Cambridge: Cambridge University Press, 1982)

Gray, Douglas, *Robert Henryson* (Leiden: E.J. Brill, 1979)

Green, Richard Firth, *Poets and Princepleasers: Literature and the English Court in the Late Middle Ages* (Toronto: University of Toronto Press, 1980)

Greenblatt, Stephen, 'Murdering Peasants: Status, Genre and the Representation of Rebellion', *Representations* 1.1. (1983), 1-29

Greetham, D.C., 'Self-Referential Artifacts: Hoccleve's Persona as a Literary Device', *Modern Philology* 86 (1989), 242-51

Guthke, Karl S., *The Gender of Death: A Cultural History in Art and Literature* (Cambridge: Cambridge University Press, 1999)

Hale, J.R., *Arts and Warfare in the Renaissance* (New Haven: Yale University Press, 1990)

Hamilton, A.C., *The Early Shakespeare* (San Marino: The Huntingdon Library, 1967).

Hanawalt, Barbara A. and David Wallace, eds., *Bodies and Disciplines: Intersections of Literature and History in Fifteenth-Century England* (Minneapolis: University of Minnesota Press, 1996)

Hand, Sean, ed., *The Levinas Reader* (Oxford: Blackwell, 1989)

Hanks, D. Thomas, jr., *The Social and Literary Contexts of Malory's Morte Darthur* (Cambridge: D.S. Brewer, 2000)

Hanna, Ralph III, *William Langland: Authors of the Middle Ages 3* (Aldershot: Ashgate, 1993)

Harrison, Robert Pogue, *Forests: The Shadow of Civilization* (Chicago: University of Chicago Press, 1992)

Hasler, Anthony J., 'Hoccleve's Unregimented Body', *Paragraph* 13 (1990), 164-83

Hattinger, Franz, *The Duc de Berry's Book of Hours* (Berne: Hallwag, 1962)

Havely, Nick, ed., *Dante's Modern Afterlife: Reception and Response from Blake to Heaney* (London: Macmillan, 1998)

Hawkins, Anne Hunsaker, 'Yvain's Madness', *Philological Quarterly* 71 (1992), 377-397

Hegel, G. W. F., *The Philosophy of History*, trans. by J. Sibree (New York: Dover Publications 1956)

Henryson, Robert, *The Testament of Cresseid*, ed. by Denton Fox (London: Nelson, 1968)

----- *Poems*, ed. by Denton Fox (Oxford: Clarendon Press, 1981)

----- *Selected Poems*, ed. by W.R.J. Barron (Manchester: Carcanet, 1991)

Herlihy, David, *The Black Death and the Transformation of the West* (Cambridge, Mass.: Harvard University Press, 1997)

Hershkowitz, Debra, *The Madness of Epic: Reading Insanity from Homer to Statius* (Oxford: Clarendon Press, 1988)

Hewett-Smith, Kathleen M., *William Langland's Piers Plowman: A Book of Essays* (New York: Routledge, 2001)

Heyworth, P.L., ed., *Medieval Studies for J.A.W.Bennett* (Oxford: Clarendon Press, 1981)

Hillgarth, J.N., *The Spanish Kingdoms 1250-1516* vol.1 (Oxford: Clarendon Press, 1981)

Hilton, Rodney, *Bond Men made Free: Medieval Peasant Movements and the English Rising of 1381* (London: Methuen, 1973)

Hirsh, James, 'Shakespeare and the History of Soliloquies', *Modern Language Quarterly* 58 (1997), 1-26

Hitchcock, Walter R., *The Background of the Knights' Revolt* (Berkeley: University of California Press, 1958)

Holbein, Hans, *The Dance of Death: 41 Woodcuts by Hans Holbein the Younger* (New York: Dover Publications, 1971)

Hölderlin, Friedrich, *Essays and Letters on Theory*, trans. and ed. by Thomas Pfau (Albany: State University of New York Press, 1988)

Hollington, Michael, ed., *Charles Dickens: Critical Assessments*, 4 vols (London: Helm Information, 1995)

Homans, Peter, *The Ability to Mourn: Disillusionment and the Social Origins of Psychoanalysis* (Chicago: University of Chicago Press, 1989)

Horowitz, Gregg M., *Sustaining Loss: Art and Mournful Life* (Stanford: Stanford University Press, 2001)

Howard, Bloch, R., *Medieval Misogyny and the Invention of Western Romantic Love* (Chicago: University of Chicago Press, 1991)

Howard, Donald R., *The Three Temptations: Medieval Man in Search of the World* (Princeton: Princeton University Press, 1966)

----- *The Idea of The Canterbury Tales* (Berkeley: University of California Press, 1976)

Hunt, Tony, 'The Emergence of the Knight in France and England 1000-1200', *Forum for Modern Language Studies* 17 (1981), 93-114

Husband, Timothy, *The Wild Man: Medieval Myth and Symbolism* (New York: Metropolitan Museum, 1980)

Hussey, S.S., *Piers Plowman: Critical Approaches* (London: Methuen, 1969)

Jackson, Stanley W., *Melancholia and Depression: From Hippocratic Times to Modern Times* (New Haven: Yale University Press, 1986)

Jacob, E.F., *The Fifteenth Century* (Oxford; Clarendon Press, 1961)

James, Henry, *Literary Criticism: Essays on Literature: American Writers, English Writers* (Cambridge: Press Syndicate of the University of Cambridge 1984)

Jennings, Michael W., *Dialectical Images: Walter Benjamin's Theory of Literary Criticism* (Ithaca: Cornell University Press, 1987)

Jones, Terry, *Chaucer's Knight: The Portrait of a Medieval Mercenary* (London: Metheun, 1980)

Justice, Steven, *Writing and Rebellion: England in 1381* (Berkeley: University of California Press, 1994)

Justice, Steven and Kathryn Kerby-Fulton, *Written Work: Langland, Labor and Authorship* (Philadelphia: University of Pennsylvania Press, 1997)

Kane, George, ed., *Piers Plowman: The A Version* (London: Athlone, 1960)

Kane, George and E.T. Donaldson, eds., *Piers Plowman: The B Version* (London: Athlone, 1975)

Karras, Ruth Mazo, *Common Women: Prostitution and Sexuality in Medieval England* (Oxford: Oxford University Press, 1996)

Kaske, R.E, 'The Knight's Interruption of *The Monk's Tale*', *English Literary Histoty* 25 (1957), 249-268

Kay, Sarah and Miri Rubin, eds., *Framing Medieval Bodies* (Manchester: Manchester University Press, 1994)

Keen, Maurice, 'Huizinga, Kilgour and the Decline of Chivalry', *Medievalia et Humanistica* n.s. 8 (1977), 1-20

----- *Chivalry*, (New Haven: Yale University Press, 1984)

Kelly, Henry Ansgar, *Ideas and Forms of Tragedy from Aristotle to the Middle Ages* (Cambridge: Cambridge University Press, 1993)

----- 'Bishop, Prioress, and Bawd in the Stews of Southwark', *Speculum* 75 (2000), 342-388

----- *Chaucerian Tragedy* (Cambridge: D.S. Brewer, 1997)

Kerby-Fulton, Kathryn, *Reformist Apocalypticism and Piers Plowman* (Cambridge: Cambridge University Press, 1990)

Kindrick, Robert L., 'Henryson's "Uther Quair" Again: A Possible Candidate and the Nature of the Tradition', *Chaucer Review* 33 (1998), 190-220.

Kirk, Elizabeth D., *The Dream Thought of Piers Plowman* (New Haven: Yale University Press, 1972)

Klibansky, Raymond; Erwin Panofsky and Fritz Saxl, *Saturn and Melancholy* (London; Dent, 1964)

Knapp, Ethan, 'Bureaucratic Identity and the Construction of the Self in Hoccleve's *Formulary* and *La male regle*', *Speculum* 74 (1999), 357-376

Koerner, Joseph Leo, *The Moment of Self-Portraiture in German Renaissance Art* (Chicago: University of Chicago Press, 1993)

Kohl, Stephen, 'More than Virtues and Vices: Self-Analysis in Hoccleve's "Autobiographies"', *Fifteenth-Century Studies* 14 (1988), 115-127

Kolve, V.A., *Chaucer and the Imagery of Narrative* (Stanford University Press, 1984)

Koonce, B.G., *Chaucer and the Tradition of Fame: Symbolism in The House of Fame* (Princeton: Princeton University Press, 1966)

Kristeva, Julia, *Powers of Horror: An Essay on Abjection*, trans. by Leon Roudiez (New York: Columbia University Press, 1982)

----- *Black Sun: Depression and Melancholia*, trans. by Leon Roudiez (New York: Columbia University Press, 1989)

Krochalis, Jeanne E., 'Hoccleve's Chaucer Portrait', *Chaucer Review* 21 (1986), 234-245

Kruger, Steven F., 'Mirrors and the Trajectory of Vision in *Piers Plowman*', *Speculum* 66 (1991), 74-95

----- *Dreaming in the Middle Ages* (Cambridge: Cambridge University Press, 1992)

Lacan, Jacques, 'Desire and the Interpretation of Desire in *Hamlet*', *Yale French Studies* 55/56 (1977), 11-52

----- *Écrits: A Selection*, trans. by Alan Sheridan (London: Tavistock, 1977)

----- *The Four Fundamental Concepts of Psychoanalysis*, trans. by Alan Sheridan (Harmondsworth: Penguin, 1979)

Laharie, Muriel, *La folie au moyen age, xi-xiii siècles* (Paris: Le Leopard d'or 1991)

Lambdin, Laura C. and Robert T. Lambdin, eds., *Chaucer's Pilgrims: An Historical Guide to the Pilgrims in The Canterbury Tales* ed. (Westport, Conn.: Greenwood Press, 1996)

Langland, William, *The Vision of Piers Plowman*, ed. by A.V.C. Schmidt (London: Dent, 1987).

Larner, John, *Culture and Society in Italy, 1290-1420* (London: Batsford, 1971)

Lawton, David, 'Lollardy and the 'Piers Plowman Tradition'', *Modern Language Review* 76 (1981), 780-793

----- 'Dullness and the Fifteenth-Century', *English Literary History* 54 (1987), 761-799

----- 'The Subject of Piers Plowman', *The Yearbook of Langland Studies* 1 (1987), 1-30

Le Goff, Jacques and Pierre Vidal-Naquet, 'Lévi-Strauss en Broceliande', *Critique* 30 (1974), 541-571

Leicester, H. Marshall, jr., *The Disenchanted Self: Representing the Subject in The Canterbury Tales* (Berkeley: University of California Press, 1990)

Lerer, Seth, *Chaucer and his Readers: Imagining the Author in Late Medieval England* (Princeton: Princeton University Press, 1993)

Lewis, C. S., *The Allegory of Love* (Oxford: Oxford University Press, 1936)

Longnon, Jean and Raymond Cazelles, *The Très Riches Heures of Jean, Duke of Berry: Musée Condé, Chantilly* (New York: George Braziller, 1969)

Löwith, Karl, *Meaning in History* (Chicago, Chicago University Press, 1949)

Lydgate, John, *Fall of Princes*, ed. by Henry Bergen (Washington: Carnegie Institution of Washington, 1923)

Lynch, Terence, 'The Geometric Body in Dürer's "Melencolia I"', *Journal of the Warburg and Courtauld Institute*, 45 (1982), 226-231

Macaulay, G. C., ed., *The Complete Works of John Gower* (Oxford: Clarendon Press, 1901)

Machiavelli, *The Prince*, ed. and trans. by Quentin Skinner and Russell Price (Cambridge: Cambridge University Press, 1988)

MacLennan, George, *Lucid Interval: Subjective Writing and Madness in History* (Leicester: Leicester University Press, 1992)

MacQueen, John, *Robert Henryson: A Study of the Narrative Poems* (Oxford: Clarendon Press, 1967)

----- *Allegory* (London: Methuen, 1970)

Malcolm Godden, *The Making of Piers Plowman* (London: Longman, 1990)

Mann, Jill, *Chaucer and Medieval Estates Satire: The Literature of Social Classes and the General Prologue to The Canterbury Tales* (Cambridge: Cambridge University Press, 1973)

Maravall, José Antonio, *Culture of the Baroque: Analysis of a Historical Structure*, trans. by Terry Cochran (Minneapolis: University of Minnesota Press, 1986)

----- *Utopia and Counterutopia in the "Quixote"*, trans. by Robert W. Felkel (Detroit: Wayne State University Press, 1991)

Margherita, Gayle, 'Criseyde's Remains: Romance and the Question of Justice', *Exemplaria* 12 (2000), 257-297

Marlowe, Christopher, *King Edward II*, ed. by Charles R. Forker (Manchester: Manchester University Press, 1994)

------ *The Complete Works of Christopher Marlowe*, ed. by Richard Rowland (Oxford: Clarendon Press, 1994)

Marrow, James H. and Alan Shestack, eds., *Hans Baldung Grien: Prints and Drawings* (New Haven: Yale University Art Gallery, 1981)

Martindale, Andrew, *Heroes, Ancestors, Relatives and the Birth of the Portrait* (The Hague: Gary Schwarz, SDU Publishers, 1988)

----- *Simone Martini* (Oxford: Phaidon, 1988)

Maxwell, Richard, *The Mysteries of Paris and London* (Charlotteville: University Press of Virginia, 1992)

McCall, John P., *Chaucer Among the Gods* (Pennsylvania State University Press 1979)

McKisack, May, *The Fourteenth Century, 1307-1399* (Oxford: Clarendon Press, 1959)

Medcalf, Stephen, *The Later Middle Ages* (London: Methuen, 1981)

Meiss, Millard, *Painting in Florence and Siena after the Black Death: The Arts, Religion and Society in the Mid-Fourteenth Century* (Princeton: Princeton University Press, 1951)

Meiss, Millard with Sharon Off Dunlap Smith and Elizabeth Home Beatson, *French Painting in the Time of Jean de Berry: The Limbourgs and their Contemporaries*, 2 vols (London: Thames and Hudson, 1974)

Metzger, Erika A. and Michael M. Metzger, *Reading Andreas Gryphius: Critical Trends 1664-1993* (Columbia, SC: Camden House, 1994)

Meyer-Lee, Robert J., 'Hoccleve and the Apprehension of Money', *Exemplaria* 13 (2001), 173-214

Minnis, Alistair with V.J. Scattergood and J.J. Smith, *Oxford Guides to Chaucer: The Shorter Poems* (Oxford: Clarendon Press, 1995)

Mitchell, Jerome, *Thomas Hoccleve: A Study in Early Fifteenth Century English Poetic* (Urbana: University of Illinois Press, 1968)

Moore, R. I., *The Formation of a Persecuting Society: Power and Deviance in Western Europe, 950-1250* (Oxford: Blackwell, 1987)

Morris, Helen, 'Shakespeare and Dürer's Apocalypse', *Shakespeare Studies* 4 (1968), 252-62

Morse, Ruth and Barry Windeatt, eds., *Chaucer Traditions* (Cambridge: Cambridge University Press, 1990)

Moulton, Ian Frederick, '"A Monster Great Deformed": The Unruly Masculinity of Richard III', *Shakespeare Quarterly* 47 (1996), 251-68

Muscatine, Charles, *Poetry and Crisis in the Age of Chaucer* (Notre Dame: University of Notre Dame Press, 1972)

Neaman, Judith S., *Suggestions of the Devil: Insanity in the Middle Ages and the Twentieth Century* (New York: Octagon Books, 1978)

Neill, Michael, *Issues of Death: Mortality and Identity in English Renaissance Tragedy* (Oxford: Clarendon Press, 1997)

Nerlich, Michael, *The Ideology of Adventure: Studies in Modern Consciousness 1100-1750, vol.1* (Minneapolis: University of Minnesota Press, 1987)

Newman, Francis X., ed., *Social Unrest in the Middle Ages* (Medieval and Renaissance texts and studies, Binghamton, New York, 1986)

Newman, Jane O., *The Intervention of Philology: Gender, Learning and Power in Lohenstein's Roman Plays* (Chapel Hill: University of North Carolina Press, 2000)

Niesz, Anthony J., *Dramaturgy in German Drama: From Gryphius to Goethe* (Heidelburg: Carl Winter: Universitätsverlag, 1980)

Nietzsche, Friedrich, *The Gay Science*, trans. by Walter Kaufmann (New York: Vintage, 1974)

----- *Human, All Too Human: A Book for Free Spirits*, trans. by R.J. Hollingdale (Cambridge: Cambridge University Press, 1996)

Nissé, Ruth, '"Our Fadres Olde and Modres": Gender, Heresy and Hoccleve's Literary Politics', *Studies in the Age of Chaucer* 21 (1999), 275-99

Nolan, Edward Peter, *Now Through a Glass Darkly: Specular Images of Being and Knowing from Virgil to Chaucer* (Ann Arbor: University of Michigan Press, 1990)

North, J.D., *Chaucer's Universe* (Oxford: Clarendon Press, 1988)

Ober, William B., 'Can the Leper Change His Spots? The Iconography of Leprosy' pts 1 and 2, *American Journal of Dermatopathology* 5 (1983), no. 1 pp. 43-58, no. 2 pp. 173-186

von der Osten, Gert, *Hans Baldung Grien: Gemälde und Documente* (Berlin: Verein für Kunstwissen 1983)

Otten, Charlotte F., *A Lycanthropy Reader: Werewolves in Western Culture* (New York: Syracuse University Press, 1986)

Owens, Craig, *Beyond Recognition: Representation, Power and Culture* (Berkeley: University of California Press, 1994)

Panofsky, Erwin, *The Life and Art of Albrecht Dürer* (Princeton: Princeton University Press, 1955)

----- *Tomb Sculpture: Its Changing Aspects from Ancient Egypt to Bernini* (London: Thames and Hudson, 1964)

----- *Early Netherlandish Painting: Its Origins and Character*, 2 vols (1953; New York: Icon Editions, 1971)

----- *Studies in Iconology: Humanistic Themes in the Art of the Renaissance* (New York: Harper and Rowe, 1972)

Parr, Johnstone, 'Cresseid's Leprosy Again', *Modern Language Notes* 60 (1945), 487-491

----- 'The Date and Revision of Chaucer's *The Knight's Tale*' *PMLA* 60 (1945), 307-24

Pascal, Roy, *German Literature in the Sixteenth and Seventeenth Centuries: Renaissance, Reformation, Baroque* (London: Cresset Press, 1968)

Patch, Howard R., *The Goddess Fortune in Mediaeval Literature* (Cambridge, Mass.: Harvard University Press, 1927)

Patrides, C.A. and Joseph Wittreich, eds., *The Apocalypse in English Renaissance Thought and Literature* (Manchester: Manchester University Press, 1984)

Patterson, Lee, "Christian and Pagan in *The Testament of Cresseid*," *Philological Quarterly* 52 (1973), 696-714

----- *Negotiating the Past: The Historical Understanding of Medieval Literature* (Madison: University of Wisconsin Press, 1987)

----- ed., *Canterbury Tales, Literary Practice and Social Change in Britain 1380-1530* (Berkeley: University of California Press, 1990)

----- ed., *Literary Practice and Social Change in Britain, 1380-1530* (Berkeley: University of California Press, 1990)

----- 'On the Margin: Postmodernism, Ironic History and Medieval Studies', *Speculum* 65 (1990), 87-108

----- *Chaucer and the Subject of History* (London: Routledge, 1991)

Patty, James S., 'Baudelaire and Dürer: Avatars of Melancholia', *Symposium*, 38 (1984), 244-57

Paxson, James J., *The Poetics of Personification* (Cambridge: Cambridge University Press, 1994)

Pearlman, E., 'The Invention of Richard of Gloucester', *Shakespeare Quarterly* 43 (1992), 410-29

Pearsall, Derek, *John Lydgate* (London: Routledge and Kegan Paul, 1970)

----- 'Hoccleve's *Regement of Princes*: The Politics of Royal Self-Presentation', *Speculum* 69 (1994), 386-410

----- ed., *Piers Plowman: An Edition of the C-Text* (Exeter: University of Exeter Press, 1994)

Pendleton, Thomas A., ed., *Henry VI: Critical Essays* (London: Routledge, 2001)

Peters, Edward and Walter P. Simons, 'The New Huizinga and the Old Middle Ages', *Speculum,* 74 (1999), 587-620

Pinti, Daniel J., *Writing After Chaucer: Essential Readings in Chaucer and the Fifteenth Century* (New York: Garland, 1998)

Pittock, Malcolm, 'The Complexity of Henryson's *The Testament of Cresseid*', *Essays in Criticism* 40 (1990), 198-221

Pratt, John H., 'Was Chaucer's Knight Really a Mercenary?', *Chaucer Review 22* (1987) 8-27

Quétel, Claude *History of Syphilis*, trans. by Judith Bradock and Brian Pike (Oxford: Polity Press, 1990)

Rawcliffe, Carol, *Medicine and Society in Later Medieval England* (Stroud: Sutton Publishing, 1995)

Reijen, Willen von, ed., *Allegorie und Melancholie* (Frankfurt: Suhrkamp Verlag, 1992)

Reiman, Donald H., ed., *The Triumph of Life* (Urbana: University of Illinois Press, 1966)

Ribner, Irving, *The English History Play in the Age of Shakespeare* (London: Methuen, 1965).

Ricci, Pier Giorgio, *Giovanni Boccaccio: Opere in Versi* (Milano-Napoli: Riccardo Ricciardi)

Rice, Eugene F., jr., *St.Jerome in the Renaissance* (Baltimore: Johns Hopkins University Press, 1985)

Richards, Peter, *The Medieval Leper and his Northern Heirs* (Cambridge: D.S. Brewer, 1977)

Richardson, Malcolm, 'Hoccleve in his Social Context', *Chaucer Review* 20 (1986), 313-22

Richter, Gerhard, *Walter Benjamin and the Corpus of Autobiography* (Detroit: Wayne State University Press, 2000)

Rigg, A.G., 'Hoccleve's *Complaint* and Isidore of Seville', *Speculum* 45 (1970), 564-74

Rigg, A.G. and Charlotte Brewer, eds., *Piers Plowman: The Z Version* (Toronto: Pontifical Institute, 1983)

Robbins, Jill, *Prodigal Son, Elder Brother: Interpretation and Alterity in Augustine, Petrarch, Kafka, Levinas* (Chicago: University of Chicago Press, 1991)

Robertson, D.W., jr., *A Preface to Chaucer; Studies in Medieval Perspectives* (Princeton: Princeton University Press,1962)

----- 'Chaucerian Tragedy', *English Literary History* 19, (1952) 1-37

Roney, Lois, *Chaucer's Knight's Tale and Theories of Scholastic Psychology* (Tampa: University of South Florida Press, 1990)

Robertson, D.W., jr. and Bernard F. Huppé, *Piers Plowman and Scriptural Tradition* (Princeton: Princeton University Press, 1951)

Rosaldo, Renato, 'Imperialist Nostalgia', *Representations* 26 (Spring 1989), 107-122

Rossiter, A.P., *Angel with Horns: Fifteen Essays on Shakespeare*, ed. by Graham Storey (London: Longman, 1989)

Rox, Henry, 'On Dürer's Knight, Death and the Devil', *Art Bulletin* 30 (1948), 67-70

Ruggiers, Paul G., 'Notes Towards a Theory of Tragedy in Chaucer', *Chaucer Review* 8 (1973) 89-99

Russell, George and George Kane, eds., *Piers Plowman: The C Version* (London: Athlone, 1988-1997)

Sacks, Peter M., *The English Elegy: Studies in the Genre from Spenser to Yeats* (Baltimore: Johns Hopkins University Press, 1985)

Sackville, Thomas and Thomas Norton, *Gorboduc or Ferrex and Porrex*, ed. by Irby B. Cauthen, jr. (Lincoln: University of Nebraska Press, 1970)

Salter, Elizabeth, *The Knight's Tale and the Clerk's Tale* (London: Edward Arnold, 1962)

Sass, Louis, *Madness and Modernism* (New York: Basic Books, 1992)

----- *Paradoxes of Delusion: Wittgenstein, Schreber and the Schizophrenic Mind* (Ithaca: Cornell University Press, 1994)

Saunders, Corinne J., *The Forest of Medieval Romance: Avernus, Broceliande, Arden* (Woodbridge: Boydell and Brewer, 1993)

Scanlon, Larry, *Narrative, Authority and Power: The Medieval Exemplum and the Chaucerian Tradition* (Cambridge: Cambridge University Press, 1994)

Scarry, Elaine, *The Body in Pain: The Making and Unmaking of the World* (Oxford: Oxford University Press, 1985)

Scase, Wendy, *Piers Plowman and the New Anticlericalism* (Cambridge: Cambridge University Press, 1989)

Scattergood, V.J. and J.W. Sherborne, *English Court Culture in the Later Middle Ages* (London: Duckworth, 1983)

Schiesari, Juliana, *The Gendering of Melancholia: Feminism, Psychoanalysis and the Symbolics of Loss in Renaissance Literature* (Ithaca: Cornell University Press, 1992)

Schmidt, A.V.C., ed., *The Vision of Piers Plowman: A Complete Edition of the B-Text* (London: Dent, 1987)

----- *William Langland, Piers Plowman: A Parallel-text Edition of the A, B, C, and Z Versions* (London: Longman, 1995)

Schmitt, Jean-Claude, *Ghosts in the Middle Ages: The Living and the Dead in Medieval Society*, trans. by Teresa Lavender Fagan (Chicago: University of Chicago Press, 1998)

Schweitzer, Edward C., 'Fate and Freedom in *The Knight's Tale*', *Studies in the Age of Chaucer 3* (1981)

Scriber, Bob and Gerhard Benecke, eds., *The German Peasant War of 1525: New Viewpoints* (London: Allen and Unwin, 1979)

Seymour, M.C., *Selections from Hoccleve* (Oxford: Clarendon Press, 1981)

Shakespeare, William, *King Henry V*, ed. by J.H. Walter (London: Methuen, 1954)

----- *King John*, ed. by E.A.J. Honigmann (London: Methuen, 1954)

----- *King Henry VI*, pts. 1-3, ed. by Andrew S. Cairncross, (London: Methuen, 1957-1964)

----- *King Henry IV*, pt. 1, ed. by A.R. Humphreys (London: Methuen, 1960)

----- *King Richard III*, ed. by J. Dover Wilson (Cambridge, Cambridge University Press, 1961)

----- *The Riverside Shakespeare*, ed by G. Blakemore Evans (Boston: Houghton Mifflin 1974)

----- *Twelfth Night*, ed. by J.M. Lothian and T.W. Craik (London: Methuen, 1975)

----- *King Richard III*, ed. by Antony Hammond (Arden Shakespeare, London: Methuen, 1981)

----- *Much Ado About Nothing*, ed. by A.R. Humphreys (London, Methuen, 1981)

----- *Hamlet*, ed. by Harold Jenkins (London: Methuen, 1982)

----- *Troilus and Cressida,* ed. By Alan Palmer (London: Methuen, 1982)

----- *King Henry VI*, pts. 1-3, ed. by Michael Hattaway (Cambridge, Cambridge University Press, 1990-1993)

----- *The First Quarto of King Richard III*, ed. by Peter Davison (Cambridge, Cambridge University Press, 1996)

----- *King Henry VI*, pt. 2, ed. by Ronald Knowles (London: Thomson Learning, 1999)

----- *King Richard III*, ed. by Janis Lull (Cambridge: Cambridge University Press, 1999)

----- *King Henry VI*, pt. 1, ed. by Edward Burns (London: Thomson Learning, 2000)

----- *King Henry VI*, pt. 3, ed. by John D. Cox and Eric Rasmussen (London: Thomson Learning, 2001)

----- *King Henry VI*, pt. 3, ed. by Randall Martin (Oxford: Oxford University Press, 2001)

----- *King Richard II*, ed. by Charles R. Forker (London: Thomson Learning, 2002)

----- *King Henry VI*, pt. 2, ed. by Roger Warren (Oxford: Oxford University Press, 2003)

Simpson, James, 'The Transformation of Meaning: a Figure of Thought in Piers Plowman', *Review of English Studies*, n.s. 37 (1986), 1-23

----- *Piers Plowman: An Introduction to the B Text* (London: Longman, 1990)

----- *Sciences and the Self in Medieval Poetry: Alan of Lille's Anticlaudianus and John Gower's Confessio amantis* (Cambridge: Cambridge University Press, 1995)

----- 'Grace Abounding: Evangelical Centralisation and the End of Piers Plowman', *Yearbook of Langland Studies*, 14 (2000), 1-25

----- 'The Power of Impropriety: Authorial Naming in Piers Plowman', in *William Langland's Piers Plowman: A Book of Essays*, ed. by Kathleen M. Hewett-Smith (New York: Routledge, 2001), 145-65

Singleton, Charles, ed., *Interpretation: Theory and Practice* (Baltimore: Johns Hopkins University Press, 1969)

Skeat, W.W., *The Vision of William Concerning Piers the Plowman*, 2 vols (Oxford: Clarendon Press, 1886)

Smart, Alastair, *The Dawn of Italian Painting, 1250-1400* (London: Phaidon, 1978)

Smith, Gary, *On Walter Benjamin: Critical Essays and Recollections* (Cambridge, Mass.: MIT Press, 1988)

----- ed., *Benjamin: Philosophy, Aesthetics, History* (Chicago: University of Chicago Press, 1989)

Spahr, Blake Lee, *Andreas Gryphius: A Modern Perspective* (Columbia SC: Camden House, 1993)

Spearing, A.C., *Criticism and Medieval Poetry* (London: Edward Arnold, 1964)

----- *Medieval to Renaissance in English Poetry* (Cambridge: Cambridge University Press, 1985)

Spivack, Bernard, *Shakespeare and the Allegory of Evil: The History of a Metaphor in Relation to his Major Villains* (New York: Columbia University Press, 1958)

Spivak, Gayatri Chakravorty, *A Critique of Postcolonial Reason: Toward a History of the Vanishing Present* (Cambridge, Mass.: Harvard University Press, 1999)

Statius, *Thebaid*, trans. by J.H.Mozley, (Loeb, Harvard University Press, 1929)

Stearns, Marshall W., 'Robert Henryson and the Leper Cresseid', *Modern Language Notes* 59 (1944), 265-9

Stechow, Wolfgang, 'State of Research: Recent Dürer Studies', *Art Bulletin*, 56 (1974), 259-70

Steinberg, Michael P., *Walter Benjamin and the Demands of History* (Ithaca: Cornell University Press, 1996)

Stillinger, Thomas C., ed., *Critical Essays on Geoffrey Chaucer* (New York: G.K. Hall, 1998)

Stoekl, Allan, ed., *Visions of Excess: Selected Writings 1927-1939*, (Minneapolis: University of Minnesota Press, 1985).

Stoichita, Victor I., *The Self-Aware Image: An Insight into Early Modern Meta-Painting* trans. by Anne-Marie Glasheen (Cambridge: Cambridge University Press, 1997)

Strauss, Walter L., ed., *Albrecht Dürer: Woodcuts and Woodblocks* (New York: Abaris Books, 1980)

Strieder, Peter, *Dürer*, (London, Francis Muller, 1982)

Strohm, Paul, *Social Chaucer* (New Jersey: Harvard University Press, 1989)

----- *England's Empty Throne: Usurpation and the Language of Legitimation* (New Haven: Yale University Press, 1998)

Szittya, Penn R., *The Antifraternal Tradition in Medieval Literature* (Princeton: Princeton University Press, 1986)

Talbot, Charles W., ed., *Dürer in America: his Graphic Work* (National Gallery of Art, Washington, 1971)

Tambling, Jeremy, *Dante and Difference: Writing in the Commedia* (Cambridge: Cambridge University Press, 1988)

----- 'Dante and Benjamin: Melancholy and Allegory', *Exemplaria* 4 (1992), 341-63

----- 'Dante and the Modern Subject: Overcoming Anger in the *Purgatorio*', *New Literary History* 28 (1997), 401-20

----- ed., *Longman Critical Readers: Dante* (London & New York, Longman, 1999)

----- 'We are Seven: Dante and the Serial Killer', *Paragraph* 22 (1999), 293-309

----- *Becoming Posthumous: Life and Death in Literary and Cultural Studies* (Edinburgh: Edinburgh University Press, 2001)

----- *Confession: Sexuality, Sin, the Subject* (Manchester: Manchester University Press, 1990)

Tassone, Giuseppe, *A Study on the Idea of Progress in Nietzsche, Heidegger and Critical Theory* (Lewiston: Edwin Mellen Press, 2002)

Taylor, Karla, *Chaucer Reads the Divine Comedy* (Stanford: Stanford University Press, 1989)

Tillyard, E.M.W., *Shakespeare's History Play* (1944; Harmondsworth: Penguin, 1962).

Torti, Anna, *The Glass of Form: Mirroring Structures From Chaucer to Skelton* (Cambridge: Cambridge University Press, 1991)

Tristram, Philippa, *Figures of Life and Death in Medieval English Literature* (London: Paul Elek, 1976)

Tuck, Anthony, *Crown and Nobility 1272-1461* (Oxford: Blackwell, 1985)

Ulmer, Bernhard, *Martin Opitz* (New York: Twayne, 1971)

Vale, Malcolm, *War and Chivalry: Warfare and Aristocratic Culture in England, France and Burgundy at the End of the Middle Ages* (Athens, GA.: University of Georgia Press, 1981)

Vance, Eugene, *From Topic to Tale: Logic and Narrativity in the Middle Ages* (Minneapolis: University of Minnesota Press, 1987)

Veith, Liza, *Hysteria: The History of a Disease* (Chicago: Chicago University Press 1965)

Vickers, K.H., *Humphrey, Duke of Gloucester* (London, A. Constable, 1907)

Villon, Francois, *The Poems of Francois Villon*, trans. by Galway Kinnell (New York: New American Library, 1965)

----- *Francois Villon: Complete Poems*, ed. by Barbara N. Sargent-Baur (Toronto: University of Toronto Press, 1994)

Wack, Mary Frances, *Lovesickness in the Middle Ages: The Viacticum and its Comentaries* (Philadelphia: University of Pennsylvania Press, 1990)

Waetzoldt, Wilhelm, *Albrecht Dürer* (London: Phaidon, 1950)

Wallace, David, *Chaucerian Polity: Absolutist Lineages and Associational Forms in England and Italy* (Stanford: Stanford University Press, 1997)

Warminski, Andrzej, ed., *Aesthetic Ideology* (Minneapolis: University of Minnesota Press, 1996)

Wasserman, Julian N. and Robert J. Blanch, eds., *Chaucer in the Eighties* (New York: Syracuse University Press, 1986)

Weber, Samuel, 'Genealogy of Modernity: History, Myth and Allegory in Benjamin's *Origin of the German Mourning Play*' *Modern Language Notes*, 106 (1991), 465-500

Weese, Walter E., 'Vengeance and Pleyn Correcioun', *Modern Language Notes* 63 (1948), 331-33

Weimann, Robert, *Shakespeare and the Popular Tradition in the Theatre: Studies in the Social Dimension of Dramatic Form and Function* (Baltimore: Johns Hopkins University Press, 1978)

Weiss, Roberto, *Humanism in England During the Fifteenth Century* (Oxford: Basil Blackwell, second edition, 1957)

Wells, Stanley and Gary Taylor, eds., *William Shakespeare: A Textual Companion* (Oxford: Clarendon, 1987)

Wetherbee, Winthrop, 'Romance and Epic in Chaucer's *Knight's Tale*', *Exemplaria* 2.1 (March 1990), 303-328

Whaley, Joachim, ed., *Mirrors of Mortality: Studies in the Social History of Death* (London: Europa, 1981)

White, Hayden, *Figural Realism: Studies in the Mimesis Effect* (Baltimore: Johns Hopkins University Press, 1999)

Williams, Raymond, *Writing in Society* (London: Verso, 1983)

Windeatt, Barry, *Oxford Guides to Chaucer: Troilus and Criseyde* (Oxford: Clarendon Press, 1992)

Wittgenstein, Ludwig, *Tractatus Logico-Philosophicus*, trans. by Bertrand Russell (London: Routledge & Kegan Paul, 1971)

Wittig, Joseph S., *William Langland Revisited* (Boston: Twayne, 1997)

Wolfflin, Heinrich, *The Art of Albrecht Dürer* (1905, London: Phaidon, 1971)

Wood, Chauncey, *Chaucer and the Country of the Stars* (New Jersey: Princeton University Press, 1970)

Woolf, Rosemary, *The English Religious Lyric in the Middle Ages* (Oxford: Clarendon Press, 1968)

Wright, Herbert G., *Boccaccio in England from Chaucer to Tennyson* (London: Athlone, 1957)

Yeager, Robert F., ed., *Fifteenth-Century Studies: Recent Essays* (Hamden, Conn.: Archon Books, 1984)

Zafran, Eric, 'Saturn and the Jews', *Journal of the Warburg and Courtauld Institutes* 42 (1979), 16-27

Index

This index is selective, and so inevitably may appear arbitrary. It comprises primarily authors discussed in the main text or in footnotes, but includes salient topics, as much as these can be distinguished from 'allegory' and 'melancholy'.